CW00522312

Warfare in History

THE PLACE OF WAR IN ENGLISH HISTORY
1066–1214

Warfare in History
ISSN 1358–779X

Editorial Board
Matthew Bennett, Royal Military Academy, Sandhurst
David Parrott, University of Oxford
Hew Strachan, University of Oxford

This series aims to provide a wide-ranging and scholarly approach to military history, offering both individual studies of topics or wars, and volumes giving a selection of contemporary and later accounts of particular battles; its scope ranges from the early medieval to the modern period.

New proposals for the series are welcomed; they should be sent to the publisher at the address below.

Boydell and Brewer Limited, PO Box 9, Woodbridge, Suffolk, IP12 3DF

*Previously published volumes in this series
are listed at the back of this book*

THE PLACE OF WAR IN ENGLISH HISTORY
1066–1214

J.O. Prestwich

edited with an Introduction by Michael Prestwich

THE BOYDELL PRESS

© Estate of J. O. Prestwich 2004
Editorial matter © Michael Prestwich 2004

All Rights Reserved. Except as permitted under current legislation
no part of this work may be photocopied, stored in a retrieval system,
published, performed in public, adapted, broadcast,
transmitted, recorded or reproduced in any form or by any means,
without the prior permission of the copyright owner

First published 2004
The Boydell Press, Woodbridge

ISBN 1 84383 098 1

The Boydell Press is an imprint of Boydell & Brewer Ltd
PO Box 9, Woodbridge, Suffolk IP12 3DF, UK
and of Boydell & Brewer Inc.
668 Mt Hope Avenue, Rochester, NY 14620, USA
website: www.boydellandbrewer.com

A catalogue record for this book is available
from the British Library

Library of Congress Cataloging-in-Publication Data
Prestwich, J. O.
   The place of war in English history, 1066–1214 / J.O. Prestwich ; edited
with an introduction by Michael Prestwich.
       p. cm. – (Warfare in history, ISSN 1358–779X)
   Includes bibliographical references and index.
   ISBN 1-84383–098–1 (hardback : alk. paper)
   1. Great Britain – History, Military – 1066–1485. 2. Great Britain –
History – Norman period, 1066–1154. 3. Great Britain – History – Angevin
period, 1154–1216. 4. Military art and science – Great Britain – History –
Medieval, 500–1500. I. Prestwich, Michael. II. Title. III. Series.
   DA60.P74 2004
   355'.00942'09021 – dc22   2004004462

This publication is printed on acid-free paper

Printed in Great Britain by
Cromwell Press, Trowbridge, Wiltshire

Contents

General Editor's Preface

I only met JOP once, some twenty years ago, at a lecture he gave to the London Medieval Society at the Institute of Historical Research in Senate House. His topic then was military intelligence in the Norman and Angevin period. He spoke with clarity and dry wit, living up to his reputation as an excellent lecturer. It was not difficult to see why he had such a significant influence upon a generation of scholars that included my own supervisor R. Allen Brown and other luminaries such as Sir John Holt and John Gillingham. It was the latter pair who gained the title of *l'equipe Prestwich* during the Rome conference of 1981 when JOP spoke on Richard the Lionheart.

It is quite clear that John Prestwich possessed presence and the ability to create a loyal following amongst the academics whom he inspired. This Aristotelian influence was matched by his Socratic teaching technique. But where would the Greek philosophers have been without someone to record their words and ideas? Unusually, perhaps, for a don of his generation, JOP did not seek to establish a school of history through an extensive list of publications. In fact, his approach was the opposite – he published very little. What he did produce was of the highest quality and helped me, amongst many others, to focus upon the study of the medieval world, especially the Anglo-Norman period.

His work on the organisation and financing of warfare, together with his studies of the royal military household, form the keystone for understanding the processes of military history in the twelfth century. From the point of view of those not lucky enough to be a student at Oxford in the second half of the twentieth century, it is little less than a tragedy that such a talented historian left so little published work. Not least, he was a good generation before his time in deconstructing the concept of feudalism.

We are indeed fortunate that his son, himself a distinguished professor with a bent towards military history, has been able to bring together the Ford Lectures of two decades ago and other papers that shed light upon JOP's interpretation of history.

This volume enables a multitude of readers to encounter his ideas for the first time in print, and so to meet him many times over.

Matthew Bennett
Royal Military Academy Sandhurst

Acknowledgements

This book is not what its author would have wanted to publish, but it is, I hope, what many want to see. In 1983 the electors to the Ford Lectureship in Oxford thought that they had found the ideal way to persuade John Prestwich to go into print on a more substantial scale than he had done in writing articles for scholarly journals. By giving him the Lectureship, he would surely follow convention, and publish the lectures. They were sadly mistaken. This volume, however, now provides the text of the lectures as they were delivered in the Examination Schools in Oxford in 1983, along with two supplementary chapters as appendices.

It is not known what acknowledgements John Prestwich would have included, had he published his work as a book. Undoubtedly he would have expressed his gratitude to his wife Menna, with whom he shared so much, and who was so anxious to see his work in print. Theirs was a unique partnership. He would surely also have expressed his gratitude to his college, Queen's. The wealth of its library is one reason why he was so exceptionally well read in the sources for the eleventh and twelfth centuries. He gained much from his pupils, and would undoubtedly have wished to thank them. There would have been others; I can only apologise for not including them. For help in preparing this edition of John Prestwich's work, I would like to thank Lucy Rhymer for her assistance in assembling the footnotes, and David Carpenter for helpfully reading a draft of the introduction. Chris Prestwich provided invaluable assistance with the proofs. My chief thanks are, of course, due to my wife Maggie for her constant support.

Michael Prestwich

J.O. Prestwich

Foreword

John Prestwich had an immense reputation among medieval historians for his scholarship. His published articles, for all that they are few in number, are seminal, but it was also well known that he had a vast store of knowledge and of ideas which he did not publish. Chief among the items which did not appear in print are the six Ford Lectures given in 1983, by invitation. These summarise much of his thinking about the nature of war and society in the Anglo-Norman period, and form the bulk of this volume.

Leigh, Lancashire, was the unlikely birthplace of John Prestwich, who as a boy was known as Jack. By the time he went to Oxford he was John; there he would become known by his initials, JOP. He was born in 1914, and came from a reasonably well-to-do family. The family firm was an architectural practice; his father was a quantity surveyor. Thought to be a somewhat sickly child, Jack was sent away to school, to a preparatory school at Penmaenmawr, and then to Sedbergh School. In that period Sedbergh had a reputation for an extremely Spartan regime. On winter mornings the ice had to be broken for the compulsory cold baths. Hills were there to be run up before breakfast. It does not sound ideal for a boy thought, wrongly as it turned out, to have had a weak heart, but Jack Prestwich thrived at Sedbergh, particularly when he discovered that he was a good shot. Sport then became a matter of adopting a prone position, and remaining as still as possible. Skill at shooting meant that he acquired school colours at an early age, and he was always proud of the chocolate-coloured blazer this entitled him to.

In academic terms, Jack Prestwich was exceptional, winning prizes for every conceivable subject. He could have chosen any discipline to take forward, but the history teaching at Sedbergh was clearly superb at that time, and it is unlikely that there was much doubt in his mind as to what course he should take in the sixth form. He was also well trained in languages, both the classics and French and German. When he left school, he spent time in Germany, living with a family in Bonn, and seeing at first hand the way in which people could be taken over by the Nazi ideology.

From Sedbergh, John Prestwich went to Hertford College, Oxford, to read Modern History. There is no indication that any one of his tutors was a notable inspiration to him, though Felix Markham remained a friend for life. What was perhaps most important in his intellectual development was his decision to put in for the Lothian Prize Essay. This was on 'Feudal Society in the Latin States of Palestine and Syria and its Relations to the Saracens', and was an astonishing piece of work. It showed many of the hall-marks of the later scholar, with a remarkable attention to the primary sources, and a high degree of scepticism about feudalism. The concept that the Latin States represented an ideal feudal society, constructed *de novo*, came in for particular criticism. When it came to his final examinations, John wrote down what mark he thought he had obtained on each paper. Modestly, he considered that his paper on the most modern period of English history would only merit a β++, though he anticipated first class marks for everything else. In fact, he obtained an alpha mark on every paper he took, with a pure unadulterated alpha for the prize essay.

After his finals, JOP won a prize fellowship by examination at Magdalen. The papers he wrote survive, written in the clear, elegant hand he retained throughout life. The opening of one answer anticipates much of his future work: 'Feudalism is an unsatisfactory term which has seldom been defined adequately or used effectively as an instrument for analysing the complex and changing social structure of medieval Europe.' There was no question of his starting on a doctorate at Magdalen; in those days, there was no need for such qualifications. There were clearly some thoughts of continuing with the work on the crusader states, for there was correspondence with R.C. Smail at Cambridge, to make sure that their research did not overlap. Whether it was because of Smail's work or for some other reason is not clear, but JOP decided to work on Anglo-Norman England, leaving the Latin East for a later project (which he never began). He was also thinking hard about teaching. 'There is a clear distinction', he wrote in the *Oxford Magazine*, 'between history as understood by the trained researcher and the history which can be profitably studied by the undergraduate.' He further noted that 'The multiplication of books and the additions to knowledge have inflated the syllabus to a size which intimidates both tutors and pupils.'[1] The sentiment is interesting both in the light of the immense quantity of material published since 1937, and of the limited number of articles he himself would publish.

When a fellowship was advertised at Queen's in 1938, four candidates were interviewed, and the post duly went to JOP. It is striking that he did not belong to, nor did he join, the dominant school of medievalists at Oxford. The leading figure at the time was F.M. Powicke. 'It had always been the special aim of this school', wrote R.W. Southern, one of its members, 'to assert the normative role of the twelfth and thirteenth centuries in the development of European civilization.'[2] The church had a leading position in that analysis. An awkward meeting of JOP with Powicke took place over tea; it is clear that there was no meeting of minds. Among the possible reasons for this the fact that JOP had no interest in religion, either as a personal faith or as a historical factor, stands out. His view of the Middle Ages was determinedly secular and rational. Further, he was exceptional among the Oxford medievalists of that period in knowing German, and he was capable of making it clear that he regarded this as an essential qualification.[3] The year 1938 was very important for JOP in another way, for it was then that he married Menna Roberts; theirs was to be a remarkable partnership of two historians, both dedicated teachers and both devoted to Oxford.

The brilliant academic career was interrupted by the war. JOP was commis-

---

1   *Oxford Magazine*, 4 March 1937.
2   R.W. Southern, *Robert Grosseteste* (Oxford, 1986), 23.
3   An undergraduate essay he wrote began: 'Sitting in the observatory of history, surrounded by the elaborate precision instruments of research (many of them "made in Germany"), the newcomer is a little bewildered by the range and complexity of the science.'

sioned in the Oxford and Buckinghamshire Light Infantry. With his academic background, and his knowledge of German, not to mention his wife's networking skills, it was inevitable that he should soon have been selected to work at Bletchley Park, the central hub of British intelligence. He worked there in Hut 3, not decoding German signals, but interpreting decodes once they had been worked out. In 1944 he was sent on an exchange scheme to Washington, where he spent the rest of the war. It was not for many, many years that he spoke of his work in intelligence, such was the power of the Official Secrets Act. The tasks he performed were ideally suited to a historian, particularly a medievalist. He was engaged in sorting and evaluating difficult evidence, some of it only partially readable, and then in establishing from it hypotheses about German troop movements. In Washington he became the leading expert on Japanese troop dispositions on some particularly obscure Pacific islands. Had these featured significantly in the American reconquest of the Pacific, his knowledge would have played a vital part in the final stages of the war effort.

It is unfortunate that JOP never wrote up his experiences at Bletchley; but he did not spend as long there as most of his contemporaries did, and he felt that he had little to add to what his old friend Ralph Bennett had to say.[4] A letter to Bennett explained something of his duties as military adviser (MA) at Bletchley:

> As you know very well the MA's main duty was to draft clear and accurate signals to commands in the field which needed the intelligence, together with any essential comments; fuller annotation of the teleprints came second, And the MA had to decide on the urgency of the signal; ZZZZ was, I think, our top priority. Sometimes it was simple enough: a Fuehrerbefehl to Rommel in a nice clear text needed no comment. But, to take a real instance, an imperfect decrypt showed that something was to happen to 21 Panzer Division in two days time, the key word being A,F,RI,.,U,G, After discussion the watch thought AUFFRISCHUNG a probable emendation, and 'rest and refit' the right rendering. The MA then had to decide whether this was 'strong' 'fair' or 'slight' and whether to add a comment on a recent tank strength return from 21 Panzer Divison and the last known location of the division. Apparently trivial information might be significant, e.g. a scrap showed that a general last heard of as an army commander on the central Russian front was being booked in at Rome. He might just be going there on leave. But since we knew that Rommel was ill this might be his replacement, and it was worth a cautious signal.

When JOP returned to Oxford, it was to face a very heavy teaching load, as emergency arrangements were made to speed demobilised servicemen through the university. In those years research had to take second place. In 1954, however, he was invited to address the Royal Historical Society. His article on 'War and Finance in the Anglo-Norman State', published in the *Transactions* for

---

[4] R.F. Bennett, *Ultra in the West: The Normandy Campaign 1944–45* (1974); *Ultra and Mediterranean Strategy 1941–5* (1989); *Behind the Battle: Intelligence in the War with Germany* (1994). Bennett's work depended in part on work in the Public Record Office, an institution with which JOP was wholly unfamiliar.

that year, became a classic. His intention then was to develop his ideas further into a book on the same theme. This was to have begun with a chapter on Edward I's reign, and then look back into the Anglo-Norman period, to show that military organisation, with a strong emphasis on paid troops, had not greatly changed. Chapters of this book were written, but it was never sent to a publisher. The article he published in 1981 on 'The Military Household of the Norman Kings', however, represents a significant part of this book, and follows a similar framework of argument.[5] There is little doubt that publication of this article was prompted by the appearance of Marjorie Chibnall's article on a similar topic in *History*.[6] There were, of course, over the years many distractions from the task of writing a book. There was the help that John provided for his wife in preparing her major book on Lionel Cranfield.[7] Also, there was the discovery, as a result of teaching first-year undergraduates, that what appeared to be a minor point about punctuation in one chapter of Bede might help to transform the political history of the seventh century, and indeed provide strong hints as to the identity of the king commemorated in the Sutton Hoo burial.[8]

It is, even so, puzzling that with so much written, the book was not completed. One explanation could be that JOP strongly believed that everything had to be right. When Hugh Trevor-Roper, giving his inaugural lecture, made reference to the value of the 'fertile error' in taking the study of history forward, JOP made much fun of this.[9] Much earlier, R.H. Hodgkin, in his *A History of the Anglo-Saxons*, had expressed the hope that his maps, though far from 'satisfactory', were at least better than previous ones. He believed that 'it is better to make mistakes than to leave complete blanks'. JOP's copy of the book bears the annotation 'Shocking statement' in the margin.[10] There is no question, however, of his having any self-doubt about what he had written; he knew that he was right. It may be, however, that he felt that there was more evidence that could be brought to bear to demonstrate the truth of his arguments, and perhaps more points towards which his formidable intelligence could be directed.

Further, JOP was content that his views were being sufficiently disseminated through his teaching. He put immense care into this. The floor of his room would be spread with maps and books; volumes from the Rolls Series would be brought down from the shelves, to fall open conveniently at the page where there was some conclusive piece of evidence to prove a point. He had his mannerisms; there was the clearing of the throat, but it was perhaps the tapping of the cigarette on the cigarette box that was most memorable for those who suffered it. The success of a tutorial could be measured by the time that elapsed before the

---

5   J.O. Prestwich, "The Military Household of the Norman Kings', *EHR* xcvi (1981), 1–35.
6   M. Chibnall, 'Mercenaries and the *familia Regis* under Henry I', *History* lxii (1977), 15–23.
7   M. Prestwich, *Cranfield: politics and profits under the early Stuarts: The career of Lionel Cranfield, Earl of Middlesex* (Oxford, 1966)
8   J.O. Prestwich, 'King Æthelhere and the Battle of the Winwaed', *EHR* lxxxiii (1968), 89–95.
9   This concept is referred to below, XXX.
10   A. Jones, *Catalogue 127. History, June and July 2003* (Banbury, privately printed, 2003), 27.

somewhat battered cigarette was eventually lit. The importance of sources, and of reading them accurately, was hammered home. 'What's your evidence?' was the key question which he asked of his pupils.[11] The lecturing load he bore was, by the standards of other universities and of more recent times, not a substantial one, but it was one he carried most conscientiously. With sixteen lectures to give a year, it was necessary that each should be of the highest standard. All were written out in typescript, and even relatively minor changes from one year's version to the next involved a laborious process of retyping. Lecture courses on 'Personalities and Politics' and 'Evidence and Controversies' provided many generations of undergraduates with invaluable assistance for their papers on English medieval history; JOP believed that lectures should be relevant to the syllabus, an attitude which was distinctly unusual in the Oxford of his day.

JOP was devoted to Oxford, and to the Honour School of Modern History. It had, in his view, no equal, and he was proud of the two years he spent as Chairman of the Faculty. Within the faculty, wisdom for him naturally lay with the college tutors, not the professors. He was for many years loyal to the Stubbs Society, a strange, and now defunct, society which had both senior and junior members. Undergraduates could only join when introduced by their tutor. It must have been a terrifying experience to speak to this body in the 1950s, when discussion might take the form of an interrogation from JOP, and the object of the exercise was to display the intellectual superiority of the Oxford history tutors.

Conferences are often a way of persuading people to go into print, but JOP attended very few, surprisingly avoiding attendance even at the Battle Abbey gatherings which were so directly engaged with his field.[12] One exception was when in 1981 he went to Rome, a quite irresistible venue. JOP went there with his former pupils J.C. Holt and John Gillingham, and gave a lecture on Richard I, which enabled him to set out his ideas on Richard as a military commander.[13]

In 1983, a couple of years after he retired, JOP gave the Ford Lectures. He was deeply appreciative of the honour that was done to him by the electors in inviting him to do this, and he thoroughly enjoyed the experience of giving what was for the audience, by all accounts, a highly successful series of lectures. He planned to put the lectures into book form, but that involved extensive rewriting. He revised the first two of the lectures, trebling them in length, and annotating them extremely fully, but he stopped at that point. The task of revision was not one he enjoyed, and he was easily diverted into other, smaller projects. As a result, he began to publish far more than he had previously.

There was the question of Geoffrey de Mandeville's charters. R.H.C. Davis published an article in the 1960s, correcting J.H. Round's ordering of the

---

[11] John Edwards, 'JOP', in *War and Government in the Middle Ages*, ed. J. Gillingham and J.C. Holt (Woodbridge, 1984), p. x.

[12] He would have been delighted to know that *Anglo-Norman Studies* xxv (Woodbridge, 2003), is dedicated to his memory.

[13] 'Richard Coeur de Lion: Rex Bellicosus', in *Riccardo Cuor di Leone Nella Storia e Nella Legende* (Accademia Nazionale dei Lincei, Rome, 1981), 1–15.

charters granted to Geoffrey de Mandeville.[14] JOP was convinced that his friend Ralph Davis was mistaken, and devoted much time and attention to demonstrating this. He published his views in 1988, and then engaged in a controversy with Davis in the pages of the *English Historical Review*.[15] The importance of what he wrote on this topic lies less in the somewhat arcane problems of the charters, their guarantors and the precise dating of the documents, as in the fact that this controversy provided him with the opportunity to set out his views on Stephen's reign. Interestingly, however, he told one of his former pupils that the one thing he regretted about his academic achievements was that he had not persuaded everyone that he was right about the Mandeville charters. If any scholar, even in a footnote, suggested that Davis had been correct, they would receive a lengthy further exposition of the case from JOP in the post. He was always very clear that the arguments he had with Davis were purely academic; they were not the product of any personal animosity whatsoever, a point which he always claimed was incomprehensible to Cambridge academics. As Davis said to him, 'A debate is not a quarrel.'[16]

The fact that he had been in Intelligence in the Second World War inspired JOP to write about military intelligence in the twelfth century for the Festschrift presented to his pupil, Sir James Holt. This was a part of the planned book that was to come out of the Ford Lectures.[17] Another Festschrift to which he contributed was that for W.L. Warren which came out as a volume of *Peritia*.[18] This is an important article, which contains many of the gems of his teaching. His demonstrations of the way in which historical misinterpretations are so often based on mistranslations of the sources reveals much of his historical method. Publishing the article caused him much irritation; he could see no reason why a journal should prefer its own well-established footnote conventions to his own somewhat old-fashioned style. Somehow, he was later persuaded to go to a conference on Anglo-Norman Durham, and his lively exposition of the career of one of his heroes, Ranulf Flambard, duly graces the pages of the published proceedings.[19]

It was typical of JOP that he should have spent his final years thinking not about the book which should have summed up his thinking about war, the state and the economy in the Anglo-Norman period, but about a riposte to an article

14 R.H.C. Davis, 'Geoffrey de Mandeville Reconsidered', *EHR* lxxix (1964), 299–307.

15 J.O. Prestwich, 'The Treason of Geoffrey de Mandeville', *EHR* cii (1988), 283–312; 'Geoffrey de Mandeville: a Further Comment', *EHR* ciii (1988), 960–7; 'Last Words on Geoffrey de Mandeville', *EHR* cv (1990), 670–2.

16 Letter of 24 August 1992 to Edmund King. In a letter of 7 January 1992 to Ralph Bennett JOP commented that Marjorie Chibnall 'supposed, quite wrongly, that I had some personal vendetta with Ralph Davis: in fact we had been friends for a great many years'.

17 'Military Intelligence under the Norman and Angevin Kings', in *Law and Government in the Medieval England and Normandy: Essays in Honour of Sir James Holt*, ed. G. Garnett and John Hudson (Cambridge, 1994), 1–30.

18 'Mistranslations and misinterpretations in medieval English history', *Peritia, Journal of the Medieval Academy of Ireland* x (1996), 322–40.

19 'The Career of Ranulf Flambard', in *Anglo-Norman Durham*, ed. David Rollason, Margaret Harvey and Michael Prestwich (Woodbridge, 1994), 299–310

by a young scholar, Stephen Church, on the household knights of King John.[20] JOP considered that this challenged some of his basic assumptions, and to make matters worse, its author claimed an *imprimatur* from two of his former pupils and his son. Part of the issue turned on the interpretation of some detailed evidence; the broader problem was that he believed that Church had neither properly appreciated his own views, nor realised the depth of evidence that supported them.[21]

JOP was not a manuscript scholar; there was more than enough printed material for his period without the need to search out fresh sources. Nor was he even a habitué of the Bodleian Library. Almost all the works he needed were kept in his room, first at college, and after retirement in his home. Relatively few were his own; the Queen's College Library had a remarkably fine collection, and provided him with virtually all the research materials he needed. On one occasion in the 1960s, he told a student to go and consult something to be found in Migne's *Patrologia Latina*. Upon repairing to the college library, the student was told firmly that the volume in question 'had been taken out by Mr Prestwich in 1938'. No doubt, in his role as College Librarian, JOP was able to avoid the problems presented by regular recalls of books.

JOP had a strong belief in the careful analysis of sources, without assumptions or prejudices derived from the application of models taken from the social sciences. This does much to explain his rejection of the concepts of feudalism. His view of the duty of the historian was set out in a paper he gave to a group at Queen's in the 1970s.

> He must believe, as an historian, in the virtues of truth or probability and in the exposure of error and myth. No professional historian can afford to say that in the interests of his religion or his country – or his class – he is prepared to suppress or represent the evidence. He is likely to believe that the full truth is desirable, beneficial or even positively good: that good intentions are not enough and that it is necessary to take a realistic view of the probable consequences of acting upon them. He is likely to believe that the manipulation or misrepresentation of history for religious or political ends has had demonstrably harmful consequences and to hold that his own work may make it a little more difficult to misuse history in this way; though he is unlikely to suppose that his efforts will produce rapid or extensive results.

His scholarship was meticulous. He had, above all, an extraordinary knowledge of the chronicle sources, and an ability to read them in a fresh way, deducing new conclusions from the way in which events were reported.

There was no Prestwich school of history, but over the years JOP supervised many postgraduates, encouraging them to adopt his careful approach to the evidence. The attention he put to the process of supervision was immense; a very substantial file was built up about each research student, containing carbon copies of the carefully composed letters sent to them with advice and references.

---

[20] S.D. Church, 'The rewards of royal service in the household of King John: a dissenting opinion', *EHR* cx (1995), 277–302.
[21] See below, 131.

Those he supervised included Emilie Amt, R. Allen Brown, David Carpenter, Judith Green, J.C. Holt, Simon Lloyd, Marie-Therese O'Flanagan and Hilary Waite.

*

The main part of this book consists of the Ford Lectures, as given in 1983. There have been many requests that they should be published, but it must be stressed that JOP never intended them to come out in this form. The necessary limitation of the lecture format, with just six lectures, each given in no more than an hour, meant that a great deal had to be left out. This was not the place for a repetition of arguments about the vital role of the royal household knights in twelfth-century warfare, still less for discussion of the question of whether knights under Henry I were paid 8d or 6d a day. JOP was also keen to open some new horizons, hence his discussion of sea power in one of the lectures. His intention was that the published version of the lectures would be very much fuller, and that the volume would be the full-scale demonstration of his views that he had always intended to write. When he wrote a revised version of the first lecture, very significantly longer than the original, it contained a substantial exposition of his views on feudalism. This was very important as part of the general argument he was presenting, and it therefore forms an appendix to this volume. The question of the composition of military forces was not dealt with in the lectures in any detail. It is, however, of fundamental importance to the subject matter, and so a further appendix is included which derives from JOP's first book project. This was written in the early 1960s, and covers the period up to 1135; later chapters, which would have taken the analysis on to the end of the twelfth century, were never written.

The extent to which the material in this volume needed editing has been limited, for the typescripts were meticulously prepared. Where there was duplication between the Ford Lectures and the related pieces, the principle adopted has been to leave the text of the lectures intact, but to adapt the appendices on feudalism and the composition of military forces so as to limit repetition of evidence and examples as far as possible, though inevitably some duplication remains. In the original text, scholars were, where entitled, given their professorial titles. This, in JOP's case, may on occasion have been a form of abuse; the more often he titled someone 'Professor', the more likely it was that he disagreed with him. It seemed right to omit such titles from the published text. In other respects, JOP's style has been left intact.[22] There are occasional informalities, and it is important to remember that the lectures were intended to be read out aloud. The reader would do well to imagine them punctuated by a distinctive clearing of the throat. In the typed text of the lectures, the notes were given in brief form in brackets in the text; these have been converted into fuller

---

[22] He clearly did not believe that it is wrong to start sentences or even paragraphs with the word 'But'. In doing this he followed the example of that great stylist, F.W. Maitland: see for example F. Pollock and F.W. Maitland, *The History of English Law* (2nd edn, reissued 1968), i. 82–3.

footnotes. In the final two chapters, the format of the notes has been updated in line with more modern conventions than those JOP used; he would not have been happy with this.

Some of the chronicles JOP drew on so extensively have been re-edited in recent years. Where he was using Rolls Series editions, it seemed proper to leave the references unchanged, for these are readily available. In other cases, where he was using old editions which are difficult to obtain, citations have been altered to new versions. Those to the *Chronicle of Battle Abbey*, for example, have been changed to Eleanor Searle's edition. References to William of Poitiers's *Gesta Guillelmi* and to the *Vie de Suger* have also been altered to modern editions. Where a note has been added by the editor, his initials are given in square brackets. At the end of each chapter, a brief note provides a guide to work published since JOP wrote.

Michael Prestwich

Abbreviations

Ambroise	*The Crusade of Richard Lion-Heart by Ambroise*, trans. M.J. Hubert, ed. J. L. La Monte (New York, 1941)
Ann. Mon.	*Annales Monastici*, ed. H.R. Luard (4 vols, Rolls Series, 1864–67)
Ann. Wint.	'Annales monasterii de Wintona', in *Ann. Mon.* ii.
Coggeshall	*Radulphi de Coggeshall Chronicon Anglicanum*, ed. J. Stevenson (2 vols, Rolls Series, 1875)
Chron. Abingdon	*Chronicon Monasterii de Abingdon*, ed. J. Stevenson (2 vols, Rolls Series, 1858)
Chron. Battle	*The Chronicle of Battle Abbey*, ed. E. Searle (Oxford, 1980)
DB	*Domesday Book*
De Expugnatione	*De Expugnatione Lyxbonensi. The Conquest of Lisbon*, ed. C.W. David (New York, 1936)
Devizes	Richard of Devizes, *Chronicon*, ed. and trans J.T. Appleby (London, 1963)
Diceto	*Radulphi de Diceto Decanai Lundoniensis Opera Historica*, ed. W. Stubbs (Rolls Series, 1875)
Eadmer, *Historia Novorum*	Eadmer, *Historia Novorum in Anglia*, ed. M. Rule (Rolls Series, 1884)
EcHR	*Economic History Review*
EHR	*English Historical Review*
Florence	Florence of Worcester, *Chronicon ex Chronicis*, ed. B. Thorpe (Eng. Hist. Soc., 1848–49)
Foedera	T. Rymer, *Foedera, Conventiones, Litterae, et Acta Publica*, ed. A. Clarke and F. Holbrooke (London, 1816–69)
Gerald of Wales, *Opera*	*Giraldus Cambrensis, Opera*, ed. J.S. Brewer, J.F. Dimock and G.F. Warner (Rolls Series, 1861–91)
Gesta Guillelmi	*The Gesta Guillelmi of William of Poitiers*, ed. R.H.C. Davis and M.M. Chibnall (Oxford, 1998)
Gesta Stephani	*Gesta Stephani*, ed. K.R. Potter and R.H.C. Davis (Oxford, 1976)
Howden, *Chronica*	*Chronica Rogeri de Hoveden*, ed. W. Stubbs (4 vols, Rolls Series, 1868–71).
Howden, *Gesta*	*Gesta Regis Henrici Secundi*, ed. W. Stubbs (2 vols, Rolls Series, 1867).
Huntingdon, *Historia Anglorum*	Henry of Huntingdon, *Historia Anglorum*, ed. T. Arnold (Rolls Series, 1879)
Hyde Chronicle	'Chronica monasterii de Hida iuxta Wintoniam', in *Liber monasterii de Hida*, ed. E. Edwards (Rolls Series, 1866)
Laurence of Durham	*Dialogi Laurentii Dunelmensis monachi ac prioris*, ed. J. Raine (Surtees Society 70, 1880)
Letters, Lanfranc	*The Letters of Lanfranc, Archbishop of Canterbury*, ed. H. Clover and M. Gibson (Oxford, 1979).

Malmesbury, *Gesta Regum*	William of Malmesbury, *De Gestis Regum Anglorum*, ed. W. Stubbs (2 vols, Rolls Series 90, 1887–89)
Malmesbury, *Gestis Pontificum*	William of Malmesbury, *De Gestis Pontificum Anglorum*, ed. N.E.S.A. Hamilton (Rolls Series 52, 1870)
Malmesbury, *Historia Novella*	William of Malmesbury, *Historia Novella,* ed. G.R. Potter (1955)
Migne, *Patrologia Latina*	*Patrologia cursus completes, series Latina*, ed. J-P. Migne (221 vols, Paris, 1844–64)
MGH	*Monumenta Germaniae Historica*
Newburgh, *Historia*	William of Newburgh, *Historia Rerum Anglicarum*, ed. R. Howlett, in *Chronicles of the Reigns of Stephen, Henry II and Richard I*, i and ii (Rolls Series, 1884)
Orderic	*The Ecclesiastical History of Orderic Vitalis*, ed. M. Chibnall (6 vols, Oxford, 1969–80)
PRS	Pipe Roll Society
Rot. Lit. Claus.	*Rotuli Litterarum Clausarum in Turri Londinensi asservati*, ed. T. Duffus Hardy (Record Commission, 1833–34)
Rot. de Oblatis	*Rotuli de Oblatis et Finibus in Turri Londinensi asservati*, ed. T. Duffus Hardy (Record Commission, 1835)
Rot. Lit. Pat.	*Rotuli Litterarum Patentium in Turri Londinensi asservati*, ed. T. Duffus Hardy (Record Commission, 1835)
Suger, *Vie de Louis VI*	Suger, *Vie de Louis VI le Gros,* ed. H. Waquet (Paris, 1964)
Torigny	Chronicle of Robert of Torigni, in *Chronicles of the Reigns of Stephen, Henry II, and Richard I*, iv, ed. R. Howlett (Rolls Series, 1889)
TRHS	*Transactions of the Royal Historical Society*
Walter of Coventry	*Memoriale Walteri de Conventria*, ed. W. Stubbs (Rolls Series, 1872–73)
VCH	*Victoria County History*

Bibliography of John Prestwich's Articles

'War and Finance in the Anglo-Norman State', *Transactions of the Royal Historical Society*, 5th ser., iv (1954), 19–43; reprinted in *Anglo-Norman Warfare*, ed. M. Strickland (Woodbridge, 1992), 93–127.

'Anglo-Norman Feudalism and the Problem of Continuity', *Past and Present* 26 (1963), 39–57.

'King Æthelhere and the Battle of the Winwaed', *EHR* lxxxiii (1968), 89–95.

'Richard Coeur de Lion: Rex Bellicosus', *Riccardo Cuor di Leone Nella Storia e Nella Legende* (Accademia Nazionale dei Lincei, Rome, 1981), 1–15; reprinted in *Richard Coeur de Lion in History and Myth*, ed. J.L. Nelson (London, 1992).

'The Military Household of the Norman Kings', *EHR* xcvi (1981), 1–35; reprinted in *Anglo-Norman Warfare*, ed. M. Strickland (Woodbridge, 1992), 93–127.

'The Treason of Geoffrey de Mandeville', *EHR* cii (1988), 283–312.

'Geoffrey de Mandeville: A Further Comment', *EHR* ciii (1988), 960–7.

'Last Words on Geoffrey de Mandeville', *EHR* cv (1990), 670–2.

'The Place of the Royal Household in English History, 1066–1307', *Medieval History* i (1991), 37–52.

'Military Intelligence under the Norman and Angevin Kings', *Law and Government in the Medieval England and Normandy: Essays in Honour of Sir James Holt*, ed. G. Garnett and John Hudson (Cambridge, 1994), 1–30.

'The Career of Ranulf Flambard', *Anglo-Norman Durham*, ed. David Rollason, Margaret Harvey and Michael Prestwich (Woodbridge, 1994), 299–310.

'Mistranslations and misinterpretations in medieval English history', *Peritia, Journal of the Medieval Academy of Ireland*, x (1996), 322–40.

1

The Problem of Interpretation

The invitation to give these lectures, which were founded well over a century ago by James Ford, is accompanied by a list of those who have given them in the past two decades. The intention is presumably to encourage the recipient; but a glance at that list and a little reflection on how much our knowledge and interpretation of English history has been advanced and shaped by the published lectures, not merely in those two decades, aroused in me considerable feelings of trepidation. I can only suppose that in these days of financial stringency and suspended posts the electors decided to bring back a college tutor from retirement in order to get some more service out of him and to give more length, if not body, to the relevant section of the lecture list. I hope that I have not misunderstood the intention of the electors; and I am deeply sensible of the honour they have paid me.

My general theme, the place of war in English history from 1066 to 1214, will seem to many to be both unedifying and old-fashioned, and the title requires some explanation. By war I mean not merely – or indeed mainly – active hostilities, but how armed forces were raised, maintained, supplied, disciplined and transported. I shall have something to say about the ends for which they were used, the relations between war and diplomacy, propaganda and morale, military intelligence, and economic warfare.

It is a requirement of these lectures that they should be on English history, but here too I propose to take rather wide terms of reference: indeed the evidence requires them. To two men writing in the 1120s it seemed that the history of the English had almost come to an end. 'There is today', wrote William of Malmesbury, 'no Englishman who is an earl, bishop or abbot. Strangers devour the wealth and entrails of England; and there is no hope of the misery coming to an end.'[1] Similarly Eadmer commented sourly that no Englishman could hope for preferment in the church, while an alien needed only the semblance of virtue and the support of his friends to be judged worthy of the highest honour.[2] We do indeed hear of the employment of English troops as early as 1068.[3] But in the general record of this period we hear far more of troops drawn from Normandy, Brittany, Maine, Anjou, Poitou, Flanders and Wales than of distinctively English forces.

---

[1] Malmesbury, *Gesta Regum*, i. 278.
[2] Eadmer, *Historia Novorum*, 224.
[3] *Orderic*, ii. 212.

Towards the end of this period the term 'English' was coming to be applied to those who had been born and lived in the country, irrespective of language or descent, though it is with a little surprise that we find Richard I at Jaffa in 1192 represented as describing himself and his forces there as 'we Englishmen'.[4] But even then the balance of political power in England was being related to the capacity to raise troops from outside England. We are told that in the struggle for power in England between William Longchamp and Count John in 1191 the former took a much more confident line as soon as he heard that the foreign mercenaries for whom he had sent were beginning to land in the country. Count John's answer, according to Richard of Devizes, was to hire 4,000 Welsh troops; and when Longchamp finally met Count John outside Winchester on 28 July it appeared that he too had taken the useful precaution of hiring Welsh troops in order to level the odds if it came to a fight. It did not come to a fight: it seldom did. Far more was involved than the mobilization of rival military forces. But the episode is a reminder that Wales, alongside the better-known recruiting grounds on the continent, was and had long been a large reservoir of military manpower. We may reasonably suspect Richard of Devizes's figure of 4,000 Welshmen as too high, even though he was on the spot at Winchester; but the Pipe Rolls establish that over 1,800 Welsh troops had been sent to Normandy three years previously and that at least 2,100 were dispatched there five years later.[5]

If English history cannot be reduced to the history of the English in this period it is equally unrealistic to confine it to the bounds of England. The Conqueror's own operations took him to Maine, Brittany, the Tay estuary in Scotland, St David's in Wales, and, at the very end of his life, to within thirty-odd miles of Paris. Contemporaries credited him with designs on the old Carolingian capital of Aachen and on Ireland, while his half-brother, Odo, and his eldest son, Robert, were believed to have framed ambitious or desperate designs for intervening in Italy.[6] And towards the end of our period, in what has been called the first of the international wars in the west, the theatre of operations extended from Limerick to Ascalon and from the Pyrenees to Norway.[7]

My limiting dates are those of two battles, Hastings and Bouvines. But I do not intend to tell the story of campaigns and engagements in the century and a half separating these two battles: indeed I shall have more to say about the battles which were declined than of the few that were fought. My purpose in choosing so long a period is rather to consider how war was conducted during

---

4   Devizes, 82.
5   Newburgh, *Historia*, i. 559; Devizes, 55; *Pipe Roll 34 Henry II* (PRS, 1925), 8, 95, 106, 210; *Chancellor's Roll 8 Richard 1* (PRS, 1930), xvii–xviii.
6   For Aachen see *Lamperti monachi Hersfeldensis opera*, ed. O. Holder-Egger (Monumenta Germaniae Historica, 1894), 195 (in the copy of this in the Durham University Library, which belonged to the economic historian Eileen Power, this passage about ambitions on Aachen is underlined, and in the margin Power noted that 'Freeman says no other authority mentions this story. Prob. however a crystallized rumour embedded in L.') [MCP]; for Ireland *Anglo-Saxon Chronicle s.a.* 1087; for Odo *Orderic*, iv. 38–40, Malmesbury, *Gesta Regum*, ii. 554, *Hyde Chronicle*, p. 296; for Robert Malmesbury, *Gesta Regum*, ii. 552.
7   For the dispatch of troops to Norway by John in 1201 see *Pipe Roll 3 John*, ed. D.M. Stenton (PRS, 1936), 157, 264.

the period, to ask whether the changes which took place were those of kind or of degree, and to consider how war influenced and reflected the changes in English society and government. Large claims have been made for the significance of the battle of Hastings: England then received 'a new royal dynasty, a new aristocracy, a virtually new Church, a new art, a new architecture and a new language'.[8] And of Bouvines, taken in conjunction with the battles of Las Navas de Tolosa and Muret in the two preceding years, a distinguished French historian (and of the school of the *Annales* at that) has recently claimed that it 'fixed for centuries the destiny of all the states of Europe'.[9] For my purposes it is enough to take these two dates merely as enclosing the history of what historians call the Norman and the Angevin empires.

The Regius Professor recently told us (in his previous capacity as Chichele Professor of the History of War) that until comparatively recently past wars were studied in order to deduce either immutable principles or lines of development as guides to the efficient conduct of war in the future. But, he continued, the historian's task is very different: he has to study war not merely in the framework of political history but in that of economic, social and cultural history as well.[10] Historians of early modern and modern Europe have been especially vocal in urging that the history of war is too important to be left to staff colleges or institutes of strategic studies (e.g. G.N. Clark on the modern state; Lewis Namier on social history, 'the social history of nations is largely moulded by the forms and development of their armed forces'; and Richard Pares's statement that the Second World War should have 'destroyed some of the blinkers which historians wore when they considered the subject of war', calling particular attention to the evidence which war and the preparations for war offer about the state of society and the economic effects of war on society).[11]

If, attentive to these admonitions, we consider war in its wider aspects, seeking to link it with the forms and methods of government, the social structure, the economy and habits of thought, there is a strong *prima facie* case for giving a large place to war in the years and in the area I have chosen to consider. Three periods stand out conspicuously in respect of the scale, duration and intensity of warfare. The forty years between the battles of Hastings and of Tinchebray were years of almost continuous military effort in the making, defence and maintenance of the Norman empire. Historians have not yet reached agreement, and they probably never will, on the precise effects of this military effort on society and government. But it is difficult to agree with Richardson and Sayles that the effects were minimal, that changes in the character of the English monarchy were 'more apparent than real', that 'the structure of the state remains essentially as it was', and that 'below the seat of power the changes at first were few or none'.[12] The Domesday Survey was carried out

---

8   R.H.C. Davis, *The Normans and their Myth* (London, 1976), 103.
9   Georges Duby, *Le Dimanche de Bouvines* (Paris, 1973), 183.
10 M. Howard, *War in European History* (Oxford, 1976), ix–x.
11 R. Pares, 'Recent British Works on Modern British History', *Bulletin of the Institute of Historical Research* 21 (1946–8), 116–127.
12 H.G. Richardson and G.O. Sayles, *The Governance of Mediaeval England from Conquest to Magna Carta* (Edinburgh, 1963), 33.

under the shadow of a threatened invasion of England. If it was merely a routine administrative operation of a kind long familiar, it is difficult to understand why contemporaries, ordinarily uninterested in such matters, should have described the carrying out of the Survey in such detail and with such mixed emotions of awe and consternation. And it requires a remarkably callous disposition, or an undiscerning eye, to emerge from a reading of Domesday Book persuaded that for those below the seat of power life went on much as it had done under the Confessor. It was not so here at Oxford which Salter found to present in 1086 'a striking picture of poverty, depopulation and misery'; it was not so at York, Norwich, Lincoln and Shrewsbury; and it was conspicuously not so at Chester where Domesday, for once not content with the figures, emphasised that when Earl Hugh received the city it was indeed wasted, *valde enim erat vastata*.[13]

Military considerations also entered into the reorganization of the English church during this period. Archbishop Lanfranc's concern with matters of defence and internal security are well known.[14] Less familiar perhaps is the evidence showing that considerations of defence entered into the policy of transferring bishops' sees from vills to cities. When Bishop Leofric moved his see from Crediton to Exeter in 1050 the contemporary documents referred to the frequent devastation of Devon and Cornwall by pirates and to the consequent need to place the cathedral within the walls of Exeter where it would be safe – or safer – against enemies (*ab hostilitatis incursu liber; infra moenia eiusdem urbis . . . tutiorem munitionem adversus hostes*).[15] No such direct evidence exists for the more numerous transfers of sees after the Conquest, but the very choice of Norwich, Lincoln, Chester, Salisbury and Chichester in place of Elmham, Dorchester, Lichfield, Sherborne and Selsey is suggestive. And it is significant that when William of Malmesbury, who had a good eye for sites and buildings, noted the move to Salisbury he should have described the new site as 'a castle instead of a city, on high ground, and protected by a substantial wall'.[16] Similarly Henry of Huntingdon, writing from local knowledge, described the new cathedral of Lincoln as 'on the high ground of the city next to the castle . . . a strong church in a strong place and a beautiful church in a beautiful site . . . both acceptable to those serving God and, as the times required, impregnable by enemies'.[17]

The second of my periods conspicuous for the scale and duration of warfare is that of the nineteen years of, to choose a reasonably neutral term, the reign of Stephen. Here the problem of interpretation is particularly acute. Historians have recently argued that it does not deserve all the harsh things said at the time and since, that conditions of anarchy were neither universal nor continuous, that the governmental machine survived in some sort of working order, and that the

[13] *DB*, i. 262b.

[14] See e.g. *Letters, Lanfranc*, 31–6; *The Vita Wulfstani of William of Malmesbury*, ed. R.R. Darlington (Camden 3rd ser. xl, 1928), 56; *Hugh the Chanter*, 5.

[15] The *Leofric Missal* and King Edward's charter in *Councils and Synods, A.D.871–1204*, ed. D. Whitelock, M. Brett and C.N.L. Brooke, part I, no. 71.

[16] Malmesbury, *Gesta Pontificum*, p. 185.

[17] Huntingdon, *Historia Anglorum*, p. 212.

disturbances were exceptional only as contrasted with the stern rule of the Norman kings who preceded Stephen and the firm authority of Henry II who followed.[18] We must certainly make allowance, a large allowance, for the constructive energies within English society in Stephen's reign. It is certainly very tempting to apply a reductionist analysis to the civil war of Stephen's reign, the war for the succession, There is McFarlane's general consideration that only undermighty kings had overmighty subjects. Stephen, it has been argued, was conspicuously undermighty, in the eyes of the Anglo-Saxon chronicler 'a mild man, and soft and good, and did no justice',[19] and in the opinion of his modern critics vain, sly, shifty, lacking in stamina and guilty of mean perverse stupidity, a man to whom the intricacies of administration were probably so much double Dutch, guilty of blunder after blunder, weak and unstable.[20] Only a series of disastrous mistakes by Stephen enabled the Empress Matilda and her brother, Robert earl of Gloucester, to land in England in the autumn of 1139 and to dispute the succession by arms. Still more recently it has been argued that McFarlane's description of the Staffords and the Beauchamps of a later period as 'less factious backwoodsmen than watchful trimmers' can be applied with perfect justice to the aristocracy of Stephen's reign.[21] On this view the leading magnates in England sought to minimize the effects of the war of succession, aiming not at baronial autonomy but at security under lordship, a lordship finally found and gratefully accepted when in November 1153 the succession dispute was finally resolved in favour of the future Henry II.

The gains in knowledge and in sympathetic understanding of character and motives have been very substantial. And on a more general view it becomes much easier to account for the more creative achievements within English society during the civil war: the very rapid extension of the new religious orders; ecclesiastical building at Norwich, Bury St Edmunds, Romsey, Winchester and Lincoln; the patronage of art and letters; and the qualities of enterprise and organization in the expedition which captured Lisbon in 1147, an expedition containing a large Anglo-Norman contingent and which installed Gilbert of Hastings as bishop of Lisbon. If the machinery of government did indeed survive in reasonably good working order it becomes much easier to understand the apparent ease with which Henry II restored order and stability. Not all the military captains of this period were predatory opportunists. Richard de Lucy first appears as a flamboyant commander of the garrison at Falaise which he held for Stephen in 1138.[22] He was still fighting for Stephen in the summer of 1153 when he encountered Duke Henry's forces in the mid-Thames valley and was driven back to Oxford.[23] And in 1173–74 he was again actively engaged in both England and Scotland, though this time in the service of Henry II. He

---

[18] For example H.A. Cronne, *The Reign of Stephen* (London, 1970), 1–5.
[19] *Anglo-Saxon Chronicle, sub anno* 1137.
[20] R.H.C. Davis, *King Stephen* (London, 1967), 31 and *passim*; Cronne, *Reign of Stephen*.
[21] E. King, 'King Stephen and the Anglo-Norman Aristocracy', *History*, lix (1974), 180–94.
[22] *Orderic*, vi. 526 and n. 2.
[23] Torigny, 174.

succeeded to some of Geoffrey de Mandeville's offices in the south-east in 1143, and for almost a quarter of a century served Henry II as justiciar.

Nevertheless it is very difficult to accept the reductionist thesis when it is applied to the character and consequences of warfare in Stephen's reign. First, the appearance of a clear-cut civil war between two parties is illusory. As William of Newburgh put it, neither Stephen nor the empress could control their own factions.[24] Second, it was not merely a war over the succession to the throne of England. To Geoffrey of Anjou it was a war for the control of Normandy, a war which he had won by 1145. To David I of Scotland it was a war for the expansion of his kingdom into the north of England, a war which enabled him to make Carlisle his capital. And to the Welsh it was a war of revenge and recovery, a war sustained with remarkable determination and success. Gerald of Wales remembered it in the south as the great war, *guerra illa grandis*; and for Sir John Lloyd in his *History of Wales* this was the period of 'the national revival'.[25] Third, there is the cumulative force of the narrative sources cogently marshalled eighty years ago by H.W.C. Davis,[26] and these can be reinforced by those for the north of England, left out of Davis's reckoning, and by more local sources than he chose to cite. The Durham monks received detailed reports of the activities of robber bands in Nottinghamshire, where they had outlying estates; and one of these was the more formidable in that it was run by the castellan of Nottingham.[27] One of the most revealing passages is that in which the author of the *Gesta Stephani* paid reluctant tribute to the good order maintained by Robert earl of Gloucester in the west country in 1143, though with the major qualification that he made heavy demands for forced labour on castles, for troops and for money: it was, the passage continues, merely a semblance of peace, *umbra quaedam pacis*, a condition in which men worked not for themselves but for others, increasing by their efforts the causes of strife and war.[28] Henry of Anjou may finally have been accepted as the successor to the throne in November 1153 because, as Stenton put it, 'responsible persons of every class were tired of the civil war';[29] but it had taken eight months of active campaigning by Henry to make men aware of their responsibilities. Some of his troops behaved with such brutality that they had to be sent back across the Channel.[30] We seriously underestimate the difficulties and achievements of Henry II if we assume that he took over a country of which the bulk of the inhabitants, the economy and the machinery of government had been only slightly affected by the years of war, and that he found his leading subjects anxious for the smack of firm government.

24 Newburgh, *Historia*, i. 69.
25 J.E. Lloyd, *A History of Wales from the Earliest Times to the Edwardian Conquest* (London, 1912), ii, ch. xiii.
26 H.W.C. Davies, 'The Anarchy of Stephen's Reign', *EHR* xviii (1903), 630–41.
27 *Reginaldi monachi Dunelmensis Libellus de admirandis Beati Cuthberti*, ed. J. Raine (Surtees Soc. i, 1835), 127–36.
28 *Gesta Stephani*, 148–50.
29 F.M. Stenton, *The First Century of English Feudalism, 1066–1166* (2nd edn, Oxford, 1961), 248.
30 *Gesta Stephani*, 250–2.

The third of my periods of major military effort, extending from the accession of Richard I in 1189 to the battle of Bouvines on 27 July 1214, is very different in character. It saw the great Mediterranean campaign of Richard I which enabled the kingdom of Jerusalem (more properly of Acre) to survive for another century and which by the capture of Cyprus gave the west a strategic post in the eastern Mediterranean which endured for almost four centuries. The wars and diplomacy of the two decades following Richard's release from captivity in 1194 are commonly treated as centring on the loss of Normandy in 1204; ten years dominated by the efforts of Richard and John to defend it followed by ten years of efforts to recover it, efforts finally frustrated at Bouvines. That we look on these two decades in this way is a tribute to the power, scholarship and title of Sir Maurice Powicke's great book, *The Loss of Normandy*. But Sir Maurice, very properly, chose to concentrate on the fate of the duchy of Normandy: he knew very well that much more was at stake. What Philip Augustus aimed at was the destruction of Angevin power in the west. When he negotiated his marriage to Ingeborg of Denmark in 1193 he hoped to take over the old Danish claims to the English throne and, to make those claims good, to have the use of the Danish army and fleet for a year.[31] The sensible Danes had better uses for their armed forces in the Baltic, and Philip had to settle for a large cash dowry with the wife he so promptly discarded. Nevertheless England was threatened with invasion from the Channel ports in 1193 and again in 1205 and 1213. Moreover by 1206 Philip Augustus had gained not merely Normandy but, as Ralph of Coggeshall pointed out, Anjou, Brittany, Maine, Touraine and almost all of Poitou.[32]

King John's measures in the face of these threats and massive losses have been censured as 'an impossible policy of restoring his position in France', and Sir Richard Southern went on to invite us to consider 'how much more might have been won in Ireland, Scotland and Wales at a fraction of the cost of maintaining the Continental connection'.[33] But to John in these years, down to 27 July 1214, the position and the prospects appeared very differently. By successive campaigns in 1209, 1210 and 1211 he had won a great deal in Scotland, Ireland and Wales: so much that a contemporary commented that in these countries 'there was now no one who did not obey his nod, which, as is very well known, had not been the case under any of his predecessors'.[34] His diplomatic agents were active, and with a large measure of success, on a wide arc extending from Norway through Denmark, Germany, the Low Countries, Toulouse and Navarre to Aragon; and of course in Rome. In the summer of 1213 his fleet surprised the French fleet at anchor off Damme, the port of Bruges, and destroyed it. When John crossed to La Rochelle in February 1214 he could be reasonably confident. He secured the lower Garonne, won over the Lusignans, entered Angers, and his expensively subsidised allies from Germany finally wheeled into action. Their defeat at Bouvines was decisive though not inevi-

---

[31] Newburgh, *Historia*, i. 368; Howden, *Chronica*, iii. 224.
[32] Coggeshall, 146.
[33] R.W. Southern, *Medieval Humanism and Other Studies* (Oxford, 1970), 139.
[34] Walter of Coventry, ii. 205.

table. As William le Breton put it 'the goddess of battles fluttered in the air above the combatants as if uncertain to whom to give the victory'.[35] Indeed at one point Philip himself was unhorsed by the German infantry and saved only by his armour.

Certain general characteristics distinguish the warfare of these twenty-five years. First, the geographical scale on which it was conducted and the issues which were decided. Richard's Mediterranean campaign changed the balance of power in the eastern Mediterranean. The victories of Philip Augustus in the decade from 1204 to 1214 went far towards giving his kingdom its frontiers on the Channel coast, the Atlantic, the Pyrenees and the Mediterranean. Second the English royal records repeatedly strike notes of urgency, intransigence and ideological bitterness. When John asked the Irish church for an aid in 1204 he described Philip Augustus as acting against God and reason, and himself as confronting the greatest emergency which had arisen or could arise.[36] When invasion was threatened in 1205 John ordered total mobilization, and he proclaimed in almost Churchillian terms that if the aliens came (and he was careful to choose the emotive term 'aliens', later employed against his own regime in Magna Carta), all were to oppose them with force and arms.[37] Crusading ideology was beginning to be injected into the conflicts within western Europe. In 1188 it was decided, during the preparations for the Third Crusade, that the king of France and his forces should wear red crosses, the king of England and his forces white crosses, and the count of Flanders and his forces green crosses. The course of that crusade suggests that the different colours of the crosses soon came to count for more than their common shape. It was as a crusader that the king of Aragon was victorious against the Almohads in 1212; and it was by a crusader, Simon de Montfort, that he was defeated and killed in the following year. One source tells us that the Flemings wore crosses at the battle of Bouvines; and it was as crusaders bearing the white cross of the Angevins that the royalists fought and won at Lincoln in 1217.[38]

A third characteristic, the prominence of sea power, must be reserved for later discussion. One striking piece of evidence is afforded by Roger of Howden. Roger, who had had personal experience of Mediterranean waters, believed that in 1200 the Sicilian admiral Margarit offered to make Philip Augustus emperor of the west or of the east – Rome or Constantinople – whichever he preferred. On Philip's ready acceptance (though Howden does not tell us which of the two empires Philip chose) Margarit left Paris, ordered his galleys to assemble at Brindisi, but was unluckily murdered at Rome, thus putting an end to these exciting schemes.[39] But Venetian sea power was very soon to be a reality at Constantinople.

The fourth characteristic of these years is that apart from John's rebellion

---

[35] Quoted by Duby, *Bouvines*, 58.
[36] *Foedera*, I, i. 90.
[37] *Foedera*, I, i. 92.
[38] *The Political Songs of England*, ed. T. Wright (London, 1839), 25; 'The Annals of Dunstable', in *Ann. Mon.*, iii. 226; 'Annals of Waverley', in *Ann. Mon.*, ii. 287.
[39] Howden, *Chronica*, iv. 121–2.

during Richard's crusade there was no campaigning in England: it was a war base, often on a war footing, dominated by the royal castles on which so much was spent and in which, by the end of our period, a huge war reserve of about 200,000 marks had been accumulated.[40] That force played a large part in maintaining internal security within the English war base is sufficiently demonstrated by the events of the seven weeks which elapsed between the death of Richard and the coronation of John in the spring of 1199. Howden tells us that all who had castles – bishops as well as earls and barons – then fortified them with men, victuals and arms.[41] That the administration under Geoffrey fitz Peter took the threat very seriously is shown by the recorded expenditure on hiring troops, victualling, garrisoning and repairing the royal castles throughout the country from Carlisle to Dover and from Cornwall to Colchester.[42] That political management also played a large part is plain from the promises made at Northampton by Hubert Walter, William Marshal and Geoffrey fitz Peter in a meeting to which they had summoned the leading malcontents.[43] John remained to the end a highly sensitive politician. In the early months of 1213, for example, he was simultaneously buying time at home by political methods and buying allies abroad in preparation for the great assault against Philip Augustus. Here the problem of interpretation, and of judgement, is to decide how large a place to assign to military resources and how much to allow for the arts of political management and propaganda.[44]

This rapid review of warfare in the making and maintenance of the Norman empire, in the civil war of Stephen's reign, and in the ambitious strategy pursued by Richard and John has been intended to remind you of some of the salient events we have to interpret, and to establish at least a *prima facie* case for holding that a large place must be assigned to war in the general English history of this period. But medievalists may allow themselves a quiet or even a complacent smile when they hear those of their colleagues concerned with more recent periods proclaiming with the zeal of recent converts the need to recognize – to quote one distinguished authority – that 'war has been part of a totality of human experience'.[45] For medievalists have been accustomed to consider war in just this way since at least the eighteenth century, relating it to the economy, social structure, government and modes of thought by employing the general concept of feudalism.

To expound the concept of feudalism, to assess its influence, to examine the difficulties experienced in applying it, and to trace with admiration the modifications and refinements which have enabled many of its exponents to conquer

---

[40] J.E.A. Jolliffe, 'The Chamber and the Castle Treasures under King John', in *Studies in Medieval History presented to F.M. Powicke* (Oxford, 1948), 135.

[41] Howden, *Chronica*, iv. 88; and compare Coggeshall, 98 for a more dramatic account

[42] *Pipe Roll 1 John*, ed. D.M. Stenton (PRS, 1933), pp. xiii–xv for a summary of these measures.

[43] *de quibus plus dubitabant*, Howden, *Chronica*, iv. 88.

[44] Compare *Foedera*, I. i. 108 for John's dispatch of £6,000 to Otto IV with *Rot. Lit. Pat.*, 97 for John's proclamation to all in Lincolnshire and Yorkshire.

[45] Howard, *War in European History*, x.

fresh areas in time and in space would require a separate set of lectures; though I cannot resist the temptation to call attention to the work of Gilbert Stuart in the late eighteenth century, agreeably entitled *A View of Society in Europe, in its Progress from Rudeness to Refinement: or, Inquiries concerning the History of Law, Government, and Manners* (Edinburgh, first edn 1778, second edn 1792). The publishers in their preface to the second edition discouragingly observed that 'the historians of the feudal system have never been distinguished for popularity', that 'Du Cange and Spelman are sufficient to chill the nerves of the most ardent reader' and that they had accordingly supplied translations of the Latin passages full of barbarous words and 'entirely inexplicable by a common dictionary'. Evidently Stuart had something in common with John Horace Round, for his publishers found it necessary to say that 'personal animosity was, we hope, buried in his grave'. Nevertheless they were right in stressing the work's 'uncommon merit'.

Despite the difficulties experienced in defining the nature and establishing the chronology of feudalism it may seem that it is still the best, as it has long been the most favoured, model available to us for solving the general problem of interpretation in the period I have chosen to consider. The essential elements of the model, stated in its simplest terms, are as follows. First, English society in the century after the Norman Conquest was a society organized specifically for war, the basis of the conditional tenure of land. Knights trained to fight on horseback and the network of castles were the instruments of war and coercive rule. From the territorial magnates, the tenants in chief, kings obtained unpaid service in the field and in garrisoning the royal castles; and they governed with the advice of their magnates, their natural counsellors. Military and political power lay preponderantly in the hands of the greater barons; they were the immediate lords of the knights; their castles outnumbered those of the king; and their honours were feudal states in miniature. Hence, as Stenton put it, the work of the Norman kings depended to a great extent on baronial loyalty and the feudal army remained the ultimate defence of the land.[46]

Second, the model of feudalism is comprehensive: its parts interlock. Postan took it as having been established by Stenton's Ford Lectures that during the greater part of the twelfth century England suffered from 'the seizure of land by turbulent neighbours and all other incidents of feudal and civil war', 'a *malaise* which affected England as a whole', and he used this to support his view that the system of estate management during this period 'was everywhere inimical to expansion'.[47] Stenton set the famous oath of Salisbury of 1086 into the feudal framework when he taught us that it was an exaction of homage and fealty from the honorial barons, the leading followers of the tenants in chief.[48] Galbraith placed the Domesday Survey of the same year firmly in the same context, concluding that 'the Normans were never so feudal as when they first arrived in England, and Domesday Book was their supreme and successful effort to wrest

---

[46] Stenton, *First Century*, 217.
[47] M.M. Postan, 'Glastonbury Estates in the Twelfth Century: A Reply', *EcHR* 2nd ser., ix (1956), 117–18.
[48] Stenton, *First Century*, 113.

the intractable material of O.E. tenures into the feudal form in which alone they could understand it'.[49] It has even been argued that Anselm's greatest work, the *Cur Deus Homo* was irretrievably feudal in temper; and although Sir Richard Southern has rejected this view he emphasised that the feudal *servitium debitum* was at the centre of Anselm's thought about the relations of God and man.[50]

In later lectures I shall make little use of the concept of feudalism. This is with no lack of respect for the historians who have found it helpful and illuminating, least of all for Sir Frank Stenton, its most powerful and influential exponent for the first century of my period. It is not always remembered that Stenton's *First Century of English Feudalism* was not, and did not claim to be, a study of English society: it was, as he clearly explained, a study of the lay honours designed to illustrate *some* features of Anglo-Norman history, or, to put it more colloquially, history written from the records of the estate offices rather than from dispatches from the field and reports of war correspondents.[51] It is less often remembered that a few years after his Ford Lectures Stenton issued the warning that 'generalisations about the political tendencies of that super-abstraction called feudalism need to be controlled by reference to the history of individual families'. Of the rebellions of the 150 following the Norman Conquest he observed, in words that might almost have been written by Namier, that 'most of them represent the elementary instincts of simple-minded men – loyalty to a dead king's eldest son, a great lord's fear of an unfriendly king, sympathy with a king's sons held back from power, ambition for great place'.[52] Moreover when Stenton printed the text of a mid-twelfth-century agreement between two Lincolnshire barons he added a footnote in which he commented that the arrangements in question 'give a remarkable illustration of the influence of money on feudal relationships, an influence which is often underestimated'.[53]

Nevertheless when we turn from the records of the baronial honours to the wider evidence on the conduct of war under the Norman kings we find that the influence of money was conspicuous: so conspicuous that we must accuse some of our witnesses not of underestimating it but of exaggerating it. The Normans, William of Malmesbury wrote, were a warlike people who if they could not succeed by force did so by trickery and money: they were disloyal to their lords at a slight affront, judging treachery by its outcome and changing their opinions for money.[54] In 1094 the French forces entered Normandy but, according to Henry of Huntingdon, 'thanks to Rufus's cleverness and money the king of France withdrew, and so his whole army vanished in the dark clouds of

---

49 V.H. Galbraith, 'The Making of the Domesday Book', *EHR* lvii (1942), 161–77.
50 R.W. Southern, *St Anselm and his Biographer* (Cambridge, 1963), 108, 110.
51 Stenton, *First Century*, vii.
52 F.M. Stenton, 'The Changing Feudalism of the Middle Ages', *History*, xix, (1934–35), 289–301. The reference to Sir Lewis Namier's work is to his seminal study of eighteenth-century politics, L.B. Namier, *The Structure of Politics at the Accession of George III* (2nd edn, London, 1957) [MCP].
53 Stenton, *First Century*, 50.
54 Malmesbury, *Gesta Regum*, ii. 506.

money'.[55] Henry I's success in 1119 in dissolving the powerful coalition against him in Normandy and the neighbouring territories of France, Flanders and Anjou produced particularly bitter remarks on Henry's distribution of pensions, gifts and promises. The Hyde chronicler reported that avarice led all William Clito's supporters to abandon him, despite the oaths they had sworn and the faith they had pledged.[56] Suger singled out Fulk count of Anjou: despite being bound to the king of France by homage, oaths and hostages he put avarice before fealty and came to terms with Henry I.[57]

In assessing the value of these general statements we must make allowance, perhaps a large allowance, for the readiness of these writers to moralize. Avarice was a stock vice easily attached to rulers, as it was attached to the Conqueror by William of Malmesbury, to Rufus by Orderic Vitalis,[58] and to Henry I by Henry of Huntingdon.[59] Belief in the power of money to corrupt was not always well founded. Eadmer reported suspicions that gold and silver were preferred to justice in the papal court.[60] But although the archbishop of Canterbury set off for Rome in 1116 in the belief, so we are told, that everything there was for sale, his efforts proved fruitless.[61] Nevertheless the cumulative evidence is too great in volume, too widely distributed, the illustrative details too specific, and the supporting record evidence too convincing to allow us to discount or to ignore the corrosive power of money in war and diplomacy, what William of Malmesbury in an expressive phrase termed the violence of money, *violentia denariorum*.[62]

It is best therefore to begin by attending to the language of our sources with minds unencumbered by the concept of feudalism, a concept wholly foreign to those sources. William of Malmesbury tells us of the defence of the *respublica* against the barbarians in 1085, not of a feudal kingdom against the Danes.[63] The Winchester Annals describe the Domesday Survey as the product of a royal edict, not of feudal counsel,[64] and we hear much of these royal edicts by Rufus and Henry I.[65] William of Poitiers, the biographer of the Conqueror, drew extensively on his classical reading, instituting an elaborate comparison between his master and Julius Caesar, awarding the palm to the former. Our first reaction is to change Galbraith's dictum and to conclude that the Normans were never so Roman as when they first arrived. It should not be our only, or our last reaction; but it is a healthily corrective reaction.

[55] Huntingdon, *Historia Anglorum*, 217.
[56] *Hyde chronicle*, 519–20.
[57] Suger, *Vie de Louis VI*, 194–6.
[58] *Orderic*, iv. 174.
[59] Huntingdon, *Historia Anglorum*, 512.
[60] Eadmer, *Historia Novorum*, 69.
[61] Hugh the Chantor, *The History of the Church of York, 1066–1127*, ed. C. Johnson (1961), 49–51.
[62] Malmesbury, *Gesta Pontificum*, 129.
[63] *Vita Wulfstani*, 56.
[64] *Annales Monasterii de Wintonia*, in *Ann. Mon.*, ii. 34.
[65] e.g. Malmesbury, *Gesta Regum*, ii. 369, 372, 470, 476; *Orderic*, vi. 66, 182.

Note on further reading

The question of English identity has received much recent attention. See J. Gillingham's collection of papers, *The English in the Twelfth Century: Imperialism, National Identity and Political Values* (Woodbridge, 2000), in particular 'Henry of Huntingdon and the Twelfth-Century Revival of the English Nation' (123–144), where he argues for an awareness of Englishness among the rulers of England by the mid-twelfth century. Ian Short, 'Tam Angli quam Franci: Self-Definition in Anglo-Norman England', *Anglo-Norman Studies* xviii (1996) also points to the middle of the century as a time when the 'Anglo-Normans' might term themselves as English. At the same time, there has also been increased awareness of the importance of the British context; see for example Robin Frame, *The Political Development of the British Isles 1100–1400* (Oxford, 1990), and R.R. Davies, *Domination and Conquest: The Experience of Ireland, Scotland and Wales 1100–1300* (Cambridge, 1990).

The warfare of the Norman period has been the object of study by S. Morillo, *Warfare under the Anglo-Norman Kings 1066–1135* (Woodbridge, 1994), a book based on a thesis examined by JOP. The history of battles was treated with a certain disdain by JOP, but J. Bradbury, 'Battles in England and Normandy, 1066–1154', *Anglo-Norman Studies* vi (1983), 1–12 is a valuable study.

The reign of King Stephen attracts medieval historians like wasps to a honey-pot. A valuable collection of articles, many taking a revisionist line, was edited by Edmund King, *The Anarchy of Stephen's Reign* (Oxford, 1994). D. Crouch, *The Reign of King Stephen 1135–1154* (Harlow, 2000) offers a comprehensive and up-to-date coverage. Mention must also be made of M. Chibnall, *The Empress Matilda* (Oxford, 1991), and D. Matthew, *King Stephen* (London, 2002). For criticism of the term 'Anarchy' as applied to Stephen's reign, see G.J. White, 'The Myth of the Anarchy', *Anglo-Norman Studies* xxii (2000), 323–37. The end of the reign has been the object of study by G.J. White, *Restoration and Reform, 1153–1165: Recovery from Civil War in England* (Cambridge, 2000), and by E. Amt, *The Accession of Henry II in England: Royal Government Restored* (Woodbridge, 1993).

The military career of Richard I was examined more fully by JOP in his 'Richard Coeur de Lion: Rex Bellicosus', *Riccardo Cuor di Leone Nella Storia e Nella Legende* (Accademia Nazionale dei Lincei, Rome (1981), 1–15; reprinted in *Richard Coeur de Lion in History and Myth*, ed. J.L. Nelson (London, 1992). Richard also has been the subject of extensive study by John Gillingham, culminating in his major biography, *Richard I* (London, 1999).

For comments about JOP's views on feudalism, see below, 103.

2

The Conduct of War

Before considering some aspects of the conduct of war in this period (and I emphasise *some* aspects, since my treatment is necessarily highly selective), it is relevant to ask why the wars were fought. One temptingly simple answer was given by Galbraith when he warned us that the purely clerical narratives at our disposal are no good guides to what he called 'the outlook of the ruthless military adventurers who actually dictated the course of events . . . the only real realists in an age of turmoil'. Members of the baronial class, including kings, he continued, insisted that their sole business was that of fighting; and though he noted the interest which Henry II and John took in English administration, he stressed that they were far more intent upon continental adventures.[1] Other historians equally deserving the greatest respect have delivered similar judgements: Sir Richard Southern held that the Norman and Angevin kings were 'mesmerized by the prospect of Continental glory' and that for this end 'they were prepared to take every kind of risk'. Henry I's ambition to have Normandy as well as England was 'indefensible in its purpose, deleterious in its effects and unjust in its measures'.[2] Richard I has appeared as *par excellence* the irresponsible military adventurer. To Stubbs in the nineteenth century he was 'a man of blood', actuated by 'the mere delight of the struggle and the charm of victory', in short 'a bad ruler'.[3] To Stubbs's severest critics in the twentieth century, Richardson and Sayles, Richard was equally 'one of those noble knights', 'credited with vast dreams of empire', a man who had 'no conception of the relation of financial means to political ends' and 'no practical interest in administration'.[4]

It is not difficult to mobilize evidence in support of these judgements. Besides the opportunities offered to military adventurers within the Norman empire which straddled the Channel there was the example of that other Norman empire in the Mediterranean of Roger the Great of whom Orderic Vitalis wrote that 'with passionate violence he destroyed men near and far, and by cruelly causing much blood and many tears to be shed, so prospered that he was the first

[1] V.H. Galbraith, *Domesday Book: Its Place in Administrative History* (Oxford, 1974), 179–80.
[2] Southern, *Medieval Humanism*, 138–9, 213.
[3] '*Itinerarium Peregrinorum et Gesta Regis Ricardi*', in *Chronicles and Memorials of the Reign of Richard I*, i, ed. W. Stubbs (Rolls Series, 1864), xviii–xxvii.
[4] Richardson and Sayles, *Governance of Medieval England*, 328–9.

of his line to mount a royal throne'.[5] There was the prospect of adventure and gain in the Spanish peninsula which seduced one of the Conqueror's household knights[6] and, more significantly, Rotrou count of Perche on whom Henry I had bestowed one of his numerous illegitimate daughters in marriage, together with estates in England. Rotrou did good service for Henry I in three of his major campaigns; but in the intervals and afterwards he engaged in several expeditions in Spain, he and his men being tempted by the generous wages and splendid estates promised by his cousin, the king of Aragon.[7] Maritime expeditions from north-western Europe took part in several attacks on Lisbon before the successful siege of 1147 in which a large Anglo-Norman contingent took part.[8] The contemporary account of the siege of 1147 by one who took part in it put into the mouth of a Moorish defender a revealing attribution of motive. 'Neither the land nor the sea is enough for you', the Moor was made to say: 'it is not want but ambition of the mind which drives you on . . . you adjudge us to poverty and exile in order to achieve glory'.[9] And many adventurers in Normandy, including Henry I's household knight, Ralph the Red, succumbed to Bohemond of Antioch's recruiting drive in the west in 1106, tempted by promises of the rich rewards to be won by an attack on the eastern empire; though Henry I was careful to keep Bohemond out of England.[10] In the 1160s Ireland was opened up as a land of opportunity. William of Newburgh's description of Strongbow as ambitious, extravagant, impoverished, pursued by his creditors and hence the readier for great deeds presents us with the model of the adventurer.[11]

If Richard I was credited with dreams of empire he was not the first king since the Conquest to entertain wide ambitions, if we give credence to some of our witnesses. There were stories in Germany to the effect that the Conqueror was advancing on Aachen, while the Anglo-Saxon chronicler believed that if he had lived two years more he would have mastered Ireland. Suger reported that Rufus hoped to acquire the French throne; William of Malmesbury, more modestly, that he intended to acquire Poitou by the same methods as he had already acquired Normandy.[12] And Gerald of Wales alleged in a famous passage that the ambitions of Henry II extended not only to the kingdom of France but to the Roman Empire itself.[13] What made this charge plausible was Gerald's reference to Henry's agreement in 1173 (of which the text has survived) with the count of Maurienne, and which establishes beyond doubt Henry's interest in securing for the House of Anjou control of the castles, lands and passes which gave a passage into the upper Italian plain.[14]

---

5   *Orderic*, vi. 434.
6   *Orderic*, iv. 100.
7   *Orderic* vi. 396 and n. 1. See other references in the index for Rotrou's long career from his participation in the First Crusade down to his going over to Geoffrey of Anjou in 1141.
8   See the evidence assembled by C.W. David in his edition of *De Expugnatione*, 16–17.
9   *De Expugnatione*, 120.
10   *Orderic*, vi. 68–70.
11   Newburgh, *Historia*, i. 167–8.
12   Above, xx; *Suger, Vie de Louis le Gros*, 10; Malmesbury, *Gesta Regum*, ii. 379.
13   Gerald of Wales, *Opera*, viii. 157.
14   Howden, *Gesta*, i. 36–41 for the agreement; Diceto, i. 255; and especially Torigny, 250,

It is therefore tempting to ascribe the wars conducted by the Norman and Angevin kings largely to their ambition, greed and ruthlessness or to their need to satisfy or control the similar appetites of their leading subjects. And some of the evidence for the conduct of war can be used to support this interpretation of the objects of war. The harrying of the north and northern midlands by the Conqueror was certainly ruthless. Of this Stenton observed that 'the operations of 1069–70 were distinguished from ordinary warfare by a deliberate attempt to ruin the population of the affected districts'.[15] However, it is not at all clear that in so-called 'ordinary warfare' the non-combatant population was always, or indeed usually, spared. How for example had the Conqueror, as duke of Normandy, conducted his conquest of Maine in 1063? According to his biographer he did so with his usual restraint, *solita ilia temperantia*. He could have burned the city of Le Mans to the ground and have massacred his opponents. Instead he preferred to spare men's lives and to leave the city intact. His chosen method, the biographer continues, was to strike fear into the population by frequent and prolonged raids, to destroy vineyards, crops and villages, in short to afflict the population with a host of hardships. It is easier, William of Poitiers concluded, to imagine than to describe the terror produced by this treatment.[16] We may accept this account (and allow our imagination to play on the disagreeable details) partly because it was written by a man with experience of war and in praise of William's restraint, and partly because an entirely different source, the Anglo-Saxon Chronicle, gives a very similar though slightly heightened account of the Conqueror's methods in his later Maine campaign of 1073: the destruction of vineyards, the burning down of cities and the infliction of very severe damage on the country, an achievement noted with particular satisfaction on this side of the Channel since English troops were given the major credit.[17]

If Le Mans was spared from the flames in 1063 it and many other towns and cities were burnt in deliberate acts of war in campaign after campaign. It would be possible to give a very long list; but a few examples must stand for all. In 1119 Henry I attacked Evreux, strongly held by the citizens as well as by the garrison of the castle. He made no progress and finally summoned the bishop of the city, who was with him, and pointed out that the only hope of success lay in victory by fire, *victoria per incendium*. He added that this would mean that churches would be burnt and the innocent suffer great damage, but, if the bishop agreed, Henry and his magnates would pay for the rebuilding of the churches. The bishop did agree; and since the weather was dry the city was destroyed.[18] More ingenuity was shown by the Norman castellan of Bonneville in 1138. Geoffrey of Anjou's invading forces had occupied the neighbouring town of Touques (just outside Deauville). The castellan then formed a fire-raising party composed of prostitutes and poor boys and sent them into Touques at night. The

pointing out in connection with the count of Maurienne's first approach to Henry in 1171 that *nec aliquis potest adire Italiam nisi per terram ipsius.*

[15] F.M. Stenton, *Anglo-Saxon England* (2nd edn, Oxford, 1947), 596.
[16] *Gesta Guillelmi*, 60.
[17] *Anglo-Saxon Chronicle, s.a.* 1073; Florence, ii. 10; Malmesbury, *Gesta Regum*, ii. 316.
[18] *Orderic*, vi. 228.

first part of the plan worked: fires were lit in forty-six places in the four quarters of the town; the Angevin troops panicked; and their count tried to rally his men in a graveyard. But the prostitutes and boys had done their work only too well, for the smoke in Touques was too thick for the Norman castellan to deliver his intended assault on a demoralized enemy. In this period the expression 'by fire and sword' was not mere rhetoric, and it is probable that the torch was the more destructive instrument. The Conqueror's last sight on a campaign was of the town of Mantes in flames: six weeks later he died. Henry II's last sight of campaigning was of his birthplace, Le Mans, similarly destroyed; and four weeks later he was dead.[19]

Orderic Vitalis has a revealing story of Richer II de Laigle when engaged on a plundering raid in 1119. Richer and his knights were followed by distressed peasants hoping to recover, or even buy back, their livestock which Richer's men had added to the rest of their booty. Irritated by the importunate peasants the knights turned and charged them, whereupon the terrified peasants flung themselves down by a wayside crucifix. And Richer then gave orders for the lives of the peasants to be spared. Orderic's comment is that Richer's action in thus sparing about a hundred peasants, from whom he could have extorted a great price, was one that deserves to be remembered for ever; and this tells us much about the normal effects of war.[20] Indeed Orderic's account of the sufferings of the clergy, monastic communities and defenceless populace of Normandy under Robert Curthose is, as Haskins noted, convincingly illustrated by the long schedule which the nuns of Holy Trinity at Caen then compiled of their losses year after year in land, cattle, produce, rents and men, 'a matter-of-fact summary more eloquent of the Norman anarchy than are many pages of the chronicler'.[21] It is noteworthy that the schedule lists among the offenders William count of Evreux, Nigel d'Oilly, Robert of Mowbray, the future Henry I and Ranulf brother of Ilger, sheriff of Huntingdonshire.

Occasionally we are given a description of total war as a set policy. We are told that in 1149 King Stephen considered how best to break his opponents and, after taking advice from various quarters, decided 'to attack the enemy everywhere, plunder and destroy all that was in their possession, set fire to the crops and every other means of supporting human life, and let nothing remain anywhere'.[22] 'First lay waste the land, then destroy one's enemies' was the advice of the count of Flanders in 1173.[23] Hence, if the Conqueror's harrying of the north was distinguished from the ordinary methods of warfare it was in its scale and not in its methods.

Nevertheless it would be wrong to argue from the conduct of war to the objects for which wars were fought, to suppose that because many instances of ruthlessness can be cited throughout our period the Norman and Angevin kings went to war because they and their followers were 'ruthless military adventurers'

[19] *Orderic*, iv. 78; Howden, *Gesta*, ii. 67.
[20] *Orderic*, vi. 248–50.
[21] C.H. Haskins, *Norman Institutions* (Cambridge, 1918), 62–4.
[22] *Gesta Stephani*, 218.
[23] *Jordan Fantosme's Chronicle*, ed. and trans. R.C. Johnston (Oxford, 1981), ll. 449–50.

whose sole business was that of fighting, committed to aggression and dreaming of empire. When rulers went to war they considered it necessary to justify their action. They commonly did so by claiming to be asserting or defending their rights, or for a cause acceptable to, even enjoined by, the church. Frequently they claimed both legal and moral right as, notoriously, did the Conqueror when he claimed the bequest of England by the Confessor, the confirmation of this by Harold's oath, and the backing of the papacy. Sometimes a claim was very thin, as when Stephen alleged a deathbed designation in his favour by Henry I; and accordingly his claim had to be fortified by papal confirmation.[24] Sometimes a claim rested on an allegation of ancient facts, as when the Conqueror claimed the Vexin on the grounds of a supposed grant to his father fifty-four years previously.[25] Sometimes claims went back much further. It might be thought that the crusaders needed no further justification for their attack on Lisbon in 1147 than that the city was held by infidels. But the archbishop of Braga when demanding the surrender of Lisbon did so on the grounds that the original Moorish conquest 358 years previously had been fraudulent. He even made concessions to the Moorish claims by virtue of long seisin, proposing that since the Moors had indeed held Lisbon for a long time (*usu longo*) they should be allowed to remain and to follow their own customs, provided only that they surrendered the castle.[26]

We may well believe Orderic Vitalis when he tells us that those from regions outside Normandy who flocked in to join Duke William's enterprise in 1066 were panting for the spoils of England;[27] we may not believe that *all* these men were actuated by confidence in the justice of the cause as well as by Duke William's well-known generosity, as William of Poitiers claimed.[28] But it is to push scepticism too far to hold that Duke William had no belief in his cause and that he either failed to inspire a belief in its justice among *any* of his followers or did not even care to try. The claiming of rights and the advancing of justifications acceptable to the church mattered in this period, and especially to rulers and those who aspired to rule: they served both as an incentive to war when claims and justifications conflicted, as they commonly did, and as limiting the objectives of war.

William Rufus had a reputation among contemporaries as an outstanding soldier.[29] But if we consider his conduct of war it appears remarkably limited in its aims. He once told the count of Maine that he was determined to have whatever his father had held,[30] and his military operations were sensibly confined to the area thus demarcated. He did not even claim Normandy. If Orderic's account can be trusted, Rufus, when explaining his intention in 1089 to send an army to

---

[24] See Davis, *King Stephen*, 15–16.
[25] See Chibnall's discussion in *Orderic*, iv. xxx–xxxiii.
[26] *De Expugnatione*, 116–18.
[27] *Orderic*, ii. 144.
[28] *Gesta Guillelmi*, 102.
[29] e.g. *Orderic*, iv. 178 and v. 200 – *imperiosus et audax atque militaris erat; militia clarus;* Suger, *Vie de Louis VI*, 6, *usui militie aptus.*
[30] *Orderic*, v. 230.

Normandy, justified it on the grounds that he had received a tearful cry of distress from the holy church in Normandy, that the whole duchy was exposed to slaughter and rapine, and that it was his duty to succour the church, to protect defenceless widows and orphans, and to punish thieves and murderers with the sword of justice.[31] It was not until the beginning of 1091 that Rufus himself landed in Normandy, though his men and his money had preceded him, and even then Rufus chose to negotiate rather than fight. Ultimately in 1096 the whole of Normandy passed to Rufus not by conquest but in pledge for a term of years; and this perfectly proper procedure involved accepting Robert Curthose's title to the duchy. And when a lucky capture of the count of Maine encouraged Rufus to propose the invasion of Maine in 1098 he explained apologetically that he had been slow to regain his inheritance because he had been unwilling to disturb the inhabitants or cause the loss of life.[32]

If Rufus's actual campaigns are considered they will be seen to be cautious, prosaic, often indecisive and sometimes unsuccessful. He never fought a battle; he made slow work of the siege of Pevensey in 1088; he failed to take Bamburgh by arms in 1095; and in 1098, despite acting in concert with Duke William of Aquitaine, he failed to make good his father's claim to the French Vexin. It was by political methods rather than by the rough and undiscriminating use of force that Rufus triumphed in the highly dangerous crisis at the beginning of his reign. Chroniclers naturally stressed the measures of general import taken by Rufus; his promises to Lanfranc, confirmed at his coronation, his carrying out of his father's bequests to churches and the poor, and his written promises of general reforms, directed especially towards the English.[33] It is only from scattered notices that we can piece together Rufus's discreet but highly important dealings with Roger of Montgomery, William I de Warenne, Rufus's younger brother, Henry, and the twelve leading citizens of London. And there are hints that others were won over or usefully fortified in their loyalty. Hence Rufus was able to concentrate his military efforts in the south-east of England and to force the surrender of the intransigents at Rochester. Even then Rufus showed a surprising degree of restraint: he controlled his initial desire for vengeance, spared the lives of the Rochester garrison and condemned only a few to exile. Of these Robert of Bellême was reconciled with Rufus in the same year and came to enjoy his high favour.[34] William of St Calais, bishop of Durham was tried for treason in 1088 and given a safe conduct to go into exile; yet he too was restored to favour in 1091, and for the remaining four years of his life served as one of Rufus's leading advisers.

These themes of a concern with legal claims and moral justifications, the subordination of military means to political ends, great caution in the conduct of hostilities, a lack or a suppression of vindictiveness and a readiness to compromise recur frequently and sometimes where they might least be expected. When

---

[31] *Orderic*, iv. 178–80.
[32] *Orderic*, v. 238.
[33] *Florence*, ii. 21–5; Eadmer, *Historia Novorum*, 25.
[34] See J.F.A. Mason, 'Roger de Montgomery and his Sons (1067–1102)', *TRHS*, 5th ser., xiii (1963), 19–20.

in November 1191 Richard I demanded from Saladin the restoration of the whole kingdom of Jerusalem as it had existed in the time of Baldwin IV, the leper king (in whose health and prospects Henry II had shown so keen an interest in 1176[35]), he did so not as a defiant crusader but as one claiming his hereditary right.[36] It was Richard's hereditary right as head of the senior branch of the House of Anjou. The junior branch, which had produced four kings of Jerusalem, was at that time represented by one survivor, Isabella. This was no sudden or specious claim on Richard's part. Henry II had long shown a substantial interest in the fortunes of his relatives in the east and had backed that interest by transmitting to Jerusalem a sum estimated in 1187 at £20,000.[37] Richard's approach to the problems of the crusade after the fall of Acre was highly realistic. First there had to be an agreed settlement with Saladin and he opened negotiations very quickly. 'The Muslims and the Franks are bleeding to death, the country is utterly ruined and goods and lives have been sacrificed on both sides. The time has come to stop this.'[38] Second Richard recognised that Saladin would only come to terms under pressure, and that pressure was best applied not in attacking Saladin's army in the field, whence Saladin drew most of his supplies, but against Egypt. Contrary to what almost all historians of the crusades tell us Richard proclaimed Ascalon and not Jerusalem as his objective before his army left Acre (i.e. to threaten Egypt rather than to recover the holy places by direct attack.[39] Third Richard saw that any settlement – in the event a three-year truce, with the coastal strip from Tyre to Jaffa in Christian hands – could be only temporary and that any long-term solution depended upon adequate support from the west. Within a few weeks of the fall of Acre Richard warned the abbot of Clairvaux that after the crusaders had completed their task the kingdom would need both men and money by which it might be settled and defended – 'in populo, unde terra possit populari et muniri, et in pecunia'.[40]

It may be thought that Richard's policy in the east merely reflected the interests and the preferred strategy of the military orders and the native nobility. But his conduct of war in north-western Europe after his release from captivity indicates that his policy was to recover territory, not to gain it; to enforce an acceptable peace, not to commit himself to unlimited warfare and expense. William of Newburgh wrote of the concern in 1197 for an honest peace, a full peace, even of Richard and Philip Augustus as avid for peace. Hubert Walter negotiated the truce of 1197, intended to lead to a final settlement; and he was again negotiating for peace in September 1198, though the negotiations broke down over Richard's refusal to abandon his allies.[41] And we should probably accept

[35] Howden, Gesta, i. 116.
[36] Ambroise, ll. 7377–84.
[37] See H.E. Mayer, 'Henry II of England and the Holy Land', EHR xcvii (1982), 721–39.
[38] Baha ad-Din, cited by J. Gillingham, Richard the Lionheart (London, 1978), 194–6.
[39] Established on the independent evidence of Ambroise and Howden who were with the army at the time: Ambroise, ll. 5545–9; Howden, Gesta, ii. 185–6.
[40] Howden, Chronica, iii. 132.
[41] Newburgh, Historia, ii. 496; Gervase of Canterbury, Opera, i. 544; Howden, Chronica, iv. 61.

Richard's own justification for acquiring at such trouble and fortifying at such vast expense the site of Chateau-Gaillard: it had hitherto been weakly defended, offering to the enemy a gap through which to invade Normandy;[42] and Richard's remark about holding Chateau-Gaillard even if its walls had been made of butter tells in the same sense. If we judge Richard by what he did rather than in the light of the legends which so quickly gathered round him we must conclude that he fought to defend or to recover the rights of the house of Anjou, whether these lay in Sicily, Palestine, England or the continent. He was indeed prepared to surrender certain claims, as in Scotland in 1189 and in Toulouse in 1196, for the sake of what he considered more important objectives elsewhere.

Why then were both Rufus and Richard I considered as pre-eminently devoted to war and driven by dreams of empire? The short answer is that both men encouraged as well as attracted legends about themselves in their own life-times in order to maintain the morale of their own forces and in the hope of weakening the resolve of their enemies. They were not the last commanders who have found it useful to combine practical caution with personal panache. They had very different styles. Rufus liked to boast, to startle and to shock. He calculated his effects: William of Malmesbury tells us that his severity of manner in public was assumed: *affectato rigore feroci voce colloquentem reverberans* contrasted with *in triclinio cum privatis, omni lenitate accomodus.*[43] Richard relied more on his personal valour carried to the point of recklessness. He was not prepared to risk his army in the siege of Jerusalem, but he was ready to risk his own life again and again. For this he was rightly censured both by his own men and by Saladin.[44] He was wounded before the battle of Arsuf, exhausted and ill after his exertions at Jaffa, disabled for a month by a wound from a crossbow bolt in the summer of 1196, finally succumbing on 6 April 1199 to a similar wound.[45] Nevertheless it remains the case that Richard never fought on soil to which he, or a member of his house, had no claim, with the exception of Cyprus; and we shall return to a consideration of Richard's conquest of Cyprus later in the term. We do not ordinarily think of Richard as a family man, for we remember Stubbs's censure of him as a bad son and a bad husband. But we shall not understand Richard's campaigns and diplomacy unless we set them firmly in the context of his extensive family: his nephew, Otto of Brunswick, was successively earl of York, designated as heir to the throne of Scotland, then made count of Poitou, elected as king of Germany in 1198 and, as Otto IV, defeated at the battle of Bouvines which ends our story. There was Richard's youngest sister, Joan, who as the widowed queen of Sicily was collected by Richard on his crusade, together with her dowry and her husband's legacy, then used by Richard who, testing Saladin's readiness to negotiate, suggested that she should marry Saladin's brother, and finally married off by Richard to Raymond of Toulouse as part of a generous settlement which ended a long and damaging dispute. Two of Richard's nieces were employed in his negotiations for peace

[42] Diceto, ii. 154–5.
[43] Malmesbury, *Gesta Regum*, ii. 367.
[44] Ambroise, ll. 7085–175, 12146–52.
[45] Ambroise, ll. 6059–64, 11691–726; Devizes, 74, 79; Coggeshall, 95.

with Philip Augustus: in those of 1195 Eleanor of Brittany was to marry the heir to the French throne; and in those of 1199, on terms much more favourable to Richard, Blanche of Castile was substituted.[46]

We can indeed dismiss notions that any of the Norman and Angevin kings was a ruthless military adventurer dreaming of or planning empire in military conquest after military conquest, sharing the ambitions and seeking to emulate the legendary feats of Arthur celebrated by Geoffrey of Monmouth in his best-seller of the twelfth century, the *Historia Regum Britanniae*. Henry II's agreement with the count of Maurienne in 1173 on which writers from Gerald of Wales in the twelfth century down to the German scholar Hardegen[47] in the twentieth have largely founded their charges that Henry was aiming at the Roman empire, is most naturally interpreted as intended to secure for Henry's youngest son, John, marriage to an heiress and the prospect of becoming count of Maurienne (or as it came to be known, Savoy); possibly as helping to bring immediate pressure on the count of Toulouse; and at the very most as linked with Henry's cautious probing in northern Italy at a time when German power and influence there had been temporarily weakened.

In considering the place of war in the minds and recorded actions of the Norman and Angevin rulers some general statements deserve our attention. William of Malmesbury tells us that Henry I 'preferred to fight with policy rather than with the sword: he triumphed, if he could, without spilling blood; if he could not he spilt as little as possible'.[48] Of Henry II William of Newburgh wrote that 'hating the danger of bloodshed he sought to procure peace by arms if he could not do otherwise, but preferably by means of money whenever possible'.[49] Here it is relevant to ask how many battles were fought and how many were not. 'Battle' in this period is a term not susceptible of precise definition. But if we limit it to major set-piece engagements in which rulers of England were involved during our period we have the following list:

1066 Hastings (Harold and Duke William).
1079 Gerberoi (William I besieging the castle, held by Robert Curthose, and wounded in a sally by defenders).
1106 Tinchebray (Henry I and Robert Curthose).
1119 Brémule (Henry I and Louis VI).
1141 Lincoln (Stephen captured).
1143 Wilton (Stephen routed by Robert of Gloucester).
1191 Arsuf (Richard I on the march south from Acre).
1192 Jaffa (a rescue operation by Richard I).
1198 South of Gisors (Philip Augustus surprised by Richard and routed in a pursuit battle).

Three other battles of consequence can be added, though rulers of England were not involved in them: Bourg Thérould, 1124, ending the Norman rebellion; the

---

46 For all this see J.O. Prestwich, *Richard Coeur de Lion: Rex Bellicosus* (Rome, 1981).
47 F. Hardegen, *Imperialpolitik König Heinrichs II von England* (Heidelberg, 1905).
48 Malmesbury, *Gesta Regum*, ii. 488.
49 Newburgh, *Historia*, i. 282.

battle of the Standard, 1138, in which David I of Scotland's forces were defeated; and the so-called rout of Winchester, 1141, in which Robert earl of Gloucester was captured. The details of this list may well be questioned and one or two engagements added or subtracted. But its general significance is plain: twelve battles in all; nine in which rulers of England were engaged, only seven of these being fought in western Europe; no battles fought by Rufus, Henry II or John. It is a short tally for a century and a half.

Against this rough list of seven battles fought in western Europe by rulers of England we must set those in the same theatre which were not fought by these same rulers. By battles not fought I mean occasions on which opposing armies were mobilized and in contact (or a battle expected) without an engagement following. A little search gives the following:

1101	The invading army of Robert Curthose in contact with the forces of Henry I at Alton but a settlement reached.[50]
1119	Henry I very reluctant to fight at Brémule.[51]
1137	Stephen was dissuaded by his magnates from seeking a battle with Geoffrey of Anjou.[52]
1140	With only a short distance between the armies of Stephen and Robert of Gloucester the latter declined to fight and Henry withdrew to Bristol.[53]
1144	Stephen abandoned the siege of Tetbury since Roger of Hereford's forces were only two miles away and Robert of Gloucester was coming up to do battle.[54]
1153	The forces of Stephen and Henry of Anjou met twice, first at Malmesbury with only the River Avon dividing them, and than at Wallingford, separated this time by the Thames; but the result was not battle but negotiations leading to the treaty of Westminster which gave the succession to Henry of Anjou.[55]
1161	The armies of Henry II and Louis VII met. Each waited for the other to attack, and a truce followed.[56]
1173	Henry II drew up his army at Breteuil prepared to do battle against Louis VII, but the French asked for a day's truce and proposed a conference on the following day. When Henry came to the rendezvous his infantry complained that while they had been ready to fight on the previous day they were now tired from so much marching; but the more experienced soldiers praised Henry's caution. And in any event the French did not keep the rendezvous.[57]

---

[50] See C.W. Hollister, 'The Anglo-Norman Civil War: 1101', *EHR* lxxxviii (1973), 315–334.
[51] *Hyde Chronicle*, pp. 216–17, and Malmesbury, *Gesta Regum*, ii. 481.
[52] *Orderic*, vi. 484.
[53] *Gesta Stephani*, 104.
[54] *Gesta Stephani*, 172–4.
[55] Huntingdon, *Historia Anglorum*, 286–8; *Gesta Stephani*, 232, 238.
[56] Torigny, 210–11.
[57] *Howden, Gesta* i. 51–4.

1180   Both Henry II and Philip mobilized their armies, but the peace treaty of Yvry was renewed.[58]

1187   Both Henry II and Philip Augustus drew up their forces for a pitched battle ('*omnia parata essent ad pugnam*') but a truce for two years was concluded.[59]

1195   The armies of Richard I and Philip Augustus were drawn up for battle at Issoudun. It appeared, as William of Newburgh commented, that the day would determine the victor of the long struggle; but the French prudently and cautiously decided that their numbers were insufficient and that an honest peace was preferable to a retreat with Richard in pursuit.[60]

1197   William of Newburgh commented that the long and destructive war between Richard and Philip could have been brought to a swift end by the victory of one side; but both preferred to prolong it rather than to end it by staking, all on battle.[61]

This avoidance of battle is not a characteristic of ruthless military adventurers. Why then did rulers engaged in war show the caution on which contemporaries so frequently commented? Partly because battles were dangerous. Both the Conqueror and Rufus were wounded at Gerberoi.[62] Henry I had a narrow escape in Wales and was saved by his armour in 1118 and 1119;[63] Stephen was captured in the battle of Lincoln; Henry II had two lucky escapes at Limoges in 1183, saved first by his armour and then by his horse suddenly lifting its head and intercepting an arrow; and Richard was killed at Chalus-Chabrol.[64] A more important reason is that in most conflicts the object was not total victory and extensive conquest but the assertion or defence of limited rights. To mobilize forces, to besiege castles, to devastate the countryside, to burn towns and cities and to attack the enemy's supplies were all methods of demonstrating that the particular and limited claims were being seriously made and pressed with vigour, to ensure a strong position in the negotiations which would follow. In the last lecture, we saw a little of Richard de Lucy's long military career from 1138 to 1174. Jordan Fantosme gives us a closer view of him in Northumberland during the great rebellion of 1173–74.[65]

> Richard de Lucy – no better man can be found
> Gives good help to his lord in maintaining his war.
> He well understands his business in seeking truces and peace.

---

[58] *Howden, Gesta* i. 245–9.
[59] *Howden, Gesta*, ii. 6–7.
[60] Newburgh, *Historia*, ii. 460–1.
[61] Newburgh, *Historia*, ii. 492.
[62] *Anglo-Saxon Chronicle*, and Florence, ii. 15.
[63] Malmesbury, *Gesta Regum*, ii. 477–8; *Orderic*, vi. 204, 238; *Hyde Chronicle*, 318; Huntingdon, *Historia Anglorum*, 241.
[64] *Howden, Gesta*, i. 296.
[65] *Jordan Fantosme's Chronicle*, ll. 766–8.

We then hear of Humphrey de Bohun and his men burning Berwick to the ground and destroying much of the country. Richard de Lucy intervened to point out that this was madness; the rebel earl of Leicester had landed in Suffolk with a force of Flemish mercenaries and it was essential to deal with this threat and to call off hostilities with the Scots before they too heard this news. Bohun was immediately convinced and exclaimed, 'Lord Richard de Lucy, now we shall see what you are made of.' They did see, and Richard de Lucy got his truce with the Scots. Meanwhile across the Channel Henry II had been holding two meetings with Louis VII in which he proposed detailed terms of a peace settlement.[66]

In many of the wars of our period the object was not to destroy opponents but to acquire subjects. This explains the apparently surprising leniency shown by Rufus after the rebellion of 1088, as by Henry II after the rebellion of 1173–74. And it also helps to explain the terms which Stephen granted to the garrison of Exeter after the long and expensive siege in 1136, terms castigated by his most recent historians as the first of his mistakes and as demonstrating his 'fatal weakness'.[67] On this principle we should also accuse Rufus of 'fatal weakness' in granting similar terms to the garrison of Rochester in 1088; but whatever charges may fairly be levelled against Rufus, weakness is not one which is supported by or has been imposed upon the evidence.

There is then abundant evidence that the conduct of war in our period was frequently ruthless. The Welsh troops, the Flemish mercenaries of Stephen's reign, the Brabançons employed by Henry II and the mercenary captains brought back to England by King John were not men of gentle disposition. But when we seek to understand the conduct of war by the seven rulers of England of our period in relation to the objects for which they fought we are not justified in describing them as 'ruthless military adventurers', 'men of blood', 'prepared to take every kind of risk', and 'intent upon continental adventures'. They were aware of the responsibilities of kingship, fully familiar with the instruments of coercive government, and they accepted with varying degrees of intelligence, readiness and determination the need to assert and defend what they conceived to be their rights and the interests of their families by the use of force. But they, and the men around them, were also aware that the use of force, the making of war, was only one, and not always the most effective means to their ends. And they were aware too of the other and wider responsibilities of kingship, and of the pleasures such as hunting for which arduous campaigning provided few or severely reduced opportunities.

Note on further reading

The most important book to appear on this subject since JOP gave his Ford Lectures is M. Strickland, *War and Chivalry. The Conduct and Perception of War in England and Normandy, 1066–1217* (Cambridge, 1996). Strickland's

---

[66] *Howden, Gesta*, i. 59–60.
[67] Cronne, *Reign of Stephen*, 33.

emphasis is very different from that of JOP; he was concerned with the nature of chivalry in the Anglo-Norman period, and with the self-perception of knights. He demonstrated that many of the concepts familiar from study of later periods were valid for the eleventh and twelfth centuries, while not denying the importance of pragmatism and profit. John Gillingham's studies of 'William the Bastard at War', in *Studies in Medieval History presented to R. Allen Brown*, ed. C. Harper-Bill, C.J. Holdsworth and J.L. Nelson (Woodbridge, 1989), 141–58, and of 'Richard I and the Science of War', in *War and Government in the Middle Ages: Essays in honour of J.O. Prestwich*, ed. J. Gillingham and J.C. Holt (Woodbridge, 1984), 1–13, provide excellent case studies of two great commanders. There is no specific study of William Rufus as a military leader, but for a full general study, there is the biography by Frank Barlow, *William Rufus* (London, 1983). For the campaigns of Henry I, there is the biography, published posthumously, by C.W. Hollister, *Henry I* (London, 2001). Jordan Fantosme and his description of the defence of the north in the rebellion of 1173–74, is discussed by M. Strickland, 'Securing the North: Invasion and the Strategy of Defence in Twelfth-Century Anglo-Scottish Warfare', *Anglo-Norman Studies* xii (1990), 177–98.

3

Sea Power

Sea power is a rather grand term, appropriate to the days of Drake, Rodney, Howe and Nelson, to Grand Fleets and High Seas Fleets, to the American Seventh Fleet and even to a task force operating eight thousand miles from its home ports, but not, you may think, to maritime activities in the period between the battles of Hastings and Bouvines, a period in which warfare was supposedly dominated by knights and castles. However, 'sea power' is a conveniently short title for the lecture list; and my reason for devoting a lecture to maritime activities is less that I have new information to convey than that the information which is readily available does not appear to me to have received in our general histories the space, and in particular the consideration, which it deserves. I propose to take three episodes for illustrative purposes, one from each of the three periods I singled out as conspicuous for the scale, duration and intensity of warfare.

The first episode is that of the siege of Exeter in 1068. The troops which conducted that siege went by land, and there was no naval blockade; but nevertheless it has a bearing on what may fairly be termed sea power in the second half of the eleventh century. In March 1067, only three months after his coronation, William the Conqueror left England to enjoy a triumphal progress in Normandy. He returned to England on 7 December 1067 and celebrated the Christmas feast at Westminster. Easter in 1068 fell very early, on 23 March, and William celebrated this at Winchester. In the interval between these two great feasts he conducted a winter campaign, including Englishmen for the first time in his army, besieged Exeter for eighteen days suffering considerable losses, failed to storm it and finally accepted its surrender on favourable terms. He then arranged for the construction of a castle at Exeter and pushed on into Cornwall before disbanding his army and returning to Winchester. It appears as a minor tidying-up operation. Stenton devoted eighteen lines to it, Barlow eleven lines and Douglas eight lines.[1] Nevertheless there are puzzling aspects of this episode as reported by the three main sources: Orderic Vitalis (who was following the lost ending of William of Poitiers); the D version of the Anglo-Saxon Chronicle; and the Worcester chronicle. The salient problems are firstly, why should William have initiated this campaign in the south-west at a time when, as William of Poitiers tells us, disaffected Englishmen had been sending emissaries to the Danes and a Danish invasion of England was threatening, when the north of England was unsubdued and

---

[1] F.M. Stenton, *Anglo-Saxon England* (2nd edn, Oxford, 1947), 592; F. Barlow, *The Feudal Kingdom of England, 1042–1216* (London, 1972), 91; D.C. Douglas, *William the Conqueror: The Norman Impact upon England* (London, 1964), 213.

Scotland an obvious threat?[2] For it was William who initiated the campaign by demanding an oath of fealty from Exeter.[3]

Secondly, why did Exeter, through its *primores*, refuse to swear fealty or to admit William to the city? Dover, Canterbury, London, Stigand, Edwin, Morcar, Waltheof and many others had all submitted and done fealty. And what were the 'other cities' (*'aliae ciuitates'*), to which Exeter had sent emissaries, *legationes*, urging them to join in the conspiracy? On the strength of these passages Freeman supposed that Exeter aimed at becoming 'an aristocratic commonwealth', a 'republic', a 'Free Imperial City', and had formed a 'civic league' of the western towns.[4] Round, who devoted twenty-four pages to exposing the numerous errors in Freeman's account of the siege of Exeter, had no difficulty in pouring scorn on the theory of the civic league and in pointing out that Orderic's *ciuitates* could not possibly have been applied to the little boroughs of Dorset, though he did not venture to suggest which *ciuitates* Orderic may have had in mind.

Thirdly, why when William approached Exeter should the leading citizens (the *maiores*) have met William, offered to open the gates, promised full submission and produced all the hostages he demanded; and why, despite this, should Exeter have continued to resist so long and so successfully, unmoved by the spectacle of one of the hostages being blinded?

Finally, why did Exeter finally surrender on terms because, as the Anglo-Saxon Chronicle puts it, of betrayal by the thegns? And why did William grant such favourable terms? For even if Orderic, following William of Poitiers, exaggerated or invented in reporting that William prevented any looting of Exeter by his troops, Domesday establishes that the financial liabilities of Exeter remained unchanged. Round's view that the thegns had been 'the party of non-resistance from the first' is implausible: we should have expected the thegns rather than the citizens to have urged and led resistance.[5] And not the least puzzle is that Round should have found William's favourable treatment of Exeter a 'paradox' and a 'mystery', and should have emphasised that his own solution was 'conjectural'.[6] Round did not ordinarily deal in mere conjectures. And here his conjecture that William was 'in sore straits', that Swein of Denmark was in his rear and half of England on his flank, merely makes it the more puzzling that William should have ignored these threats in the first place in favour of dealing with Exeter.

There is, I believe, a hypothesis which makes sense of the admittedly unsatisfactory evidence and which is supported by further scraps of evidence, though it can be no more than a hypothesis. The basis for this is afforded by the very short account of the episode in the Worcester chronicle, and I give it in translation:

2 *Gesta Guillelmi*, 183.
3 *Orderic*, ii. 212.
4 E.A. Freeman, *The History of the Norman Conquest of England* (Oxford, 1867–79), iv. 146–51.
5 J.H. Round, *Feudal England: Historical Studies on the Eleventh and Twelfth Centuries* (London, 1895), 451.
6 Ibid., 449–54.

Then (after William's return from Normandy) he set off in arms to Devon, besieged the city of Exeter, which the citizens and some English ministers (or officials – the Latin is *ministri*)[7] were holding against him, and he quickly broke into it. Countess Gytha, that is to say the mother of Harold king of the English and sister of Swein king of the Danes, escaped from the city with many men and made for Flanders: the citizens however accepted terms (*dextris datis*) and surrendered.

Gytha was in fact the aunt, not the sister, of Swein of Denmark; but the prominence given to her presence in Exeter and her escape ultimately to Flanders (though the Anglo-Saxon Chronicle explains that she went first to the island of Flatholme in the Bristol Channel) deserves note. Freeman, unlike Round, rightly saw Gytha's importance.

Now for the hypothesis. After the battle of Hastings Gytha withdrew to the south-west partly to place herself out of William's immediate reach and especially because the House of Godwin (Gytha herself, her sons Harold, Leofwine and Tostig, her daughter, Queen Edith, and two grandchildren) had held very extensive estates in Devon and Somerset. The House of Godwin had experienced and had recovered from a previous crisis. In 1051 Godwin, his wife Gytha and three of their sons had been exiled and had taken refuge in Flanders. The other two sons, Harold and Leofwine, had sailed to Ireland. But in the following year they were back and restored to power thanks to a nicely coordinated move, Godwin sailing from Flanders and Harold from Dublin, joining up in the English Channel. What had been done in 1052 could, Gytha hoped, be done again in 1068. Harold's three sons (Godwin, Edmund and Magnus, all illegitimate) had taken refuge in Ireland after the battle of Hastings. Gytha could hope to hold the south-west as a secure base until Harold's sons could bring reinforcements from Ireland, drawing on the naval resources of Leinster, and meanwhile Gytha could urge her nephew, King Swein of Denmark, to launch a great expedition across the North Sea. Had such a plan succeeded it would not have placed a member of the House of Godwin on the English throne, but all its members could have hoped for wealth and influence under a Danish regime in England; and Gytha, Godwin's widow, would have been revenged upon the Conqueror.

The evidence which supports, or is at least consistent with, this hypothesis is as follows:

1. William of Poitiers reports that before the Conqueror's return to England at the end of 1067 the English had been sending frequent missions to Denmark and elsewhere for help.

2. Orderic's account of Exeter as being only two miles from the coast and at the shortest distance from Ireland and Brittany is geographically inaccurate in respect of Ireland but significant in respect of contacts between Gytha and her grandsons in Ireland.

3. Orderic's report of missions (*legationes*) from Exeter to other cities (*ciuitates*) cannot, as Round noted, refer to little centres of population in the West Country but might well apply to missions to Dublin and Denmark. At the very least it implies

---

[7] See Stenton, *First Century*, chap. ii for the *ministri* of the twelfth-century honours.

wide-reaching plans, for neither William of Poitiers nor Orderic ever applied the term *ciuitas* to anything less than a county town, commonly reserving it for the seats of archbishoprics and bishoprics.

4. The Worcester chronicle's description of Exeter as held against William by the citizens *and* some English officials is significant. If the officials were Gytha's, the men who managed her family's estates in the south-west, this would explain the strange course of the episode. The original refusal of fealty and of any admission of William to Exeter would come from Gytha's party, while their offer of the customary tribute would be an attempt to buy time. The offer of the citizens (maiores) to surrender as soon as William approached Exeter is natural given the earlier surrenders of Dover, Canterbury and London; the continued resistance of Exeter is natural as long as Gytha's party saw prospects of holding out until reinforcements arrived from Ireland. And the final betrayal of Exeter by the thegns is most naturally interpreted as referring to the decision of Gytha and her followers to escape by sea, first to the Bristol Channel and finally to Flanders. If this is so William had no reason to treat the citizens proper with unreasonable severity, for they had offered submission and hostages as soon as he approached the city.

5. Harold's three sons did finally sail from Ireland later in the summer of 1068, landing at the mouth of the River Avon, attacking Bristol, defeating Ednoth the Staller, taking extensive booty from Devon and Cornwall and returning to Ireland. And in June 1069 two of Harold's sons were back in a fleet put at sixty-four or sixty-six ships and landed in south Devon.[8] Orderic's account of their devastations is supported by the Domesday entries recording the waste committed by the Irish.[9] However, this force was defeated with very heavy casualties, only a few survivors returning to Ireland; and it was at this point, if Orderic is right, that Gytha finally gave up hope, gathered up her great treasure and left England never to return.

6. In the late summer of 1069 between 15 August and 8 September the Danish armada[10] finally sailed and, acting in concert with their English allies, captured York and inflicted what Stenton called 'the heaviest defeat which the Normans ever suffered in England'.[11]

7. When Orderic reported the Conqueror's arrest of his half-brother, Odo of Bayeux, in 1082 he put into the Conqueror's mouth the charge that Odo had been seducing the loyalty of his troops 'whose duty it was to defend England against Danes and Irishmen and other enemies', showing that Orderic, if not the Conqueror, linked together the major threats to England from the closer sea power of the Irish ports and the greater sea power of Denmark.[12]

8. The Anglo-Saxon chronicle for 1087 stated that if the Conqueror had lived two years more, he would have conquered Ireland by his prudence and without any weapons.

---

8   Florence, ii. 3; *Orderic*, ii. 224.
9   *Orderic*, ii. 224; Exon Domesday, f. 323.
10 *Magna classis*, *Orderic*, ii. 226; 240 ships, Florence. ii. 3, and Anglo-Saxon Chronicle D; 300 ships, *Anglo-Saxon Chronicle* E.
11 Stenton, *Anglo-Saxon England*, 595.
12 *Orderic*, iv. 42.

If this hypothesis is well founded it indicates that the Conqueror's winter campaign and siege of Exeter in 1068 was a successful pre-emptive strike against the west country base of Gytha and the party of the house of Godwin, a strike which helps to explain the failure of the sea-borne expeditions of Harold's sons in 1068 and 1069 and which enabled the Conqueror to concentrate his efforts against the Danish force when it finally landed. Was that pre-emptive strike based on good intelligence? You will forgive a former member of Hut 3 in Bletchley Park (the wartime organization which, so the press reports, later moved to Cheltenham where it appears to have been less secure than its wartime predecessor) raising this question. There are indications that William did have advance information of Gytha's intentions. First, there is Orderic's statement that reports reached William while still in Normandy in 1067 that the English with the help of the Danes were planning to inflict a major defeat on the Normans.[13] Second there is the evidence, also from Orderic, that the men of Exeter had ill-treated some troops (*milites*) sent by the Conqueror from Normandy (i.e. before the Conqueror's return to England) who had been driven by a storm into Exeter harbour.[14] Why had these men been in the English Channel off the south Devon coast? They may have been blown a long way off course by the storm; or they may have been part of an intelligence-gathering mission. Of these two possibilities the latter seems more probable. Third, when Orderic reported the dispatch of emissaries from Exeter to other cities, his next sentence tells us that when William had certain intelligence of this (*ubi haec certius comperit*) he immediately made his demand for fealty from Exeter; William, that is, had intercepted the messengers and, realising the importance of this information, took immediate action. Orderic's use of the word *certius* is important; it implies intelligence of the highest degree of reliability derived from an intercept. Intelligence of an equally high degree of reliability was passed on by Lanfranc to bishop Walcher of Durham in the autumn of 1075. 'The Danes are in truth (*reuera*) coming, as the king has informed us' was the message he passed on. 'So', Lanfranc continued, 'fortify your castle with men, arms and victuals.'[15] William's intelligence was good; the Danes did indeed come in two hundred ships and raided York, but it was too late, for the rebellion of earls Ralph and Roger had already been crushed.

Here I should like to say more, if time allowed, about military intelligence during this period. I shall content myself with two observations. First, historians have underestimated or ignored much of the information on military intelligence because they translate the Latin word *rumor*, meaning news, report, information, as 'rumour'.[16] Sometimes the meaning of *rumor* is so clear in its context that no translator can mistake it. Consider for example the action of Tancred and Count Eustace II of Boulogne at Ramla early in August 1099, as described by Orderic. They captured some of the advance guard of the Egyptian army, killed some and interrogated others in order to discover *rumores certos* about the Egyptian

---

[13] *Orderic*, ii. 208.
[14] *Orderic*, ii. 212–14.
[15] *Letters, Lanfranc* 36.
[16] e.g. *Orderic*, ii, 208–9 for *rumores* as 'rumours'.

emir and his army. The interrogators were not interested in rumours or gossip; they obtained, as Orderic explains, precise information about the composition of the Egyptian army, its size, its intentions, and where it proposed to do battle.[17] Furnished with this precious intelligence the crusaders proceeded to fight and win the battle of Ascalon, much as Sir Edgar Williams, furnished with intelligence by Bletchley, was able to tell Montgomery how to plan and win the battle of El Alamein.

Second, I choose two out of many scraps of evidence on the working of the rival intelligence services of Louis VII of France and Henry II of England. The first I owe to my old pupil, J.C. Holt. In 1167 Louis VII wrote to the dean and treasurer of St Martin's in Tours, asking for information on Henry II's intentions: would he be advancing into Poitou or returning to the Norman coast? If these ecclesiastical dignitaries had certain information it was to be reported back by Louis VII's two messengers: if the information was uncertain it was to be reported by one of the messengers, the other remaining in Tours until further information became available.[18] The second scrap is supplied by Robert of Torigny. At Easter 1174 Louis VII in support of the rebellion of Henry II's sons held a war council at Paris. The plan then decided on was to deliver a two-pronged attack: one force was to invade England at the end of June and the other was to invade Normandy, to devastate it, or even to besiege Rouen. But Henry learned of these plans, for, as Robert of Torigny explains, he had many of the French barons in his pay. Hence he gave orders for the Norman castles bordering French territory to be placed in a state of full defence, changed some of their castellans, crossed to England and then returned to relieve Rouen and complete the suppression of the great rebellion. Unluckily Robert of Torigny does not give us the names of these useful moles in the French court, and perhaps did not know them: it would be pleasant to think that Henry II's secret service, unlike some of its successors, knew how to keep its secrets.[19]

The episode of the siege of Exeter in 1068 is therefore a reminder of the vulnerability of England under the Conqueror to sea power, to the capacity of the Danes and the Irish to land troops at points of their choosing on the English coast. As Stenton observed in his Ford Lectures the danger of a Danish attack upon England has received less than its due of attention because it never materialized on a scale comparable with the invasions of 1014 and 1066. But it received its full due of attention from William the Conqueror, especially in relation to the invasion which did not happen in 1085 and 1086. Irish sea power has received even less attention, though it was important enough for Henry II to hire a fleet from Dublin for his major Welsh campaign of 1165. And Irish sea power played a large part in the history of Wales. Gruffydd ap Cynan, ruler of Gwynedd from 1098 to 1137, was born and brought up in Dublin, half-Welsh and half-Irish.[20] Before he finally established his control of Gwynedd he spent

---

[17] *Orderic*, v. 176.
[18] Note that *rumores* is mistranslated as 'rumours' by J.C. Holt, 'The End of the Anglo-Norman Realm', in J.C. Holt, *Magna Carta and Medieval Government* (1985), 55.
[19] Torigny, 263–4.
[20] I owe this information to my former pupil, Dr Marie-Therese Flanagan.

five periods of exile in Ireland, returning each time with the formidable support of Irish ships and Irish mercenaries; and this is only one instance of several.

My second episode is of a summer campaign and it takes us into a warmer climate. It is the story of the capture of Lisbon in 1147 and it rests almost entirely on a single source, the *De Expugnatione Lyxbonensi*, a source which has been described as 'perhaps the most detailed surviving record of any military expedition in the twelfth century'.[21] This source is in the form of a long newsletter or dispatch, almost certainly composed at Lisbon in the winter following the capture of the city, and addressed to a friend in Suffolk. The author was closely linked with and possibly the chaplain of Hervey de Glanvill, the leader of the East Anglian contingent; J.C. Russell supposed him to be Ranulf Glanville, the future justiciar.[22] What was the composition of the force which set sail from Dartmouth (the port of rendezvous) on 23 May 1147? It consisted of three main contingents: one from Cologne, one from Flanders and Boulogne, and one from England and Normandy. It was drawn, that is, from the ports and towns bordering the English Channel and the valley of the lower Rhine, a region united by ties of trade, an urbanized region conspicuous for its commercial enterprise and, especially in the Low Countries, industrial expansion. The Anglo-Norman contingent was itself divided into four groups, each under its own constable; one from Norfolk and Suffolk, one from Kent, a third from London and the fourth from Normandy. But within the contingent from England we hear of men from Ipswich, Hastings, Southampton and Bristol; and also of Bretons and Scots. None of the four Anglo-Norman leaders was of any social eminence. Only the Norman leader can be classed as of the lesser nobility, the three from England being drawn from the gentry or merchants; indeed Henry of Huntingdon described the whole expedition as composed of poor men without any great leader, and he drew an edifying contrast between their success and the failure in the Second Crusade of the forces led by the king of France and the German emperor.[23] It is noteworthy that the composition of the Anglo-Norman force cut right across divisions within England during the civil war. The Londoners were consistent backers of Stephen; Kent was under the control of William of Ypres, Stephen's leading captain of mercenaries; the Viels of Southampton and of course the men of Bristol backed Robert of Gloucester; and Normandy was now lost to Stephen and controlled by Geoffrey of Anjou.

How large was the total force? Our chief source tells us that about 164 ships assembled at Dartmouth. Ships at anchor, unlike armies in the field, can be counted with tolerable accuracy, and anyone who knows Dartmouth harbour will agree that the heights around it offer splendid vantage points. We have two other figures for the size of the fleet: the 'almost 200' of the Teutonic source and, from a Portuguese source, 190 ships in the besieging fleet at Lisbon. These figures are in surprisingly close accord, and may be provisionally accepted. Moreover our main source provides further figures which invite some elemen-

---

[21] G. Constable, 'The Second Crusade as seen by Contemporaries', *Traditio* ix (1953), 221.
[22] J.C. Russell, 'Ranulf de Glanville', *Speculum* xlv (1970), 69–70, 72–4.
[23] Huntingdon, p. 28.

tary calculations. After reporting the capture of the suburb of Lisbon by 3,000 of the Anglo-Norman contingent it explains that arrangements were then made for the Anglo-Normans to mount night watches, each of 500 men, so that after nine nights the first watch had to go on duty again – i.e. a total force of 4,500. Evidently the Flemish-German force was slightly larger, for it was agreed that they should contribute 160 men to the party detailed for the first entry into Lisbon after its surrender, as against 140 from the Anglo-Norman contingent – i.e. 300 in all, unequally divided. Hence we can put the Flemish-German forces at about 5,500, giving a grand total of 10,000. And if we distribute the 10,000 among the original 164 ships we have a plausible figure of 61 men on average carried by each ship: a plausible figure since the ships of Richard I's crusading fleet each carried 15 sailors, 40 horses and 80 troops;[24] while we are told of one ship carrying 80 armed men in 1190.[25] Moreover the author of our main account had a commendable interest in statistics, and these are either correct or highly plausible.[26] And there is the further consideration that since the expedition was organized in thousands, in five hundreds, and in hundreds, the calculation of totals was much simpler and did not depend on the skills of the Metropolitan police in estimating the size of a demonstration in Trafalgar Square.[27]

If we can accept the figure of 10,000 as approaching the truth for the total strength of the expedition which sailed from Dartmouth, an expedition formed by agreement and not mobilized by the coercive agencies of a major state, it is indeed impressive. Edward I conquered Wales with forces little, if at all larger than this.[28] The largest force raised by Elizabeth I's government in the years 1585–1605 was that of 12,620 sent to Ireland in 1601. Perhaps more relevant comparisons are with the naval expeditions dispatched to Spanish waters by Elizabeth. In 1589 Drake and Norris assembled 143 ships and 19,000 men at Plymouth, 'the most formidable armament that assembled at Plymouth in the reign of Elizabeth', and sailed for Lisbon.[29] Little more was achieved than Essex's characteristically futile gesture in challenging the Spanish commander of the Lisbon garrison to single combat. The humbler – and more successful – members of the 1147 expedition had no use for such chivalrous antics.[30] Again in 1596 an Anglo-Dutch expedition of c.120 ships carrying rather less than 10,000 troops succeeded in sacking Cadiz, an achievement celebrated by Black as 'a brilliant display of the might of England on sea and land'.[31] Perhaps it was. But in our enthusiasm for Elizabethan sea power we should not forget that four and a half centuries earlier our expedition of 1147 had been in these same waters

---

24 Devizes, p. 15.

25 Howden, *Gesta*, ii. 116.

26 *De Expugnatione*, 68 (depth of beach at Oporto at low tide); 94 (width of Lisbon streets); 133, 142 (height of the two siege towers); 142 (rate of fire of the siege engines, which works out at four stones per minute).

27 Ibid., 56, 128, 140, 142.

28 J.E. Morris, *The Welsh Wars of Edward I* (Oxford, 1901), 178.

29 J.B. Black, *The Reign of Elizabeth, 1558–1603* (2nd edn, Oxford, 1959), 411.

30 R.B. Wernham, 'Queen Elizabeth and the Portugal Expedition of 1589', *EHR* lxvi (1951), 1–26.

31 Black, *Reign of Elizabeth*, 419.

with a markedly larger fleet and a slightly larger number of troops; and that whereas in 1596 Essex had intended to occupy and hold Cadiz but remained there for only a fortnight, the men of 1147 captured Lisbon and placed it in western hands where it has remained ever since. Historians of the early modern period stand in need of these reminders. To Braudel it was Richard Sturmy of Bristol in the mid-fifteenth century whose Mediterranean voyages first heralded the irruption of northern enterprise into Mediterranean waters. And even Wernham, from whom I take the figures of the Elizabethan expeditions to Lisbon and Cadiz, wrote of Elizabeth's naval commanders that 'they were experimenting with a novel theory, and a very novel instrument, of war. Sea power', he continued, 'had never before been used as an independent arm operating over vast distances of ocean.'[32] We have to remember that the 1147 expedition, after wintering at Lisbon, did push on into the eastern Mediterranean. For Drake Lisbon was the objective, and one he failed to attain: for the men of 1147 it was merely a diversion, and one they successfully captured.

The success of the 1147 expedition owed much to its organization. Despite the rivalries between the Anglo-Norman and the Flemish-German contingents all members of the force were bound together in a sworn unity, *conjurata unitas*, or sworn partnership, *societas conjurata*. The common code of discipline contained many borrowings from the municipal laws of the continental communes; and for every thousand men there were two elected or chosen officers responsible both for enforcing discipline and for the distribution of moneys. Whether this last phrase, *peccuniarum distributio*, refers to a common purse from which expenses were to be met or to the sharing out of any spoils is uncertain: it was however held that the spoils of Lisbon after its surrender should be treated as common property (*omnibus communia*) before individual shares were apportioned.[33] Within this formal framework of command and discipline there was what may be called the political structure of the expedition. General issues, we are told, were put to the whole body of the forces. When the king of Portugal first met the crusaders outside Lisbon and asked who their leaders were, he was surprised to be told that although they had some chiefs whose counsel carried special weight, they all wished to hear the Portuguese proposals and would then find someone who 'with the common counsel of all would answer for them all' (*qui pro omnibus communi omnium consilio responderet*). The crusaders then held a long debate to discuss the proposal to besiege Lisbon.

In the morning debate no decision was reached, but during the break for luncheon the Flemings were won over to the Portuguese proposal because, as our source uncharitably reported, 'the hope of grabbing some money exercised its usual sway over those who were feeling the pinch of want'. When the debate was resumed after the break William Viel, speaking for the detachment from Southampton and Hastings, argued against the Lisbon plan. The siege, he contended, would be long and expensive, and it would be more profitable to sail on quickly past the coast of

---

[32] 'Elizabethan War Aims and Strategy' in *Elizabethan Government and Society: Essays presented to Sir John Neale,* ed. S.T. Bindoff, J. Hurstfield and C.H. Williams (London, 1961).
[33] *De Expugnatione*, 105, 56, 176–7.

Spain and to extort large sums of money from the merchant vessels of Africa and Spain. He added as an afterthought that the wind at that season was very favourable for the voyage to Jerusalem – which was, after all, the formal objective of the expedition. However, the Lisbon plan was accepted and representatives were chosen to negotiate and draft the agreement with the king of Portugal. In this the crusaders drove a hard bargain. All enemy possessions were to go to them alone; they were to be allowed to ransack Lisbon and to have the ransoms of all prisoners; the city was to remain theirs under the overlordship of King Alfonso; and they and their heirs were to be free in perpetuity from paying merchant tolls anywhere in Portugal. We continue to hear of decisions being taken by the common counsel of all.[34] And we also hear of discontent with the leadership. During the difficult negotiations for the surrender of Lisbon a mutiny was started among the sailors by a profane priest from Bristol, directed against Hervey de Glanvill. It was, the Bristol priest argued, wrong that so many men should be subject to the rule and authority of a few, and that what was required was not deliberation but energy and the guidance of the Holy Spirit.[35] The reason for this outbreak was, we are told, that Hervey de Glanvill had punished some offenders against the code of discipline by condemning them to have no share in the spoils of Lisbon. The leadership prevailed. But we cannot discount the evidence showing that popular sentiment counted for a good deal and that the notions of common consent, the overriding obligations of a common oath, the principle of representation and a conciliar structure entered in a practical way into the organization of the crusading forces and the methods by which decisions were taken and accepted.

Since this evidence comes from one who was a member of the East Anglian contingent and relates largely to the Anglo-Norman forces it throws considerable light on the expansive energies, qualities of rough enterprise, political ideas and forms of social organization within English society during the middle decades of the twelfth century, forces which were in part released by and in part contributed to the civil war of Stephen's reign and which Henry II was able to discipline and to use. We have seen how the expedition of 1147 borrowed its code of discipline in part, sometimes word for word, from the continental communes, and indeed its whole structure was that of a commune, *societas conjurata*. London had formed a commune by 1141, and probably as early as 1135, though we know little of its working.[36] Oxford, which came to share the customs, privileges and laws of the Londoners, had at least the name of a commune in 1147, the very year of the Lisbon expedition.[37] Henry of Oxford, a man of English descent, was certainly a man of enterprise. During the civil war he acquired lands and properties in and around Oxford from supporters of the Angevin cause: from Brian fitz Count, young Geoffrey de Clinton and the empress herself, rising to become sheriff of Oxfordshire at the end of Stephen's reign and securing a charter from Henry II in 1156 which confirmed all his

---

[34] Ibid., 110–12, 114, 140.
[35] Ibid., 166.
[36] Malmesbury, *Historia Novella*, 54; *Gesta Stephani*, 6 and n. 1.
[37] Henry II's charter to Oxford in Stubbs, *Select Charters*, p. 199; see J. Tait, *The Medieval English Borough* (Manchester, 1936).

gains. Of his sons one became lord of Ibstone and a benefactor of the Templars; another, John, did very distinguished service to Henry II as an itinerant justice and diplomat, rising to become bishop of Norwich.[38] It must however be admitted that the bishop was a less robust traveller than the crusaders of 1147. The account of his journey to Sicily in 1176 is full of agonized complaints: fleas kept him awake at night; he was terrified of pirates in the Mediterranean; voyaged down the Italian coast in a miserable boat which barely carried eight passengers; had to sleep on beaches; and arrived in Sicily to find it suffering from a drought in August.[39]

Bristol, which produced the priest-agitator who organized the mutiny of 1147, also produced the highly enterprising Robert fitz Harding, a man of English descent like Henry of Oxford and like him a man who built up a very substantial landed estate at the expense of magnates who supported the Angevin cause in the west country and thus founded the fortune of the Berkeleys of Berkeley Castle. Naturally enough for a Bristol man he was interested affairs in Irish affairs, and in 1168 he entertained at Bristol the Irish exile, Dermot, the man who became the instrument for Strongbow's intervention in Ireland. Indeed there are indications that fitz Harding financed and encouraged Strongbow and acted as an intermediary between Strongbow and Henry II. We have seen William Viel, supported by his brother Ralph, arguing in 1147 against the siege of Lisbon and proposing instead a profitable diversion to piracy in the Mediterranean. The Pipe Rolls of Henry II's reign show various members of the Viel family turning their talents to more disciplined ends in the service of Henry II, performing transport service in the Welsh campaign of 1157 and ceaselessly shipping treasure, men and munitions from England to Normandy. Indeed Ralph Viel, who took part in the expedition of 1147 was rewarded by Henry II with a grant to himself and his heirs of freedom from all customs (tallages, aids and other dues) throughout the king's extensive dominions.[40] England in the mid-twelfth century was a land of colonial enterprise, of enterprise on the sea as well as of enterprise in the more prosaic but highly important field of internal colonization.

My third and last episode is a short one and must be dealt with shortly. It is that of the conquest of Cyprus by Richard I, a conquest which took him little more than a fortnight in May 1191. This was a triumph of sea power. Richard's fleet as it left northern waters in 1190 and before it wintered in Sicily had a strength of between 104 and 114 vessels. Richard of Devizes appears to have had a correspondent in the fleet who provided him with very full details, including a detailed embarkation schedule. From this it appears that the fleet carried about 8,000 troops, 4,000 horses and 1,500 sailors, though the Pipe Roll evidence shows that the ships which sailed from English ports carried larger crews, Richard's own ship having a crew of 61 as against the 15 of the

[38] *Cartae Antiquae, Rolls 1–10*, ed. R. Landon (PRS, xvii, 1939), no.140; *Book of Fees*, 114; *Chron. Abingdon*, ii. 184–5.
[39] Ralph of Diceto, i. 416–17.
[40] *De Expugnatione*, 100, n. J.

normal complement given by Richard of Devizes. When the fleet sailed from Sicily on 10 April 1191 it had been built up to a total strength of 219 cargo vessels (156 ships, 24 large vessels and 39 galleys). The galleys of the fleet were specifically war galleys, fast, highly manoeuvrable, low in the water, capable of operating under sail as well as being driven by oars, and designed for combat and reconnaissance.

This great fleet left Messina in Sicily on 10 April, was scattered by a storm on 12 April, and finally arrived at Rhodes, where Richard landed on 22 April. Two days later three of his ships arrived at Limassol on the south coast of Cyprus, two of them being wrecked and the third, bearing Richard's sister, Joan, and his intended bride, Berengaria of Navarre, prudently anchoring outside the port. On 1 May nine days after he had landed at Rhodes, Richard sailed for Limassol, arriving there on 6 May (having been delayed by another severe storm). The campaign proper for Cyprus began on 12 May and by the end of the month its self-styled emperor, Isaac Comnenus was in chains and the island was Richard's. Its capture was decisive. Richard's gains in Cyprus from captured treasure, a 50 per cent levy on movables and the subsequent sale of the island first to the Templars and then to Guy of Lusignan gave Richard financial resources which enabled him to prolong his crusade. Above all it gave him a rich and secure naval and supply base close to the coast of Syria and Palestine. The crusading army which had been besieging Acre had suffered cruelly from famine, especially in the winter of 1190–91. After Richard's arrival at Acre we hear no more of famine or shortages, except for a brief period in January 1192 when the port of Ascalon was closed to shipping by storms. The reason for Richard's success in solving the supply problem is given by a contemporary who accompanied Richard: when Richard sailed from Cyprus he left behind men who understood war and who sent victuals in abundance to Palestine – '*viros bellatores qui ei postea transmitterent necessaria victualia . . . quibus Cyprus erat abundans*'. Roger of Howden stayed long enough after the fall of Acre to note the care with which the fleet was loaded with victuals as well as with military equipment in order to assure the provisioning of the army on its march south.

But it is generally agreed by historians that the capture of Cyprus was an accident, 'wholly fortuitous, an unforeseen accident of history' as Prawer has put it. It may have been so. Perhaps only the chance of the three ships being driven by the storm to Limassol and Richard's concern to rescue their crews and passengers led him to intervene in Cyprus. But Richard must have been remarkably incurious if he had not learned during his long stay in Sicily of the vital importance of Cyprus. Moreover there are indications pointing to intent and not to accident, while at Rhodes, and before even the three ships had reached Cyprus, Richard took two actions: he sent out galleys to search for the missing ships and he instituted inquiries about the tyrant of Cyprus. The facts that Richard immediately asked for the latest intelligence on Cyprus and that the galleys found the missing ships at Limassol so quickly (Limassol being about 280 miles from Rhodes) strongly suggest that Limassol had been given as a rendezvous before the fleet left Sicily. If so the conquest of Cyprus must have been in Richard's mind from the outset. Had the rescue of the men and women on the three ships been Richard's only purpose it would have been a needless expenditure of time and effort to conquer the whole island.

Neverthelesss Richard's own dispatch of 6 August supports the accident thesis: he had merely turned aside to Cyprus in the hope of helping those of his men who had been shipwrecked and ill-treated there. William of Newburgh accepted this version: when Philip Augustus demanded half of Cyprus, in accordance with the original agreement that they should divide their conquests, one of Richard's grounds for refusing was that he had not gone to the Christian island of Cyprus intentionally – '*non ex intentione, sed incidenter*'. But Richard had every reason to deny intention. He had attacked and conquered a Christian island; and he had insisted on completing its capture despite Philip's demand that he proceed directly to Acre. Moreover Philip sailed back to France on 3 August to disseminate in the west the charge that Richard had needlessly attacked innocent Christians in Cyprus instead of the Saracens in Acre. Hence Richard had good reason to give his own and very different version three days later, on 6 August. There can be no certainty, and those who believe with A.J.P. Taylor that accidents have counted for more than designs in history will accept Richard's despatch at its face value. If so the galleys were remarkably lucky in lighting on the missing ships so quickly. But the preparation and very skilful use of Richard's great fleet throughout his crusade was no accident; and on it depended Richard's whole conduct of his crusade and the very considerable measure of success it enjoyed.

The lessons learned during the Third Crusade in the Mediterranean were soon applied in northern waters. By 1205 King John had 51 royal galleys in his service distributed round the coast from King's Lynn to Gloucester. Two were at Exeter and five stationed in Ireland, reminding us of the changes which had occurred since 1068.[41] But time does not allow a consideration of naval history under King John. One by-product of the organization of Richard I's crusading fleet is a mark which it left on the English nobility. One of the five commanders of Richard's fleet with thirty-three ships under his command was William de Forz (or de Fortibus), described as being 'of Oléron'.[42] He was a Poitevin of obscure origin, and his connection with Oléron suggests that it was his professional skill as a sailor which brought him to Richard's notice. Evidently Richard valued his services highly, for he gave him the widowed countess of Aumale in marriage, so making him count of Aumale and lord of Holderness; and it was from this marriage that the thirteenth-century counts of Aumale descended. The widowed countess had been unenthusiastic about this marriage to a Poitevin sailor, for a Pipe Roll entry records that in 1190 livestock on her lands, valued at £115 1s 4d, had been sold off for the king's benefit because, as the entry puts it, 'the countess was unwilling to marry William de Forz'.[43]

In selecting these three episodes to illustrate the role of sea power I have

---

[41] *Rot. Lit. Claus.*, 33.
[42] Howden, *Gesta*, ii. 110, 116, 120, 124.
[43] *Pipe Roll 6 Richard I*, ed. D.M. Stenton (PRS, 1928), 163. On William de Forz generally see B. English, *The Lords of Holderness, 1086–1260: A Study in Feudal Society* (Oxford, 1979), 30–2.

omitted a very great deal: in particular the unspectacular but vital role of shipping in transporting men, treasure, victuals and arms to Wales, Ireland, Normandy and Poitou. But I hope that I have said enough to persuade you that we should occasionally deflect our attention from the formal obligations of knight-service and castle-guard to consider the scale and consequences of maritime activity in this period, activity which in my three episodes at least justifies the use of the term sea power as used against a ruler of England, by a ruler of England and, not least, by the lesser men who captured Lisbon and gave it its first bishop, the Englishman Gilbert of Hastings.

Note on further reading

On the topic of military intelligence, JOP himself expanded his thoughts in a much more detailed study, 'Military Intelligence under the Norman and Angevin Kings', in *Law and Government in the Medieval England and Normandy: Essays in Honour of Sir James Holt*, ed. G. Garnett and John Hudson (Cambridge, 1994), 1–30. The siege of Exeter and the associated events have not received any more detailed study since this lecture was written; the siege of Lisbon, however, has been usefully examined in a charter by Matthew Bennett in *The Second Crusade: Scope and Consequences*, ed. J. Phillips and M. Hoch (Manchester, 2001). For Richard I and Cyprus, see John Gillingham's *Richard I*, and for other aspects of naval power under Richard, see the same author's 'Richard I, Galley-warfare and Portsmouth', in *Thirteenth Century England* VI, ed. M. Prestwich, R. Britnell and R. Frame (Woodbridge, 1997), 1–15. A useful general discussion of naval warfare in this period is to be found in N.A.M. Rodger, *The Safeguard of the Sea: A Naval History of Britain, I, 660–1649* (London 1997).

4

War and Government

In an earlier lecture I set out the *prima facie* case for holding that a large place must be assigned to war in the general history of England between the battles of Bouvines and Hastings, and especially in the forty years following the battle of Hastings, in the civil war of Stephen's reign, and in the quarter of a century following the accession of Richard I. We have now to consider how the government of England responded to the demands and vicissitudes of war; how it raised and deployed men, money and materials; how it gained allies, constructed castles, ships and siege engines; and how – and how far – it maintained a degree of internal order sufficient to enable it to prosecute war without being distracted or deflected by discontent or rebellion.

Before turning to some of the detailed evidence it may be helpful to consider very general possibilities or models, though remembering that no simple model has ever been fully embodied in historical reality. First, in a society with a low level of economic activity in which the control of military strength and administrative authority is widely dispersed the ruler can only prosecute war as a joint-stock enterprise, relying on the loyalty or contractual obligations of his followers. Feudalism as defined by Vinogradoff is just such a model. It was appropriate to 'a time when social intercourse and political views were restricted to a very narrow horizon', when 'natural husbandry provides the broad ground on the basis of which all the institutions of the time were constructed', and when 'commercial intercourse and dealings played an entirely subordinate part'.[1] If the ruler of such a society sought to replace consent by coercion, diffused authority by centralization, reaction was inevitable. And according to Stenton this is what happened after the death of Henry I when 'the military side of feudalism at once assumed a new importance' and when 'ancient baronial claims to local office, civil and military, were soon asserted'.[2]

Second, in a more developed society in which administrative talents and techniques are more widely available, reflecting a higher level of education, a government may respond to the demands of sustained warfare by extending the range and grasp of its coercive authority, mobilizing and paying its own troops under the control of its own professional captains, building its own ships and impressing merchant ships and crews as needed, suppressing ancient liberties and privileges and putting in its own agents, financing its operations by a combination of credit and direct taxation, controlling the foreign trade of the country

[1] P. Vinogradoff, *English Society in the Eleventh Century* (Oxford, 1908), 39, 87.
[2] Stenton, *First Century*, 219, 224.

in the interests both of customs revenue and economic warfare, and relying on professional judges and attorneys to make, interpret and enforce the laws. In so far as such a government is bureaucratic it will operate under fixed rules and procedures; but if the exigencies of war are pressing it is likely to urge the doctrines of necessity and prerogative, to resort to arbitrary forms of taxation, seizure of treasure, confiscation of estates and repressive police measures. The government of Edward I may be held to approximate to this model. Earlier historians emphasized the set procedures and extending range of Edward's administration, parliaments and legislation (see Plucknett's observation in his Ford Lectures of 1947 that 'we are more interested at the moment in his statutes than in his strategy and our students pay more attention to his parliaments than to his politics').[3] More recent historians have placed the stress on the huge sums Edward accumulated to finance his wars (e.g. nearly £250,000 between June 1294 and November 1295;[4] on the huge debt he left in 1307 of approximately £200,000;[5] and on his unscrupulous treatment of English earls, Marcher lords, and the cities of London, York, Bristol, Newcastle upon Tyne and Canterbury.[6]

If the response of government to the needs of war under the early Norman kings was essentially that of our first or feudal model we should expect it to have made some progress towards our second or bureaucratic and authoritarian model by the end of our period, on the eve of the battle of Bouvines. What progress had it made? Some specimen figures indicate that in scale and character the military effort made in John's reign was similar to that of Edward I. If in 1294–95 Edward I raised from taxation, confiscation, customs, loans and ordinary revenue a total of nearly £250,000, John on the eve of Bouvines had actual cash reserves (after meeting all outgoings, including subsidies to allies) of approximately half this figure.[7] On the outbreak of war with France in 1294 Edward I ordered the construction of thirty galleys which were completed in 1295.[8] In 1205 John already had fifty-one galleys in commission, while later evidence shows old galleys being repaired and new ones being constructed.[9] Edward I spent about £80,000 on his great Welsh castles during the years 1277–1307; Richard I spent about £11,500 on Chateau-Gaillard in 1197–98. The largest labour force employed on Edward's Welsh castles at any one time was about 3,500 in 1295, while in 1277 he had used 1,800 axemen in cutting a supply road through to Rhuddlan.[10] In July 1212 in preparation for the planned

---

3   See Plucknett's observation in his Ford Lectures of 1947 that 'we are more interested at the moment in his statutes than in his strategy and our students pay more attention to his parliaments than to his politics' – *Legislation of Edward I*, 1.
4   *Book of Prests*, ed. E.B. Fryde (Oxford, 1961), lii.
5   M.C. Prestwich, *War, Politics and Finance under Edward I* (London, 1972), 221.
6   K.B. McFarlane, 'Had Edward I a "Policy" towards the Earls?', in *The Nobility of Later Medieval England*; R.R. Davies, *Lordship and Society in the March of Wales, 1282–1400*, ch. 12; M.C. Prestwich, op. cit., 228.
7   Jolliffe, 'The Chamber and the Castle Treasures', 135.
8   M.C. Prestwich, *War, Politics and Finance*, 138.
9   *Rot. Lit. Claus.*, 33; *Pipe Roll 14 John*, ed. P.M. Barnes (PRS, 1955), 75–6.
10   J.G. Edwards, 'Edward I's Castle-Building in Wales', *Proceedings of the British Academy* xxxii (1946), 59; F.M. Powicke, *The Loss of Normandy, 1189–1204* (Manchester, 1913), 204–6; Morris, *Welsh Wars*, 139.

Welsh campaign John ordered thirty counties to produce over 2,000 diggers and carpenters and over 6,000 axemen – a total of 8,450 men – presumably intended for the construction of roads and castles.[11] We do not know what the response to this order would have been, for the campaign was cancelled; but it is nevertheless an indication of how he intended to conduct the campaign and the resources he expected to be available.

The response of the government to war needs under Richard and John is best considered in terms of the measures of that great war minister, Hubert Walter. He was the nephew and assistant of Henry II's justiciar Ranulf Glanvill and within a few days of Richard's coronation his abilities were recognized and rewarded with the bishopric of Salisbury. He preceded Richard on his crusade and so won his master's confidence that Richard determined to make him his chief minister. While still a captive in Germany Richard wrote to his mother Eleanor in the following terms: 'Since I am certain that the sooner Hubert is promoted the quicker I shall be released and the more securely my lands will be defended, I want to promote him to the see of Canterbury. I want him and no one else. . . .'[12] Hubert was duly elected as archbishop of Canterbury in May 1193. In December of that year he was appointed chief justiciar; and lest anything might be wanting to this concentration of authority over church and state in the hands of one man Richard persuaded the compliant Pope Celestine III in March 1195 to appoint Hubert as papal legate.[13] Although Hubert resigned the justiciarship in July 1198 he was back in office as chancellor under John, less than a year later;[14] and until his death in July 1205 he continued to exert a major influence on administration and policy, both directly and through the men he had trained.

The measures of Hubert's ministry bear so clear and consistent a stamp that it is tempting, even permissible, to see in them the application of certain principles. These were:

1. To manage existing and unquestioned royal rights and assets on up-to-date business lines, having particular regard to the fact that the period 1180–1220 was what has been described as 'one of the three great inflationary periods of recorded English history'.[15] One measure was the appointment of coroners to ensure that the profits of crown pleas were protected and a guard provided against the corruption or complaisance of sheriffs.[16] Another was an elaborate survey and valuation of all escheats and wardships. A separate board was established, to manage these lands with instructions to purchase additional stock out of current revenue where necessary in order to increase future income. One example will illustrate the application of this policy. In 1195 the manor of Westbury in Wiltshire was farmed for £24 per annum. Of this, only £5 15s was paid in, the remaining £18 5s being spent on the purchase of additional stock,

---

[11] *Rot. Lit. Claus.*, 131.
[12] 'Epistolae Cantuarienses, 1187–1199', in *Chronicles and Memorials, Richard I*, ed. W. Stubbs (Rolls Series, 1864–5), ii. 362–5.
[13] Ibid., ii. 368–9.
[14] Foedera, I, i. 71.
[15] P.D.A. Harvey, 'The English Inflation of 1180–1220', *Past and Present* lxi (1973), 3–30.
[16] R.F. Hunnisett, 'The Origins of the Office of Coroner', *TRHS*, 5th ser., vol. 8.

including 500 sheep. And in the following year the farm was raised to £31 per annum, fully paid in.[17] For an outlay of £18 5s Hubert Walter's methods produced an increased income of £7, a yield of 38 per cent.

2. A second and more extensive principle was to survey and register the country's economic resources and transactions in order that these might be controlled, tapped or taken over as necessary. In 1194 Hubert Walter ordered an exhaustive survey of all Jewish debts, pledges, lands, houses, revenues and possessions; and he also established machinery for the registration of all future loans by Jews, placing this a little later under another separate board, the justices or exchequer of the Jews.[18] Armed with this knowledge and this machinery the administration was the better able to tax the Jews while they were alive and, on their deaths, to come down on their Christian debtors.

In November 1196 a more far-reaching decree, the Assize of Weights and Measures, was enacted. Weights and measures were standardized throughout the country and the appropriate standards (measures, gallons, iron rods, beams and weights) were made and distributed throughout the counties. Committees of four or six men in each borough and city were assigned to enforce the observance of these weights and measures in all transactions. This appeared to be benevolent legislation in the interests of the consumer, though it must be remembered that the administration was itself making very large purchases of war materials in the market. But the real importance of the decree was that it was the essential preliminary to any effective taxation of industry or trade. Today a chancellor who puts an additional 1p on the price of a pint of beer can rely on getting his money from each pint consumed; but in our period, before Hubert's Assize, any such exaction would have been countered by increasing the size of the pint. Indeed Gerald of Wales accused Hubert Walter himself of exploiting this elasticity of measures in his own commercial dealings: of buying up corn in times of scarcity with the large measure and selling with the small.[19]

Hubert Walter first tried out the fiscal possibilities of the Assize of Weights and Measures in the tin mines of Devon and Cornwall, then enjoying a virtual world monopoly. In 1195–96 these tin mines were farmed out for £166 13s 4d a year.[20] In 1197 Hubert transferred the tin mines to the control of William of Wrotham. Equal and standard weights were laid down for the tin produced for – and here the fiscal implications of the Assize of Weights and Measures are revealed – a tax of one mark per thousandweight of tin produced was to be imposed. William of Wrotham proved an extremely efficient manager. The whole process of tin production was carefully supervised. Precautions against fraud were taken. The inspectors did not collect the tax; the collectors were to be men of wealth and standing; and the proceeds were to be kept not by the collectors but by independent treasurers. All had to keep records which could be checked against each other. The ports and shipping were to be controlled to

[17] *Pipe Roll 7 Richard I*, ed. D.M. Stenton (PRS, 1929), 45; *Chancellor's Roll 8 Richard I*, ed. D.M. Stenton (PRS, 1930), 196.

[18] H.G. Richardson, *The English Jewry under the Angevin Kings* (London, 1960), ch. vii.

[19] Howden, iv. 33–4; *Pipe Roll 9 Richard I*, ed. D.M. Stenton (PRS, 1931), pp. xxi–xii, 160.

[20] *Pipe Roll 8 Richard I*, 150.

prevent smuggling, and no tin could leave the two counties save by licence. In the first eight months under the new scheme a revenue of £579 1s 0d over and above the old farm was produced. By 1214 the annual revenue from this source had risen to £799 1s 3½d, indicating a level of production only occasionally exceeded in the following three centuries.[21]

In July 1202 William of Wrotham was given the opportunity of trying out these methods in the national sphere. With two colleagues he was appointed to establish the first national customs system, known as the fifteenth of merchants. Under the customs regulations of 1204 all goods leaving or entering the ports, whether liable to duty or not and whether destined for coastal or foreign trade, had to be inspected, enrolled, valued and licensed before being loaded or unloaded. Moreover – and here again we see the derivation from the original Assize of Weights and Measures – the chief customs officials were to enforce the use of the standard weights and measures in all fairs, market towns and cities. Shipping was also strictly controlled. This system served three main purposes. First, fiscal: in the first twenty-eight months revenue of almost £5,000 was collected. Second, economic warfare: the regulations of 1204 prevented the unlicensed export of foodstuffs, banned the export of arms and the import of false or clipped currency. Third, the impressment of shipping for national defence: William of Wrotham rapidly became King John's naval administrator, not only impressing merchant shipping, but also, as at Portsmouth, the naval base recently founded by Richard I, supervising the construction of royal dock-yards, controlling the royal galleys, press-ganging and paying their crews. Economic warfare had already been practised. In 1197 Richard I gained the vital alliance of the count of Flanders who had been coerced by an embargo on the export of corn from England to Flanders.[22]

Hubert Walter's first task in 1193 had been to raise the huge sum required for Richard's ransom. One of the wide range of fiscal means then adopted was a proportionate levy on revenues and chattels (or, in modern terms, on incomes and capital assets). This was not a new, though it was a recent, device. It had been employed in the Saladin tithe of 1188. But these were exceptional and formally unexceptionable purposes: the financing of a crusade and the ransoming of the king's body. Hubert Walter's concern to base not on conventional assessments such as hides or knights' fees but on actual wealth bore fruit after his death in the thirteenth of 1207, the first effective and comprehensive tax of this type levied for ordinary purposes (the defence of the land and the recovery of the lost continental possessions), not for a crusade or one of the three regular aids. And here for the first time we can see just how effective this fiscal weapon was. By the end of the exchequer year in which the thirteenth was

---

[21] J. Hatcher, *English Tin Production and Trade before 1550* (Oxford, 1973), 20; *Pipe Roll 16 John*, ed. P.M. Barnes (PRS, 1962), 144.
[22] For the customs scheme see *Rot. Lit. Pat.*, 42–3; *Pipe Roll 6 John*, ed. D.M. Stenton (PRS, 1940), 218; N.S.B. Gras, *Early English Customs System* (Cambridge, Mass., 1926). For the embargo on corn exports in 1197 see *Pipe Roll 10 Richard I*, ed. D.M. Stenton (PRS, 1932), xiv–xv.

levied £57,421 11s 5d had been collected, leaving only £2,615 5s 10d outstanding.[23]

3. A third, obvious but important principle was that of maintaining order by the regular operation of the courts, the general eyres of 1194 and 1198, the dispatch of smaller bodies of itinerant justices to take the assizes and deliver the gaols in 1195 and 1196, and the special measure of the *Edictum Regium* of 1195 for the better apprehension and incarceration of criminals, all this directed and supervised by Hubert Walter from the court at Westminster. Hubert was a busy man. He spent four days at York in June 1195. On the first day, acting as justiciar, he deputed colleagues to hear all pleas of the crown, intervening to impose fines and charges totalling £1,876.[24] Simultaneously he and his officials held the courts Christian. On the second day, in his capacity as papal legate, he visited the abbey of St Mary's, heard the complaints of the monks and deposed the abbot. And on the two following days, again as papal legate, he held a legatine council in St Peter's and issued fifteen decrees described by their most recent editors as providing 'new detailed regulations on matters of clerical discipline, jurisdiction and the like' which 'set a new model for some English church law (especially the diocesan statutes) of the next hundred years'.[25]

4. A fourth principle was to protect his own civil servants from inconvenient scrutinies and to conciliate certain powerful interests. In 1194 it had been intended to carry out a detailed inquest into the misdeeds, illegal exactions and peculations of all royal officials during the past five years. The collection of the vast sums required for Richard's ransom had aroused much discontent. William of Newburgh wrote of the royal ministers 'cloaking clear and shameful extortion under the honest name of the royal ransom'.[26] There was much talk of money sticking to the hands of the officials. But this inquest into corruption was postponed on Hubert Walter's personal orders.[27] In 1196 doubts were again raised about the honesty and efficiency of Hubert Walter's administration. William fitz Osbert, an impoverished London knight and an ex-crusader with a flair for playing the demagogue, made much trouble in London and crossed to Normandy to put further doubts into Richard's mind. These were fortified by the abbot of St Stephen's, Caen, an officer of the Norman exchequer, who asserted that Richard was being cheated of half his revenues from England. Accordingly Richard sent the abbot, together with his clerk, Philip (who had been with Richard in his captivity and was now bishop-elect of Durham), with full powers to carry out the inquiry into corruption which Hubert had blocked two years previously.

The sequence of events in the first half of April 1196, if we can trust the dates given by our various authorities, is interesting. First William fitz Osbert raised a

---

[23] *Rot. de Oblatis*, 459. Note that the outstanding debt did not include Sussex, Cumberland and some individuals. This figure represents approximately twice King John's ordinary revenue from all sources in England (but see Gillingham, *Richard the Lionheart*, 303–4).

[24] *Pipe Roll 7 Richard I*, 91–2.

[25] *Councils and Synods*, I, ii. 1042–52.

[26] Newburgh, i. 400.

[27] Howden, *Chronica*, iii. 267.

mob in London but was driven by Hubert Walter's counter-measures to take sanctuary in Bow church. On 6 April Hubert set fire to the church, smoked out fitz Osbert, and hanged him with his associates (eight or nine). On the following day, 7 April, Hubert very civilly entertained the abbot of Caen at dinner. Unluckily, according to the reliable Roger of Howden, the abbot was taken ill during the meal and died in London five days later. This fortunate chance freed Hubert from the threatened audit of his books and investigation into his ministry; and the news quickly reached Richard in Normandy. On 15 April Richard wrote to Hubert Walter to say that he agreed with Hubert's view and had decided to postpone the inquiry yet again. 'It was not', Richard explained, 'greed which led me to order the inquest into the collection of the ransom. . . . By the grace of God I have such abundant resources of money that I do not need to seek any reason to acquire any maliciously.' He added his thanks for Hubert's action in dealing with the fellow who had disturbed the city of London. At the end of his letter, after giving practical instructions about troops and castles, and having evidently forgotten his earlier remark about his abundant financial resources, Richard added a final sentence: 'Send to me as quickly as ever you can all the money and treasure you have.'[28] Other evidence of Hubert's concern to protect or conciliate powerful interests is afforded by the Assize of Weights and Measures, in which the pill of government control was sugared by the concession of urban monopolies to the powerful dyeing interests and in the land tax scheme of 1198 which expressly provided that landlords could pass the tax on to their tenants.[29]

5. Lastly, there are signs that Hubert Walter possessed qualities which raised him above the level of an immensely hard-working and ingenious administrator. He appears to have entertained doubts about the war policy and its resultant financial and political strains (strains all the greater since the five years 1193–97 were years of famine in western Europe)[30] as early as 1196 when he resigned the justiciarship and then withdrew his resignation.[31] In July 1198 he did resign, and it is probable that this was his own decision rather than one forced on him by either pope or king.[32] In the autumn of 1198 he came close to success in negotiating peace between Richard and Philip. After Richard's death he, together with William Marshal and Geoffrey fitz Peter, prepared the way for John's acceptance as king by meeting the leading malcontents in England and promising on John's behalf that their just claims (*unicuique illorum jus suum*) would be met.[33] On the day of John's coronation Hubert resumed high secular office as chancellor, and it seems as if he hoped to exercise a restraining influence. Eleven days later John issued a decree, described unusually as being at the

---

[28] For all this see Newburgh, ii. 466–71; Howden, *Chronica*, iv. 5–6; Gervase of Canterbury, i. 552–4; Diceto, ii. 145–4, and, for Richard's letter, pp. lxxix–lxxx.

[29] E. Carus-Wilson 'The English Cloth Industry in the Late Twelfth and Early Thirteenth Centuries', *EcHR* xiv (1944), 43–4 and n.1 to p. 44.

[30] Newburgh, ii. 460, 484–5, 492; Howden *Chronica*, iii. 290, iv. 15.

[31] Howden, *Chronica*, iv. 12–15.

[32] Foedera, i. 71.

[33] Howden, *Chronica*, iv. 61, 88.

specific instance of Hubert Walter, in which the new king explained that he was anxious to provide for the welfare of the clergy and people and to extirpate the evil customs which abounded because of cupidity, evil counsel and other undesirable motives; and he went on to refer to things done against immemorial custom and by arbitrary will rather than reason.[34] In thus promising to meet the individual claims of dissident magnates and in advocating the principles of good laws and customs Hubert was outlining the principles which underlay Magna Carta. Hubert evidently continued to take an independent line, and at the close of 1200 quarrelled with John and was deprived of the chancellorship for a week or so.[35] Finally in June 1205 Hubert Walter and William Marshal led the successful opposition to John's attempt to take his great expeditionary force to France.[36] A month later Hubert died.

This consideration of the response of the government to war needs in the late twelfth and early thirteenth centuries does both too much and too little credit to Hubert Walter. Too much because he was able to build on the very solid foundations laid by Henry II and his ministers, and because he was but one, though the chief, of a very able group of ministers, judges and officials; too little because he was also archbishop of Canterbury and, for a shorter period, papal legate. Moreover some of Hubert's more ambitious measures failed or were abandoned. He failed to revive and reform the assessment of the land tax; the cloth merchants purchased exemption from his Assize of Weights and Measures; and the national customs scheme was abandoned, releasing William of Wrotham to concentrate on his duties as a naval administrator. Angevin government was never uniformly systematic. It had always contained large sectors of inertia, irregularity, caprice and expressions of the king's overriding arbitrary will. There were political reasons for this. A uniform and systematic regime, if it is also held to be an oppressive regime, tends to produce systematic opposition and resistance. An imposition which bore on all merchants was likely to be resisted by all merchants. The first measure of King John's reign was a characteristic product of Hubert Walter's methods. It was an attempt to control prices and to control the profits of middlemen, and it was tried out in respect of wine prices. Maximum prices were laid down: 20s for a tun of Poitou wine, 24s for a tun of Anjou wine and 25s for a tun of French wine, except that the finest French wine could be sold for a maximum of 26s 8d. Corresponding prices were prescribed for smaller retail measures; the usual machinery of enforcement was set up in all cities and boroughs and the usual stiff penalties for infringement stipulated. 'But', Howden's account continues, 'this first edict of the king was no sooner initiated than it was immediately brought to naught; because the merchants would not stand it . . . and so the land was filled with drink and drunkards'.[37] It would however be unreasonable to conclude that Normandy and the other continental possessions north of the Loire were lost because the money

[34] *Foedera*, i. 75–6.
[35] V.H.Galbraith, *Studies in the Public Records* (London, 1948), 127–8.
[36] Coggeshall, pp. 152–3; *Histoire de Guillaume le Marechal*, ed. P. Meyer (Paris, 1891–1907), iii. 182.
[37] Howden, *Chronica*, iv. 99–100.

which should have gone to defend them was spent instead in English wine bars and soaked up in the swollen profits of English wine merchants; but defeats of administrative policy of this kind made their contribution.

Nevertheless Angevin administration in general, and Hubert Walter's administration in particular, was, given the growing pressure of war demands, sufficiently systematic to produce the systematic clauses of Magna Carta, clauses designed not to destroy the administration but to limit and control its working. You will have noted however that I have carefully chosen my limiting dates so as to exclude a consideration of Magna Carta from my brief. I hope that I have said enough to satisfy you that the war administration of these years was very much closer to my second model of bureaucracy and autocracy than to the first or feudal model as defined by Vinogradoff and illustrated by Stenton.

If we now turn back to consider the response of government to the demands of war at the beginning of our period we should find ourselves, it seems, in a very different and a much simpler world: different because much more rudimentary and simpler because of the imposition of the feudal system by conquerors endowed with French logic and a genius for organization (see for example Frank Barlow – 'The logic and symmetry of Anglo-Norman feudalism were due to its imposition on a conquered country by a strong king').[38] The greatest military threat to England in the Conqueror's reign after 1070 came in 1085 and 1086. In 1085 Cnut II of Denmark formed a powerful coalition with Count Robert of Flanders and Olaf of Norway for the invasion of England. Cnut was credited with over a thousand ships and Count Robert with six hundred.[39] The invasion fleet never sailed from its base in the Limfjord (N. Denmark), though the threat of invasion was only finally removed when Cnut was murdered in July 1086. There can be no doubt of the seriousness with which the Conqueror treated this threat. He raised what all contemporaries agreed was an exceptionally large paid force consisting of knights, infantry and archers drawn from all parts of France, and in the autumn of 1085 shipped this across to England. According to William of Malmesbury, the Conqueror, careless of expense, even hired the services of Hugh the Great, count of Vermandois and brother of the king of France.[40] On Lanfranc's advice these forces were then quartered out on the bishops, abbots, earls, barons, sheriffs and other royal officers. We have an account of the unfortunate consequences of these billeting arrangements at Worcester where Bishop Wulfstan entertained the knights too lavishly and drunken brawls broke out. Later in 1085 the Conqueror disbanded part of this force but retained the rest throughout the winter of 1085–86.[41] The Conqueror took the further precaution of laying waste the coastal regions in order to deny supplies to the invaders if they were to land; and according to one account he adopted the deception device of ordering his English troops to shave and dress in the Norman manner: after all, Danes had had a long record of military success against the English.[42]

---

[38] Barlow, *Feudal Kingdom*, 111.
[39] Malmesbury, *Gesta Regum*, ii. 319.
[40] Malmesbury, *Gesta Regum*, ii. 320.
[41] Florence, ii. 18.
[42] Stenton, *First Century*, p. 150, n. 2.

Were any administrative measures taken in response to this great threat? Here it is natural to consider the making of Domesday Book, natural because the Anglo-Saxon Chronicle, the Worcester Chronicle and William of Malmesbury all mention the anti-invasion measures and the Domesday Survey in consecutive sentences. This is anyway not surprising since the decision to carry out the Domesday Survey was taken at Gloucester during the Christmas festivities of 1085. What then was the connection, if any, between the great paid army and the great Domesday Survey? Here it is necessary to simplify, though not, I hope, to falsify, the interpretation of a great deal of very complex evidence. If we ask first what was the purpose of the Domesday Survey we are confronted by two sharply contrasted answers. To Round and Maitland, and especially to Maitland, the Domesday Survey was a geld survey, a survey of the old Anglo-Saxon land tax ('Our record is no register of title, it is no feodary, it is no custumal, it is no rent roll; it is a tax book, a geld book').[43] It was certain, Maitland held, that Domesday was designed to ensure the due and full payment of the land tax and probable, highly probable, that the Conqueror intended to sweep away the old assessment (heavily eroded by the political pressure of great landlords) and to replace it by a new and higher assessment. To Galbraith this was nonsense. 'The whole thinking behind the Survey was Norman, and therefore feudal'; the survey was 'designed to harness the wealth of England to the new contractual system of feudal baronies'; it had nothing to do with the assessment or collection of the land tax, and the very idea of reassessing it is an anachronism. Instead the purpose of the Survey was to record the resources of his tenants-in-chief in order that he might the more efficiently exploit the feudal incidents of reliefs, wardships and marriages. 'For centuries to come, then, England became perhaps the most "feudal" country in Europe.'[44]

Galbraith's starting point was that if we wish to discover why Domesday was made we should first ascertain how it was made, and on this he did work of fundamental importance, the findings of which, though they have been modified, have not been questioned. His apparently conclusive discovery, backed by convincing proofs, was that it was intended from the beginning that the information sought should be grouped tenurially and not territorially. What the central authorities wanted, and all that they ever obtained, was information on the estates of the Norman tenants-in-chief, not information on the administrative units of the hundreds and vills. The object of the Domesday Survey was Domesday Book. Domesday Book gave the information in Oxfordshire for the estates of Odo of Bayeux, the bishop of Lincoln, Robert d'Oilly and the rest: it did not give information on Bullingdon hundred, Wootton hundred, Bampton hundred nor on the individual vills within which two or more lords might have holdings. Now since – and here came Galbraith's knock-down argument – the land tax was assessed on and collected through the territorial units of the hundreds and vills, the Domesday Survey was totally useless for any assessment, reassessment or collection of the land tax.

---

[43] F.W. Maitland, *Domesday Book and Beyond* (London, 1960), 5.
[44] Galbraith, *Domesday Book*, ch. xi.

Galbraith's second discovery, also decisively proved, was a little inconvenient. It was that in 1086, the year of the Survey, an especially searching levy of the land tax was made in the south-western counties in the light of information produced by the Survey. Nevertheless his conclusion was that the link between the Survey and the tax was coincidental and not causal.[45]

A third point made by Galbraith was not a discovery but a rediscovery. He noticed that according to Orderic Vitalis, Ranulf Flambard urged Rufus to revise Domesday (*'ut totius Angliae reuiseret descriptionem'*),[46] and that there is some documentary evidence in support of this. Here Galbraith observed that 'the first evidence of an intention to reassess the geld belongs not to the reign of William I, but to the later years of Rufus', and he made the strange suggestion that instead of the idea of reassessment being the motive for the Domesday Survey the Survey may have suggested the ideas of reassessment.[47] And a fourth point was that no reassessment of the land tax was ever made, a point which is substantially, though not wholly, true and which had already been made by Maitland.

Nevertheless it is possible to restate and to amplify Maitland's original case for Domesday as a tax book, a land tax book. First there is Maitland's general contention that the government's intention in 1086 was to assess the tax on and collect the tax through the great landlords, ignoring the old machinery of the hundreds. As Maitland put it, 'of course the state will endeavour to collect the geld in big sums. It will endeavour to make the great folk answer for the geld. . . . For one reason the king can not easily tax the rich; for another he can not easily tax the poor; so he gets at the poor through the rich.'[48] The Norman lords, that is, were practised in exploiting the peasantry in their own interests; and in the Conqueror's eyes they were the appropriate instruments to exploit the peasants in his interests.

Two pieces of evidence out of many may be cited to show that in practice the land tax was collected in the way Maitland suggested. The first levy of the land tax after the making of Domesday Book of which any detailed descriptions survive is the levy of 4s on the hide in 1096. According to the Worcester chronicle this levy was imposed on the tenants-in-chief and not on the vills and hundreds. 'The bishops, abbots and abbesses broke up the gold and silver ornaments of their churches, while the earls, barons and sheriffs despoiled their knights and villeins, and brought a great quantity of gold and silver to the king.'[49] There could be no clearer statement that after the making of Domesday Book the land tax was levied on the plan of Domesday Book. To Galbraith it was 'quite unbelievable that the whole resources of an autocratic king should have been concentrated on the details of an annual custom, paid largely by the lands of the unfree *villani*'.[50] It seems a little more believable if we remember

---

[45] For example, Galbraith, *The Making of Domesday Book*, p. 96.
[46] *Orderic*, iv. 172.
[47] Galbraith, *Making of Domesday Book*, 212.
[48] Maitland, *Domesday Book and Beyond*, 121–2.
[49] Florence, ii. 40.
[50] Galbraith, *Making of Domesday Book*, 15.

that this levy of 1096, taken on the Domesday plan, produced the 10,000 marks required to enable Rufus to achieve his ambition of acquiring the whole duchy of Normandy.

The second piece of evidence is that early in Henry I's reign, before 1105, one of the knightly tenants of the abbey of Abingdon refused to pay even a half-penny of the land tax due from his manor of Sparsholt, with the result that the abbot had to make good the deficiency from the revenues of his own lands. The prudent abbot then paid Henry I well for a writ ordering the recalcitrant tenant 'to pay his geld with Abbot Faricius of Abingdon as he was wont, so that the abbot be not distrained on for his land, on pain of £10 forfeiture'.[51] On Galbraith's interpretation a tenant-in-chief had no interest in the geld payable by a sub-tenant holding of him by knight-service: the sub-tenant should have been assessed in his own hundred and have paid his geld direct to the sheriff or his local collector.

The argument that the Domesday Survey cannot have been intended as the basis for a general reassessment of the land tax since no such reassessment followed is superficially attractive. But it is an unsound principle of historical interpretation to argue back from results to intentions: history would be very different if it were the record of smoothly fulfilled purposes. To reassess a land tax in a society in which great landowners enjoy political power is a task of exceptional difficulty. Elizabeth I complained of the notorious underassessment of so many of her richer subjects. But in 1593 again at a time of military crisis, Sir Walter Raleigh opposed the proposal for a new assessment of the subsidy: it would, he said bluntly in the debate in the Commons, be 'inconvenient to have so many men's livings surveyed'.[52] Sir Henry Knyvet had suggested 'a survey of all mens Lands and Goods in England, and so much to be yearly levied as to serve the Queen to maintain wars'. And they were not surveyed.

Nevertheless there is evidence that the policy of reassessment was pursued and that it met with considerable success in some counties: by 1130 the Domesday figures for Berkshire and Surrey had been increased by 50 per cent and a 134 per cent respectively.[53] And for some manors Henry I's administration used the threat of reassessment to exact large once-for-all capital levies: here the casual survival of late evidence prevents us from knowing on how large a scale this device had been practised. And that the purpose of Domesday was fiscal is demonstrated by the fact that its strictly contemporary and official title was *descriptio totius Anglie*. The ordinary translation of *descriptio* as 'description' is plausible but unhelpful. I pointed out many years ago that since Merovingian times *descriptio* was widely used in official documents as the term for assessment and enrolment for public taxation;[54] and the same point has recently and

---

[51] *Chron. Abingdon*, ii. 125; *Regesta*, ii. no. 576 summarizing *Abingdon Chronicle*, ii. 91.

[52] *Tudor Economic Documents*, ed. R.H. Tawney and E. Power (London, 1924), ii. 233, 238.

[53] Maitland, *Domesday Book and Beyond*, 401, and *Pipe Roll 31 Henry I*, ed. J. Hunter (London, 1833).

[54] Prestwich, 'War and Finance in the Anglo-Norman State', *TRHS*, 5th ser., iv (1954), 26 n. 1.

independently been stressed by James Campbell.[55] In fact the use of the term in this sense goes back to the late Roman empire, and it continued to keep this meaning in twelfth-century England. When Henry II had a *descriptio* made of the Jews in England in 1168 he was not interested in their physical appearance or dress: he was raising 5,000 marks, a sum urgently needed to pay for the prosecution of his campaigns in Brittany and against Louis VII.[56]

It is reasonable to assume that the response of the Conqueror's administration to the military crisis of 1085–86 can best be gauged by examining that administration in action. And fortunately the making of Domesday Book allows us to see this with unusual clarity, thanks in considerable measure to Galbraith's patient reconstruction. Reduced to its essentials the procedure was as follows:

1. The country was divided into at least seven circuits or groups of counties and each was visited by a separate body of commissioners or *legati* (William of St Calais, bishop of Durham, heading the south – western circuit and the bishop of Lincoln, Earl Walter Giffard, Henry de Ferrers and Adam, brother of Eudo Dapifer, taking the west midlands circuit.

2. All the commissioners were given a very precise and detailed questionnaire or set of articles designed to discover fiscal assessments, economic resources in terms of land, labour and capital assets, cash values and possible development values: all this in triplicate showing the position as it had been under the Confessor, when the land was granted out by the Conqueror, and at the time of the Survey.

3. The circuit returns were then consolidated centrally at Winchester and reduced as far as possible to a common and compact form, the detailed entries for each county being provided with a convenient index. Evidently the commissioners for the thickly populated counties of East Anglia found their task particularly arduous, and their return arrived too late to be redrafted at Winchester, so that it survives intact as Little Domesday.

This structure of administration and the procedures adopted strikingly anticipates, even parallels, the structure and the procedures of regular Angevin administration and which Hubert Walter, as we have seen, put to such comprehensive use. There is the same systematic and remorseless inquisitiveness, the determination to base government on tested facts. There is the same use of commissioners sent out on circuit equipped with questionnaires put to men on the spot under oath. In 1086 there were seven circuits; in 1176 there were six, very similar in their composition. In 1086 the head of the south-western Domesday circuit was William of St Calais; and in the following year he was entrusted by Rufus with what William of Malmesbury calls the *administratio rerum publicarum*, the control of the regular operations of the state, a phrase strongly suggesting that it was intended that William of St Calais should have the powers of the later chief justiciars.[57] In 1176 one of the justices of the northern circuit

[55] J. Campbell, 'Observations on English Government', *TRHS*, 5th ser., xxv (1975), 49 and n. 65.

[56] *Gervase of Canterbury*, i. 205; Torigny, 236–9.

[57] Malmesbury, *Gesta Regum*, ii. 360.

was Ranulf Glanvill, Hubert Walter's uncle. Four years later Ranulf Glanvill was appointed chief justiciar. It would be absurd to claim that the administration which had to meet the emergency of threatened invasion in 1085–86 was no different from that over which Glanvill and Hubert presided a century later: there had intervened what Lady Stenton called with reference to the common law 'the Angevin leap forward'. But it is difficult to assimilate the government of England at the close of the Conqueror's reign at all closely to our first or feudal model. The great army of 1085–86 was conspicuously not a feudal army; the great Domesday Survey of 1086 was not the product of feudal thinking, nor can it be dismissed, as Richardson and Sayles chose to dismiss it, as 'a vast administrative mistake'.[58]

Note on further reading

Much work has been done on the financing of war in the late twelfth and early thirteenth centuries. See J.C. Holt, 'The Loss of Normandy and Royal Finances', in *War and Government in the Middle Ages*, 92–105, taking issue with views expressed by J. Gillingham in *Richard the Lionheart* (London, 1978), 303–4. Gillingham has discussed administration under Richard in his *Richard I* (London, 1999), 269–82. See also R.V. Turner and R.R. Heiser, *The Reign of Richard the Lionheart, Ruler of the Angevin Empire, 1189–1199* (Harlow, 2000), 141–62. The costs of war in Normandy under Richard have been examined by V. Moss, 'The Defence of Normandy 1193–8', *Anglo-Norman Studies* xxiv (2002), 145–61.

For the earlier period covered by this lecture, work has continued on Domesday, in part inspired by the anniversary of the great Survey in 1987. Among other works, this inspired the important volume edited by J.C. Holt, *Domesday Studies* (Woodbridge, 1987). Most recently, David Roffe has provided a new analysis, in *Domesday. The Inquest and the Book* (Oxford, 2000), in which he argues that the Domesday inquest should be separated from Domesday Book. It is unlikely that this contribution will end debate about Domesday, but the book provides a valuable summary of the many theories that have been put forward. The cogent arguments advanced by JOP to the effect that Domesday was intended as a reassessment of geld are but one competing theory among many, but it is interesting that one recent scholar wrote of the purpose of Domesday that 'the weight of scholarly opinion has tended to support Maitland's view that Domesday Book was the king's geld book and (unlike the manorial accounts of the later Middle Ages) not the lords' rent book'.[59]

Presumably because of lack of time, this lecture did not move on from Domesday to look at royal finance under Henry I, and the evidence of the 1130

---

[58] Richardson and Sayles, *Governance of Medieval England*, 28.

[59] G.D. Snooks, 'The dynamic role of the market in the Anglo-Norman Economy and beyond, 1086–1300', in *A Commercialising Economy. England 1086 to c. 1300*, ed. R.H. Britnell and B.M.S. Campbell (Manchester, 1995), 30.

Pipe Roll. For this, see J. Green, *The Government of England under Henry I* (Cambridge, 1986), and for a discussion of the problems of war finance under King Stephen, the same author's 'Financing Stephen's War', *Anglo-Norman Studies* xiv (1992), 91–114.

5

War and the Economy

In reviewing the attempts of the central administration to control and exploit the economic resources of England in the interests of the war effort in the reigns of Richard and John we saw something of the structure and working of the economy itself: the tin mines of Devon and Cornwall, the volume of foreign trade, the credit operations of the Jews, the shipbuilding and cloth industries and the whole scale of production which was so effectively tapped in the levy of the thirteenth of 1207. That account of the economy could have been greatly enlarged. The scale of agricultural production for the market is revealed in the detailed accounts of estates temporarily in the king's hands and so included in the Pipe Rolls. The Stuteville lands in Yorkshire produced an income of £1,250 during six months in 1203. Only 20 cent of this came from the rents of manors, while 65 per cent came from the sale of produce (37 per cent from the sale of stock, hides and skins, 28 per cent from the sale of corn).[1] About a quarter of the revenues of the bishopric of Lincoln in 1202 and of the archbishopric of Canterbury in 1206 were similarly derived from the sale of corn.[2]

The Cistercian abbey of Meaux, favourably situated on the Humber estuary, was investing actively at this time, buying additional stock, building mills, clearing water-courses, acquiring ships and enlarging its estates. One venture proved troublesome. A neighbouring knight, William Fossard, owed over £1,200 to the Jews and offered his land at Wharrom to the monastery on condition that it settled his debt. Initially all was well: the abbot persuaded Aaron of Lincoln to accept £800 in full settlement and Wharrom came to the monastery. But on Aaron's death the crown held Meaux liable for the whole of Fossard's debts to the Jews, and the abbey was put to much trouble and expense to prove its case. More trouble followed when Richard I rewarded Robert of Thornham by granting him Fossard's daughter in marriage. Robert of Thornham was a Kentish knight who had served with Richard on his crusade, commanding a squadron of galleys in the capture of Cyprus, then being appointed co-governor of the island – and now acting as seneschal of Gascony. He promptly claimed Wharrom as his wife's inheritance, and his influence with Hubert Walter enabled him to wrest the lands from the abbey. The abbey's loss of the estate, coinciding as it did with a bad harvest, £200 in taxation for Richard's ransom and the unlucky destruction by fire of a mill and a granary led to a temporary

---

1   *Pipe Roll 5 John*, ed. D.M. Stenton (PRS, 1938), 222–3.
2   *Pipe Roll 4 John*, ed. D.M. Stenton (PRS, 1937), 277, *Pipe Roll 8 John*, ed. D.M. Stenton (PRS, 1942), 54–5.

dispersion of the monks and the resignation of the abbot. However on the suggestion of the abbot of Fountains, the mother-house of Meaux, the distressed monks elected as their new abbot a complete outsider possessing the two indispensable qualifications of being an excellent man of business and a clerk and intimate of Hubert Walter. Wharrom was duly recovered; and despite the difficulties of the interdict the monks of Meaux were able to resume their profitable policy of investment and their study of market prices.[3] It is an instructive story illustrating the effect of credit operations on the land market, the play of political influence, the vicissitudes of harvests, fire and taxation and the resilience and resourcefulness of those who managed and defended the abbey's estates.

Foreign capital was attracted by the opportunities which England offered. In 1195 the Flemish merchant, Hugh Oisel of Ypres, bought licences to trade in England for £300.[4] This evidently proved a profitable investment, for in 1199 King John acknowledged a debt of 1,700 marks to Hugh, 1,000 having been lent to Otto of Brunswick and 700 to John himself.[5] It was provided that Hugh should recover his money by farming the exchange of all England at a reduced figure, and therefore increased profit, for two years. At the same time Hugh secured further privileges as a royal merchant and a citizen of London.[6] And by 1203 Hugh was of sufficient substance to bid not only for the farm of the exchange but for the administration of the recently established national customs system.[7]

At the same time representatives of a yet more formidable financial power were appearing in England, predecessors of the Riccardi, Frescobaldi, Bardi and Peruzzi who made the great loans to Edward I and Edward III which enabled those monarchs to adopt the tempting but risky policy of fighting first and paying – or rather taxing, or even defaulting – afterwards. Richard I had acknowledged a debt of 2,125 marks to merchants of Piacenza, a debt incurred in order to gain papal support for the election of his nephew Otto as king of Germany,[8] and merchants of Piacenza were in England apparently collecting this debt in 1209 and 1210.[9] But as early as 9 September 1208 three merchants of Bologna were licensed to spend the large sum of 820 marks, derived from the repayment of a loan which they had made to Robert fitz Roger, on buying cloth of Stamford and to export it under safe conduct.[10] This is of interest for several reasons. It is the earliest known instance of an Italian loan to an English layman. It shows how a lending transaction enabled the Italian merchants to gain a foothold in English trade; and the fact that the Italians chose to invest in English

3 *Chronicon Monasterii de Melsa*, ed. E.A. Bond, Rolls Series, i. 173–8, 231–4, 289–91).

4 *Pipe Roll 8 Richard I*, 295–6

5 *Rot. Chart*, 11b–12.

6 *Rot. Chart*, 12b and 13.

7 40 marks for the exchange and 1,000 marks for the customs. *Pipe Roll 5 John*, 11–12, and *Rotuli de Liberate ac de Misis et Praestitas*, ed. T. Duffus Hardy (London, 1844), 35, where the offer for the exchange is given as 50 marks.

8 *Foedera*, I, 78; *Rotuli Chartarum in Turri Londoniensis asservati*, i, ed. T. Duffus Hardy (London, 1837), 96b.

9 *Rot. Misae 11 John*, 143, 148. See also pp. 8 and 46 for repayments in 1200 and 1203.

10 *Rot. Litt. Pat.*, 86a.

cloth is testimony to the importance of the English cloth industry at this period. Robert fitz Roger was a successful man: for the greater part of John's reign he was sheriff of Northumberland, rapidly enlarged his estates there and was also trading on his own account, for in April 1206 he had been licensed to export a shipload of corn from Tynemouth.[11] He had no difficulty in meeting the farm of Northumberland, and he may therefore have borrowed from the Italians for the purposes of investment and not for reasons of personal improvidence.[12]

Elsewhere we can see more clearly the economic policy of the more enterprising men who controlled the great estates in the late twelfth and early thirteenth centuries, a policy of centralized management, resuming lands which had been leased, concentrating corn-growing or sheep-raising in areas best fitted for them, and investing heavily in capital improvements – mills, drainage, communications and buildings. One such manager was Abbot Samson of Bury St Edmunds. His first act as abbot was to survey the lands and then to visit them himself. Takings were pushed up fourfold or fivefold,[13] expenditure rigorously controlled and audited weekly, new barns erected, a manor picked up cheaply from the crown, professional lawyers engaged, corn withheld until prices reached their peak and timber reserves vigilantly watched over. Occasionally the abbot's methods were a little rough. He was irritated by the bishop of Ely establishing a new market at Lakenheath which threatened the profits of that at Bury St Edmunds, bought a royal order for its suppression, and then, when this was slow to take effect, sent off at midnight a small army said to be six hundred strong with instructions to break up the offending market and to carry off in chains such buyers and sellers as they found at this rival establishment. These energetic methods served the monks of Bury well. Samson himself maintained a stable of twenty-six horses, ran his own huntsman and hounds, and made a number of parks for himself.

Similar qualities of enterprise were shown on the estates of the bishopric of Winchester. The Winchester accounts for 1208–9 show land being brought back into demesne, sheep imported from Lincolnshire to improve the local breed, marling of the land undertaken to increase the yield, manors grouped for specialized production, and investment made in mills, including the new-type fulling mills. Much of the surplus produce of the Winchester estates was funnelled into the export trade through the port of Southampton. There the merchant Gervase the Rich had been prospering. From 1182 to 1190 he farmed the revenues of the port and then, in Richard's absence on crusade, lent money to Count John and, prudently hedging his bets, visited Richard during his captivity in Germany to offer assistance for which he received a grant of land worth £20 per annum. He financed building developments on crown land at Portsmouth, though uncharitable jurors later reported that he had made nothing more than a heap of stones on the quayside. His activities as a merchant trading in wool, wine and corn and as a moneylender enabled him to found the hospital

---

[11] *Rot. Litt. Pat.*, 62a.
[12] See J.C. Holt, *The Northerners*, 62–3.
[13] *The Chronicle of Jocelin of Brakelond*, 33.

of Godshouse in Southampton. A Fellow of Queen's has cause to be grateful to Gervase, for in the fourteenth century Godshouse and its properties came to the college.[14]

Another indication of the expansive energies within the English economy in the reigns of Richard and John is provided by the fact that the three decades from 1191 to 1220 saw the foundation of approximately thirty-four new towns, or one fifth of all those founded in England during the Middle Ages; and, as Beresford pointed out, only two, Portsmouth and Liverpool, were founded by Richard and John for naval and military reasons, the rest such as Evesham and Leeds being due to the speculative enterprise of ecclesiastical and lay land-lords.[15] The prosperity of Lincoln and the surrounding countryside is illustrated by the financing of the great new cathedral of Lincoln, begun in 1192. For this an appeal was launched and a gild formed with an annual income put at 1,000 marks a year.[16] Another fund-raising device was the establishment of a works chantry to encourage benefactors by the inducement of prayers being offered for their souls. King John's help was enlisted, and in December 1205 he issued a general proclamation to all in the diocese urging support for the unfinished fabric (*egregia structura* and *nobile opus*) and sanctioning the work of the gild for the next five years.[17] By the end of John's reign there was 11,000 marks (£7,333) in the fund.[18]

The war effort of the reigns of Richard and John was therefore conducted in the context of a relatively developed and, despite the demands of that war effort, a still developing economy. In some sectors the war demands operated as a forced draught rather than as a damper. Mining was one such sector. In 1194, faced with Richard's urgent demands for money, Hubert Walter had a silver mine at Careghofa in Wales opened up, a castle built to protect the workings, a garrison provided and arrangements made to mint the silver into coins at Shrewsbury.[19] In 1201 manorial rights in Devon and Cornwall were overridden in favour of the tinners who 'were given to prospect freely in search of new deposits'.[20] A useful stimulus was given to the iron industry in the Forest of Dean when it was required to produce 50,000 horseshoes and £100 worth of iron for Richard's ships when his crusading forces were being made ready in 1190;[21] and a greater stimulus was given to the English shipbuilding industry when it was required to construct and repair ships and galleys under the direction of John's naval administrator, William of Wrotham. Against the drain of treasure from England must be set the effects of land transfers resulting from war taxa-

---

14 For the career of Grervase see J.M. Kaye, *The Cartulary of Godshouse*, introduction to vol. 1.

15 M.W. Beresford, *New Towns of the Middle Ages*, 330–7; and see E.M. Carus-Wilson, 'The First Half-Century of the Borough of Stratford-upon-Avon', *EcHR*, 2nd ser., xviii (1965), 46–63.

16 Coggeshall, 111.

17 *Rot. Litt. Pat.*, 57.

18 J.W.F. Hill, *Medieval Lincoln* (Cambridge, 1948), 112–13.

19 *Pipe Roll 6 Richard I*, ed. D.M. Stenton (PRS, 1928), 141.

20 G.R. Lewis, *The Stannaries*, appendix B, Stannary charter of 1201.

21 *Pipe Roll 2 Richard I*, 53.

tion and the need of both Richard and John to reward their servants, transfers which often meant that land passed from the hands of the inefficient to the efficient. The monks of Meaux were far better equipped to manage Wharrom than was its improvident and indebted former owner, William Fossard. William Brewer had a long career in the service of the crown under Richard and John. He was one of the associate justiciars of England during Richard's crusade, a baron of the exchequer, and under John was sheriff of eleven counties at different times. He was efficient to the point of being oppressive. One of the concessions purchased from the crown by the men of Dorset and Somerset in 1210 for 1,200 marks was that William Brewer should never again be their sheriff.[22] If he was efficient in the crown's interests he was also efficient in furthering his own interests. He built up a substantial barony and was prompt in this age of urban expansion to convert two of his manors into boroughs.[23]

The demands of the war in respect of English manpower appear to have been relatively small. In the letter of April 1196 in which Richard instructed Hubert Walter to send to Normandy all the money and treasure he had, he also gave instructions for the dispatch of troops. All who owed military service in England with the exception, a large exception, of William de Braose, William d'Aubigny and all barons of the Welsh march were to cross to Normandy, prepared for a long campaign. None however was to burden himself with many knights: indeed Richard prescribed for each a maximum of seven knights.[24] But in the same year at least 2,100 Welshmen were sent over to Normandy.[25] A clearer numerical indication of the number of knights Richard expected to be able to raise from England is afforded by his demand at the end of 1197 for 300 knights to serve for a year, or money in lieu at the rate of 3s a day for each knight.[26] It is probable that the greatest deflection of productive manpower in England to military ends occurred when a general impressment of ships and their crews was made for an overseas campaign. In May 1206 John ordered an impressment of this kind for his expedition to Poitou, and William of Wrotham's accounts show that approximately 3,000 sailors were taken onto the royal payroll. Of these only just over 500 were galleymen and hence presumably permanently in the king's service.[27]

It must also be remembered that between 1153 and 1214 England was not a theatre of war. There was a brief campaign against Hugh Mortimer in 1155 entailing the sieges of three castles in the Welsh march. There were the limited operations in England during the rebellion of 1173–74, though these left the south of England untouched. And there was the rebellion of John in 1193–94, suppressed relatively easily by the sieges of Windsor, Tickhill, Nottingham and Marlborough. We hear nothing of the harrying of whole provinces, of what has

---

22 *Pipe Roll 12 John*, ed. C.F. Slade (PRS, 1951), 75.
23 S. Painter, *The Reign of King John*, 72–8.
24 *Diceto*, ii. lxxx.
25 *Pipe Roll 8 Richard I*, xvii.
26 Howden, *Gesta*, iv. 40.
27 *Pipe Roll 8 John*, 148 gives 2,889 sailors; *Pipe Roll 9 John*, ed. A.M. Kirkus (PRS, 1946), 168 gives 72 sailors from Ipswich; and *Pipe Roll 11 John*, ed. D.M. Stenton (PRS, 1949), 124 accounts for 11 ships on this expedition.

been called 'government by punitive expedition',[28] of the burning of towns, or of the policy of total war adopted by Stephen in 1149. Henry II's three major campaigns, the Toulouse expedition of 1159, the Welsh campaign of 1165 and the Irish expedition of 1171 were conducted in the knowledge that the problem of security in England had been solved. Indeed it was in connection with the first of these expeditions that Robert of Torigny made his observation that Henry II, unwilling to trouble the knights engaged in farming pursuits (*agrarii milites*), or the townsmen or peasants, relied on his leading barons with their small retinues and a vast host of mercenaries. What Henry II required from the knights in England was not knight-service but jury service.

One indication of the wealth which could be accumulated in England during the quieter times of Henry II's reign is given in an account of the treasure left by Roger of Pont l'Evêque, archbishop of York from 1154 to 1181. On Roger's death the crown seized the cash and plate found in his chests and, according to Ralph of Diceto, this amounted to £11,000 of old money (old because there had been a recoinage in 1180) together with 300 gold pieces and a quantity of plate which included 1 gold cup, 16 silver cups, 3 silver salts, 40 silver spoons, 8 silver saucers and a great silver dish.[29] The precision of this list suggests that it is taken from an inventory made by the royal officials. Indeed we know from Howden that Henry II had ordered the justices to make a careful inquest into the money left by the archbishop. Ralph of Diceto was well placed to see the inventory. He had recently become dean of St Paul's where several royal clerks held canonries; and he was a friend of Richard of Ilchester, bishop of Winchester, Henry II's great minister and a leading member of the exchequer.[30] If indeed Ralph of Diceto's figures and list were taken from an official inventory they are impressive indeed, especially when we remember that the archbishop of York died on the eve of the great inflation of the four decades 1180–1220. For comparative purposes we may note the emphasis which McFarlane laid on a similar inventory of the liquid assets of Richard Fitzalan, earl of Arundel, made almost exactly two centuries later and giving a total in cash or bullion of just over £60,000.[31] William of Newburgh, whose priory lay only fifteen miles north of York, commented that although Archbishop Roger had been inattentive to his pastoral duties he left his successors nothing to worry about in respect of revenues or buildings (*de augmentis reddituum vel amplitudine aedificiorum*).[32] Members of some Oxford governing bodies must wish that their predecessors had left them so happily placed.

We have now to turn back to the first century of English feudalism and to ask two general questions: what was the economic context within which the wars of

---

[28] W.E. Kapelle, *The Norman Conquest of the North* (London, 1979), ch. 5.
[29] Diceto, ii. 12.
[30] Diceto, ii. 319–20.
[31] K.B. McFarlane, *The Nobility of Later Medieval England* (Oxford, 1973), 88–91. See *Gesta,* i. 289 for evidence that the inventory was incomplete, the bishop of Durham having had 300 marks from the archbishop of York; and see the Pipe Roll for other action against clerks at York.
[32] Newburgh, i. 225.

the reigns of the Conqueror, Rufus, Henry I and Stephen were conducted? And what effects did those wars have upon the English economy? No one would now answer these questions as did Vinogradoff when he said of post-Conquest England that it was predominantly a land of natural husbandry in which commercial intercourse and money dealings played an entirely subordinate part and that accordingly land tenure was the main condition of military service. Mercenary bands did appear in the Norman and Angevin periods, Vinogradoff conceded, but they were merely 'casual combinations of men': they could not assume a leading part on account of the lack of money in the royal treasury. His argument was largely *a priori*: since men were granted land in return for the obligation to find troops when it would have been more efficient to have hired professional soldiers, the kings must have been driven to this expedient by the lack of money. And the lack of money was explained by the natural economy, a cellular and self-sufficient agricultural husbandry.[33]

A much more sophisticated account of the economic structure and changes of this period has been given by Postan, the most influential and the most enlivening of the economic historians of medieval England during the last half-century. He rejected the whole concept of 'natural economy' for any period of English history for which written evidence exists. And he rejected too the assumption of steady and evolutionary economic growth: periods of expansion and boom have been followed by periods of stagnation and recession. It is highly probable, he held, that there had been an agricultural boom at some period in the Anglo-Saxon era and possible that the turn of the Anglo-Saxon and Norman periods saw a slump. But while Postan taught us that the English economy of the eleventh century was more developed than earlier historians had allowed, he also stressed that it was not until the late twelfth century that favourable conditions – settled times, buoyant markets and prices and improved, commercial and financial techniques – conspired in 'breaking up the self-sufficiency of local markets and in commercializing the economic activities of men'. Land was certainly farmed out and leased for money rents in the twelfth century; but while to Gilbert Stuart these practices indicated the rise of commerce, to Postan they indicated the sensible preference of landlords for fixed yields to fluctuating profits in difficult times. Indeed this whole system of indirect management of land was 'everywhere inimical to expansion': rapacious or inefficient farmers wasted the precarious assets of stock and equipment. To Postan the best indicator of the nature of the twelfth-century English economy lay in the practice of farming out land. The Latin term *firma* means fixed or settled. And since farming contracts became more general in the twelfth century this proves that landlords saw no prospect of increasing their incomes but used their coercive authority to make their tenants, free and unfree, suffer all the evils of bad harvests, predatory neighbours and disturbed conditions.

Moreover this interpretation of the evidence for the economic structure is supported in a singularly reassuring way by an interpretation of the evidence for military organization and the conduct of war. The first century of English

---

[33] Vinogradoff, *English Society in the Eleventh Century*, 21–2, 208, 213.

feudalism when military needs were largely met by unpaid service coincides with the period when the volume of production and exchange was low. The introduction of knight-service and the process of subinfeudation disrupted the greater estates; the scattered holdings discouraged centralized management and production for the market; and feudal particularism militated against the establishment and maintenance of order within which alone economic enterprise could flourish. And the apparent rigidity of the Norman land settlement as recorded in Domesday seems to forbid, or to restrict very narrowly, any commercial dealings in land itself. There are many references in Domesday such as that which tells us that three sokemen at Grantchester who had been free to sell their land in King Edward's day had been succeeded by two knights holding of Count Eustace.[34] If the land itself was largely removed from the market and firmly appropriated for the support of those who fought and those who prayed, we may conclude that the Norman Conquest arrested, and perhaps even reversed, an earlier movement towards specialization and market exchanges. Postan laid particular emphasis on the disruption caused by war: 'the seizure of land by turbulent neighbours and all other incidents of feudal and civil war . . . appear as local manifestations of a *malaise* which during the greater part of the twelfth century affected England as a whole'.[35] He noted the highly adverse conditions during the civil war between Stephen and Matilda (strangely dated as between 1130 and 1175) in which both sides recruited by subinfeudating local followers and when 'a swarm of strong men capable of preying on their neighbours' was let loose upon the country'.[36]

This account of the English economy and of the effects of war upon it has been subjected to criticism, and especially by Edward Miller;[37] and it appears to me substantially mistaken. First, we may dispose of Vinogradoff's contention that during this period the lack of money in the royal treasury meant that mercenary troops (or, to use a preferable term, paid troops) were used only occasionally as casual combinations of men. I do not wish to repeat in detail what I have written elsewhere, and many years ago, but a few pieces of evidence may be given. William of Poitiers, the Conqueror's biographer, a man with personal military experience writing within a few years of the event, tells us how the Conqueror held his invasion force together on the Norman coast for a month in the autumn of 1066 while awaiting a favourable wind. Good order was maintained for, William of Poitiers continues, tillage was utterly forbidden, and fifty thousand troops were maintained by the duke's pay (*stipendio ipsius alebantur*). The number of troops is greatly exaggerated, and it is unlikely that the whole invasion army was in receipt of regular pay from the Conqueror; but it is even more unlikely that the pay was the product of William of Poitiers's imagination

---

[34] *DB*, i. 196a
[35] Postan, 'Glastonbury Estates in the Twelfth Century: A Reply', *EcHR.*, 2nd ser., ix (1957), 117.
[36] Postan, *Medieval Economy and Society*, 97.
[37] E. Miller, 'England in the Twelfth and Thirteenth Centuries: An Economic Contrast', *EcHR*, 2nd ser., xxiv (1975), 1–14.

and not of the Conqueror's purse.[38] Paid troops continued to be used regularly in the Conqueror's reign by himself, by William fitz Osbern, who incurred a severe rebuke for paying troops too generously,[39] and by the earl of East Anglia in his rebellion of 1075.[40] Rufus was notorious for his extravagant expenditure on troops; William of Malmesbury tells us that 'sellers sold to him at their own prices and knights fixed their own rates of pay'[41] while Suger described him as 'a wonderful merchant and paymaster of troops'.[42] It is significant that in these contexts William of Malmesbury should have used the words *commercium* and *mercimonium*, trade and merchandise, and that Suger should have employed the term *mercator,* merchant: for Rufus war was indeed a trade and troops, castles and allies its merchandise. As for Henry I it is enough to note Robert of Torigny's statement that even in the relative tranquillity of Henry's last ten years his wealth allowed him to defend his frontiers with large forces which he paid adequately and rewarded.[43]

In his Ford Lectures McFarlane noted that with few exceptions historians had failed to grasp the first essential point of warfare in the late Middle Ages: the opportunities for profit presented by pay, ransoms and booty. The same observation holds good for the earlier period which is my concern. Suger noted that Rufus's knights when captured were so anxious to get back on the payroll that they speedily ransomed themselves, while the impecunious French suffered long periods of imprisonment.[44] And the pages of Orderic Vitalis are studded with references to the constant traffic in ransoms. Nor was it merely the rank and file of the armies who served for pay. The earls of Edward I's reign may have stood out against receiving pay in what McFarlane called an expensive self-denial, but the counts of this period showed no such reluctance.[45] The count of Flanders was retained by Henry I for an annual money fee, and if William of Malmesbury is right the arrangement went back to the Conqueror's time and had been kept up by Rufus.[46] The count of Maine was hired by Henry I for the campaign which finally gave him Normandy.[47] In 1136 the two brothers, Waleran count of Meulan and Robert earl of Leicester, hired the services of Theobald count of Blois for 100 marks,[48] while in 1139 Rotrou count of Mortagne was similarly taken into King Stephen's pay.[49]

Contemporaries did not fail to notice the connection between the wars of this period and the taxation which sustained them. We need look no further than the Anglo-Saxon Chronicle. In 1103, 1104 and 1105, the years in which Henry I set

---

[38] *Gesta Guillelmi*, 102.
[39] Malmesbury, *Gesta Regum*, ii. 314.
[40] Lanfranc, Letters, no. 35.
[41] Malmesbury, *Gesta Regum*, ii. 368.
[42] Suger, *Vie de Louis VI*, 8.
[43] Interpolation in William of Jumièges, *Gesta Normannorum Ducum*, ed. J. Marx, 296.
[44] Suger, *Vie de Louis VI*, 10.
[45] McFarlane, *Nobility of Later Medieval England*, 162.
[46] Malmesbury, *Gesta Regum*, ii. 478–9.
[47] *Orderic*, vi. 78, and see the mistranslation of *conduxit* as 'took with him'.
[48] *Orderic*, vi. 464.
[49] *Orderic*, vi. 534.

about reducing Normandy, we hear of 'all sorts of taxes', of 'taxes that never ceased or diminished' and, very explicitly, of 'the various taxes that never ceased, before the king crossed over [to Normandy], and while he was there, and after he came back again'.[50] Similarly in 1118, after reporting Henry I's campaigns against the king of France and the counts of Anjou and Flanders, the chronicler added gloomily that 'England paid dear for all this, because of the various taxes that never ceased in the course of all this year.'

How dearly did England pay for the wars of this period? And what kind of economy supported the war effort? At first sight it appears from Domesday that the campaigns, castle-building, taxes and extortions of the conquerors together with deliberate devastation and the operations of pirates in the Channel had combined to throttle urban life and to disrupt the pattern of trade: the evidence of the entries for York, Norwich, Chester, Shrewsbury and Oxford, for example, is decisive in its picture of abandoned houses, reduced population, and poverty. But even in 1086 there were more encouraging signs of growth, especially in the southern counties and along the south coast. Sandwich and Chichester expanded;[51] within the abbey of Fécamp's holdings in Sussex there was a new borough, possibly Winchelsea;[52] while Rochester quadrupled in value during the Conqueror's reign, and in 1086 was being farmed for twice its valuation.[53] At the exposed outpost of Rhuddlan, which had been raided by the Welsh in 1075, eighteen burgesses had been established alongside the castle, and the Normans were actively prospecting for iron mines in the neighbourhood.[54] Bury St Edmunds was a conspicuous instance of successful and planned development. It more than doubled its population in the Conqueror's reign; and the Domesday entry complacently records the construction of 342 houses on land which had been under the plough in the Confessor's time.[55]

Occasionally pride in individual achievement breaks through the ordinarily colourless formulae of Domesday. At Bermondsey the entry records a church and adds that it was new and beautiful, *nova et pulchra*;[56] and on Edward of Salisbury's manor of Wilcot in Wiltshire we are told of a new church, a fine house and a good vineyard.[57] It is significant that feeling should colour these entries in connection with buildings, for the Conqueror's reign saw the beginning of what has fairly been called 'a revolution in the art of building to which no parallel can be found at any other period of history'.[58] Indeed the scale and nature of these new buildings was not always controlled by careful estimates of the revenue available or by a prudent balancing of the aspirations of the church

---

[50] *Anglo-Saxon Chronicle*, entries for 1103, 1104 and 1105.
[51] *DB*, i. 3a, 23a.
[52] *DB*, i, 17a.
[53] *DB*, i. 2a.
[54] *DB*, i. 269a.
[55] *DB*, ii. 372a
[56] *DB*, i. 30a.
[57] *DB*, i. 69a.
[58] D. Knowles, *The Monastic Order in England* (2nd edn, Cambridge, 1963), 120.

against the needs of defence (though, as we saw earlier, some cathedrals were sited with both considerations in mind).

Domesday is however an inadequate guide to the English economy of 1086 and almost useless as an indicator of the forces of economic change which were to operate in the following half-century. It is inadequate because it is casual in mentioning markets; centres of trade and industry are often half-concealed in its manorial entries; and, as Lennard showed so convincingly, apparently conventional valuations turn out to be money rents and apparently precise statements of money rents turn out from other evidence to understate the yield. Landlords were not ordinarily disposed to boast of their achievements nor to volunteer a comprehensive statement of their resources and income. Although the Domesday questionnaire required the commissioners to estimate future development possibilities by asking 'if more can be got than is being got', the answers were usually unhelpful. At the end of the long account of the bishop of Worcester's three hundreds of Oswaldslaw Domesday records the comprehensive claim that on all the manors there could be no more plough-teams than those listed. As Maitland commented, this account was so favourable to the bishopric that it might have been dictated by its representative; and it probably was.[59]

Domesday is largely useless, or at least inadequate, as an indictor of the forces of economic change for two main reasons. First, it conveys an unnaturally rigid impression of the control of economic resources and of the return from them. Even where Domesday does show changes at work it does not reveal their full force. We learn from Domesday for example that Sandwich had paid a farm of £40 when Lanfranc received it (i.e. in 1070) and 40,000 herrings; while in 1086 it was paying £50 and the herrings as before – a useful increase in the money farm of 25 per cent in sixteen years. But Domesday Monachorum records a further increase in one year from £50 to £70, the herring element remaining constant – an increase of 40 per cent in one year.[60] This instance of rent revision throws doubt on Postan's fundamental assumption that whenever we find assets being farmed for a fixed sum this proves that the holder of these assets saw no prospect of increasing his income and was content to settle for a fixed return from a long-term contract. Where we can compare Domesday valuations or renders with later figures from the reign of Henry I Postan's assumption appears highly doubtful. Five royal manors in Herefordshire paid £50 in 1086 and £80 in 1130. Five Derbyshire manors were rented out for £40 per annum in 1086, while one of these alone, Wirksworth, was bringing in £80 per annum in 1130, though here the existence of lead mines strongly suggests that we are dealing with the expanding profits of industry and not merely of agriculture. The great estate of Necton in Norfolk was farmed out for £60 in 1086. In about 1115 the son of the Domesday holder granted it in fee farm for £80 per annum, though reserving the right to lease individual vills, compensating the tenant at the ruling market rate. He added the further and significant assurance that even if any third party should offer more than £80 he would keep to his orig-

---

[59] Maitland, *Domesday Book and Beyond*, 423–4.
[60] *DB*, i. 3a; *Domesday Monachorum*, 89.

inal bargain. This would have been pointless unless lords, tempted by rising land values, had been in the habit of breaking their contracts.[61] Indeed a greater man than the lord of Necton had already set an unedifying example, repeatedly breaking his lease in order to secure the highest possible return. This was the Conqueror himself. 'When he had given his lands at farm as dearly as he could he gave them to another who offered yet more, and then to yet another, always careless of his pact and intent on greater gains'.[62]

The second reason for Domesday's inadequacy as an indicator of economic trends lies in its date. The Conqueror's reign had seen much campaigning and devastation. But from 1088 until 1136 the internal peace and order in England was broken only by the brief Mowbray rebellion of 1095 and by the equally brief Montgomery rebellion of 1102. Rufus was notorious for his severity against those who infringed the king's peace, and after 1096 was equally effective in bringing order to Normandy. English writers may be thought sycophantic in their praise of the peace and security enforced by Henry I; but Suger similarly praised Henry for the firmness of his administration, emphasizing that not a single English magnate so much as dared to mutter against Henry throughout his administration. He added revealingly that under Henry the security of the countryside meant full barns and that full barns meant an abundance of money.[63]

Within Britain, Norman military power in the reigns of Rufus and Henry created and protected new areas for colonization and developments. Rufus seized Carlisle from the Scots, built and garrisoned a castle there and settled the region with peasants drawn from the south of England.[64] This proved a profitable as well as a defensively useful venture. By 1130 Carlisle produced a net annual revenue of over £200 for the crown. The lead and silver mines of Alston Moor were farmed by the burgesses for £40 per annum, almost covering the cost of the paid garrison of Carlisle castle (£42 7s 7½d; note that there was no feudal castle-guard). Three years later the exciting news reached Normandy that a new vein of silver had been discovered at Carlisle and that the prospectors were paying £500 per annum to King Henry.[65] This was an exaggeration, though by 1190 the Carlisle mines were being farmed for £100 per annum, an increase of two and a half fold over the 1130 figure.[66]

Even wider opportunities were created and exploited in South Wales. The castle and borough of Cardiff were established by Robert fitz Hamo, the conqueror of Glamorgan; Swansea by the earl of Warwick; Kidwelly by Roger of Salisbury; and the plantation of Carlisle paralleled by the plantation of Flemings in Pembrokeshire. The results of this military and colonial enterprise were enthusiastically described by the author of *Gesta Stephani*, well placed as an observer if he was indeed the bishop of Bath:

---

61 D.C. Douglas, *The Social Structure of Medieval East Anglia* (Oxford, 1927), 254.
62 Huntingdon, *Historia Anglorum*, 209, based on the Anglo-Saxon Chronicle.
63 Suger, *Vie de Louis VI*, 98–102.
64 *Anglo-Saxon Chronicle*, s.a. 1092.
65 *Pipe Roll 31 Henry I*, 140–2; Torigny, 123.
66 *Pipe Roll 2 Richard I*, 52.

the Normans . . . added Wales to their dominion and fortified it with countless castles; they perseveringly civilized it after they had vigorously subdued its inhabitants; to encourage peace they imposed laws and decrees upon them; and they made the land so productive and abounding in all kinds of resources that you would have reckoned it in no way inferior to the most fertile part of Britain.[67]

Perhaps the most convincing evidence for the structure of and changes in the English economy in the period between the making of Domesday Book and the outbreak of civil war in Stephen's reign is afforded not by Domesday itself, the Pipe Roll of 1130 and the manorial surveys but by the more general comments of contemporaries: William of Malmesbury, Symeon of Durham, the bishop of Bath, the poet Lawrence of Durham, Henry of Huntingdon, and the compilers of local accounts at Abingdon, Evesham, Battle abbey and Canterbury. Looking back from the last quarter of the twentieth century we are inevitably struck by the primitive, relatively uniform and predominantly agrarian nature of the English economy in the late eleventh and early twelfth centuries. Yet to William of Malmesbury, writing in the 1120s, England was distinguished from its more backward neighbours by the very characteristics we think of as modern. Commenting on the dependence of Ireland on goods imported from England he pointed out that the Irish were an agrarian people leading a poor and squalid life, whereas the English, like the French, enjoyed a more civilized way of life, living in towns and practising trade.[68] And it is significant that he chose the word *inurbanus* to describe unseemly talk or conduct in his own monastery: his values were drawn from an urban civilization.[69] Throughout the *Gesta Pontificum* William of Malmesbury repeatedly noted the regional variations in agriculture and the range, volume and importance of trade: the wealth of London, the orchards and vineyards of the Vale of Gloucester, the volume of Bristol shipping, the pastoral economy of Cheshire and its dependence on trade with Ireland, the prosperity of Lincoln, en emporium for those coming by land and sea, and Henry I's good sense in founding his abbey at Reading, at a point where almost all travellers could turn off to the more populous cities of England. He was keenly interested in the new buildings which were transforming the appearance of the towns and cities in his own day; he noted with envy the very high annual cash income of the bishop of Ely (£1,400) and with disapproval the small proportion of this (£300) which went to the monks of Ely; and he singled out for particular mention Henry I's measures on currency, trade, the cloth industry and purveyance.[70]

What then was the relation between the wars of this period and the fortunes of the English economy? The Norman Conquest was both destructive and disrup-

---

[67] Lloyd, *History of Wales*, ii. 423–46; *Gesta Stephani*, 14.

[68] *cultiori genere vitae, urbes nundinarum commercio inhabitant* – Malmesbury, *Gesta Regum*, ii. 485.

[69] Malmesbury, *Gesta Pontificum*, p. 432; and compare *Chron. Abingdon*, ii. 44–5 for praise of Abbot Faricius's *urbanitas*.

[70] Malmesbury, *Gesta Pontificum*, 69, 138, 140, 145, 152, 156, 172, 183, 195, 201, 206, 208, 274, 291–2, 295, 308, 300, 311–12, 324; *Gesta Regum*, ii. 305, 306, 374, 484, 489, 547.

tive. To very many of the Englishmen who survived the campaigns it meant poverty, flight from the towns, exploitation and oppression: in our concern with extracting statistical information from Domesday we should not ignore its occasional use of more emotive language and the contrast between Edward of Salisbury with his new church, fine house and good vineyard and the Englishman who had once had his own small manor and was now holding it under his French lord, heavily and miserably, *graviter et miserabiliter.* And there were very many who were no longer on the land which had once been theirs. The forty years after the battle of Hastings were years of severe and almost constant military activity, activity which imposed a severe strain on English resources and on the administrative skills and political dexterity of those who sought to hold together the new Anglo-Norman state. But England was already a rich and relatively developed country before the Conquest; and the Normans had crossed the Channel to enjoy its riches and not merely to loot and despoil them. By the end of Henry's reign the controlled use of their military strength in England and its extension into the colonial territories of the north and into Wales had helped to create the framework for renewed economic growth and expansion. In some respects more than a framework had been created. The administrative skills needed to back the war effort could be and were applied to the more productive management of the economy. 'Survey your lands and tenements' was Walter of Henley's advice to improving landlords in the thirteenth century; and the landlords of late-eleventh-century England were taught that lesson by the Domesday survey of 1086, a lesson they learned and applied in the private surveys such as those which have survived from Ely and Peterborough.

Moreover the royal administration, long primarily concerned with providing the means for waging war, also acted as a medieval school of business management. The bishopric of Durham was ruled in succession by William of St Calais, a Domesday commissioner, by Flambard, Rufus's former war minister, and by Geoffrey Rufus, chancellor to Henry I; and a similar sequence can be traced in most of the bishoprics. And it is perhaps no accident that the earliest recorded baronial exchequers are those of the earls of Leicester and Gloucester, for the first earl of Leicester was the leading adviser of Henry I during the earlier part of his reign and the first earl of Gloucester a dominant member of his court in Henry's later years, the man who with Brian fitz Count carried out the audit of the royal treasure in 1129. But an even greater contribution to the skills of management was made by the immensely rapid growth of schools and education during this period. The poet Lawrence of Durham complained that his duties in managing Flambard's courts and keeping his accounts at Durham left him little time for his poetry; but in his poetic dialogue he pointed to the highly practical applications of learning: to the use of arithmetic in the reckoning up on money and to the use of geometry in the surveying and division of lands. An anonymous writer of the middle of Henry I's reign noted that throughout France, Germany, Normandy and England there were almost as many highly learned masters of schools as there were royal tax-collectors and ministers, not only in towns and castles but also in villages. The comparison is significant, for the growth of education and of government went hand in hand. We cannot however ascribe the growth of education to the need to train up men capable of collecting the taxes required to finance war and maintain the military establishments: education then, and I hope now, was not meekly responsive to the requirements of governments.

Note on further reading

Several general surveys provide important commentaries on this period. C. Dyer's *Making a Living in the Middle Ages: The People of Britain 850–1520* (London, 2002) and R.H. Britnell's *The Commercialisation of English Society 1000–1500* (Cambridge, 1993) are both valuable, as is E. Miller and J. Hatcher, *Medieval England: Towns, Commerce and Crafts* (London, 1995). A wealth of material is to be found in *The Agrarian History of England and Wales, ii, 1242–1350*, ed. H.E. Hallam (Cambridge, 1988). For towns, there is *The Cambridge Urban History of Britain, I, 600–1540*, ed. D.M. Pallister (Cambridge, 2000). Although the main theme of his lecture was the relationship of the economy to war, JOP also stressed the expanding nature of an increasingly commercial economy. This is a theme which anticipated later work; see *A Commercialising Economy: England 1086 to c. 1300*, ed. R.H. Britnell and B.M.S. Campbell (Manchester, 1995).

A question to which JOP did not give much attention, but which is relevant to the issue of the commercialization of the economy, is that of the quantity of coin in circulation. A useful discussion is provided by Nicholas Mayhew, 'Modelling medieval monetisation', in *A Commercialising Economy: England 1086 to c. 1300*, 55–77. He suggests that in William I's day the volume of the English currency was no more than about £37,500, in contrast to some £900,000 for the end of the thirteenth century. This does not counter the ample evidence for the widespread use of money in the eleventh and twelfth centuries, but it puts an important perspective on the levels of payments, and the way in which government could conduct its business. In the later twelfth century a rise in the amount of coin in circulation was one of the main elements in the inflation which began at that time, and which has been discussed in a classic paper by P.D.A. Harvey, 'The English Inflation of 1180–1220', *Past and Present* lxi (1973), 3–30. This rise was particularly striking in view of the heavy expenditure on overseas war, and on Richard I's ransom. See also J.L. Bolton, 'The English Economy in the Early Thirteenth Century', in *King John: New Approaches*, ed. S.D. Church (Woodbridge, 1999), and Paul Latimer, 'Early Thirteenth-Century Prices', in the same volume.

6

Some Conclusions

It occurs to me that in giving to this last lecture the short title 'Some Conclusions' I may have aroused expectations which I do not intend to fulfil: expectations that I shall now proceed to elicit general truths on the nature of war, the causes of war, the place of war, even to offer what a distinguished French historian has termed the seductive novelty of the sociology of war.[1] I have no such general truths to offer, even for the limited period of a century and a half I have chosen to consider; and my short title is to be taken as meaning merely 'some observations by way of conclusion'. Maitland once commented that in the healthy growth of historical knowledge the new truth generally turns out to be but a quarter-truth and yet one which must modify the whole tale, and Lord Dacre, better remembered here as Hugh Trevor-Roper, made much the same point when he spoke in his inaugural lecture of the value of fertile errors.[2] Those familiar with the returns to the Inquest of Knight service of 1166, the *Cartae Baronum*, will remember the frequent occurrence of fractional fees: halves, quarters, sixths, twelfths and twenty-fourths.[3] I shall be well content if I can contribute any fractional truths.

We may begin by asking whether during this century and a half the changes which took place in the organization for and conduct of war were those of kind or of degree. The old, and perhaps still the most favoured, answer is that the changes were fundamental. Feudalism, the organization of society for war on the basis of land tenure, was introduced by the Conqueror. It provided the Norman kings with their field armies, their castle garrisons, their advisers in the persons of the tenants-in-chief, the natural counsellors, and through the feudal incidents it gave them such revenue as they required. English society was in effect a federation of baronial honours, feudal states in miniature, and hence, as Stenton stressed, 'the essential fact in the history of English feudal society, the original interdependence of king and baronage'.[4] The Oath of Salisbury of 1086, which for Stubbs was a major precaution against the disintegrating power of pure feudalism, was for Stenton of much more limited importance, designed to secure to the Conqueror the loyalty of the barons, the honorial barons as well as

1 P. Contamine, *Guerre, Etat et Société à la fin du Moyen Age*, vi.
2 F.W. Maitland, *Selected Essays*, 242.
3 e.g. return of Everard de Ros, *The Red Book of the Exchequer*, ed. H. Hall (Rolls Series, 1896), i. 452–5.
4 Stenton, *First Century*, 213.

the tenants-in-chief.[5] The balance of military power in the Anglo-Norman state is illustrated by the fact, established by R.A. Brown, that as late as 1154 225 baronial castles outnumbered the 49 royal castles by a proportion of almost 5 to 1.[6]

Most historians hold that by the close of the twelfth century a decisive transformation of society and government had taken place, a transformation characterized by a military revolution. 'Already in this period', A.L. Poole wrote, 'a society based on tenures and services is beginning to pass into a society based on money, on rents and taxes.' And he went on to emphasize that by 1200 the feudal levy had ceased to be an effective fighting force and that it had been superseded by an army chiefly composed of men paid to fight.[7] Barlow contrasted the position in 1087 when, as he put it, 'the Norman barons and knights were still living precariously in a conquered land' with that in 1216 by which date 'the barons had failed in their duties, the serjeants had fallen by the wayside, and the knights had grown as rusty as their old swords', when indeed 'English society was no longer organized for war'.[8] Barlow was deliberately exaggerating: English barons and knights did sail with King John for his Poitou campaign of 1214, though not in the numbers for which he had hoped, and the civil war which followed the grant of Magna Carta was not fought merely between Louis of France and John's alien mercenaries.[9]

Nevertheless no one now doubts the substantial justice of the statement that Angevin government was based on money, on taxes and on the use of paid troops. 'It is', wrote Henry II's treasurer Richard FitzNigel in about 1179, 'wealth which raises up and the lack of it which casts down the power of princes', and he went on to emphasize that money was indispensable in war, being poured out in fortifying castles, paying soldiers' wages and in innumerable other expenses for the defence of the realm.[10] The nature of Angevin government was shaped by the ways in which its range and grasp were extended and tightened in order to meet the demands of its masters for money. FitzNigel's hope, shared by Hubert Walter after him, was that the necessary money could be raised in accordance with fixed and rational procedures. In this way, he told Henry II in his dedicatory preface, the interests of individuals (*iura*) would be preserved and Henry would receive in full his due revenue. But FitzNigel had also, tactfully though uneasily, recognized another principle of government: princes could acquire wealth not merely lawfully but also by the exercise of their arbitrary will; and their subjects had no right to oppose or condemn their actions.[11] The exercise of arbitrary will, always present in Angevin government, was increasingly apparent in the methods by which John accumulated the great war chest which enabled him to launch his own campaign and that of his allies in

5   Stenton, *First Century*, 112–14.
6   R.A. Brown, 'A List of Castles, 1154–1216', *EHR* lxxiv (1959), 249.
7   Poole, *Obligations of Society in the XII and XIII Centuries*, 3–4, 52.
8   F. Barlow, *The Feudal Kingdom of England, 1042–1216*, 440.
9   J.C. Holt, *The Northerners* (Oxford, 1961), 98–100.
10 *Dialogus de Scaccario*, 1–2.
11 *Dialogus de Scaccario*, 1, 5.

1214; and the defeat of his allies at Bouvines meant that opposition and condemnation could no longer be evaded.

The breadth of that opposition and the comprehensiveness of its programme reflect the breadth and comprehensiveness of Angevin administration as it developed in response to the demands of war. One obvious example may be given, for although obvious it has not always been understood. Clause 12 of Magna Carta of 1215 provided that no scutage or aid, apart from the three regular aids, should be levied except by the common counsel of the realm. Clause 14 went on to define the requisite common counsel: archbishops, bishops, abbots, earls and greater barons were to be summoned individually; all other tenants-in-chief were to be summoned generally. A minimum of forty days notice was to be given, a fixed place for the assembly named, and the reason for the summons given. Moreover the business was to go forward on the day fixed even if not all those summoned had appeared, thus denying the need for individual consent. Holt in his admirable book on Magna Carta has strangely condemned clause 12 as one of the least satisfactory in the whole Charter, in particular because it ignored the new forms of taxation and especially the immensely lucrative tax of a thirteenth in 1207.[12] But these two clauses might well have been drafted with the writ for the assessment of the thirteenth before them: indeed they probably were. That writ spoke of an aid, and of its assessment, as did clauses 12 and 14. It made it plain that the aid was a war tax for the defence of the realm and the recovery of lost continental territories. And it claimed as authorization the undefined counsel and assent of the royal council. In its careful definition of the procedure by which a general subsidy should be authorized Magna Carta took a step, and an important step, in the direction of later parliamentary practice. The insistence on the cause of the summons being specified, the period of notice, the denial of the need for individual consent, and the distinction between those individually summoned, the greater lords, and those generally summoned were all embodied in later procedures. What remained to be determined was the identity and representative capacity of those generally summoned. Just as the First World War gave us the Representation of the People Act of 1918, introducing women's suffrage and almost trebling the electorate, and just as the Second World War gave us the Beveridge Report and all that followed from it, so the wars of John's reign led to the vigorous if imperfect assertion of the principles of subjecting general taxation to general consultation, of the rule of law and of the majority principle.

Another reason for the breadth and the content of Magna Carta lay in King John's political astuteness in conciliating local interests and in seeking to divide his opponents. In May 1204, when Normandy was being lost, John disafforested the county of Devon, laid down rules for the conduct of the sheriff and undertook to remove and punish any sheriff who failed to treat the men of the county well and lawfully. For this he charged 5,000 marks (£3,333) and it seems that this arrangement was made with the lesser men of Devon; for it was expressly provided that if the bishop of Exeter and the earl of Devon should wish to share

---

12 J.C. Holt, *Magna Carta* (Cambridge, 1965), 219–22.

in the benefits they would have to bear a proportionate share of the purchase price. It is a testimony to the wealth of the county that the price was paid within four years.[13] Grants of this type – and the grant to Devon is but one of many – strengthened the demand for general disafforestation and for the general reform of local administration, not for a price but as of right.

More striking moves were made by John after he learned of the baronial plot of August 1212. On 16 August he suddenly cancelled the Welsh campaign, and within two days began to bid for the support of the lesser men in order to detach them from the disaffected magnates. On 18 August he ordered all sheriffs to send to him as quickly as possible all those indebted to the Jews, with the major exception of earls and barons, since he intended to relax their debts by abolishing all the accumulated interest due. Further each sheriff was to bring with him six knights from his county to receive John's instructions.[14] Six months later John turned his attention to the counties of Yorkshire and Lincolnshire, the areas where discontent was greatest. In a letter addressed to all in those parts from archbishops and earls down to knights, free tenants and all others John explained that he had just learned of frequent complaints of the oppressive exactions of his sheriffs and other ministers and of their general evil conduct. John added that he had in no way profited personally from these exactions and that he was deeply moved by the complaints (*unde non modicum movemur*). Accordingly he was sending down a commission of four men to obtain detailed evidence on the wrongful exactions, emphasizing that it would not be his fault if matters were not put right.[15] The commissioners were carefully chosen. All four were later prominent in the moves for Magna Carta.[16] Evidently John's calculation was that if the investigation led to practical redress the credit would be his, and that if, as was more probable, little or nothing were achieved he could hope to blame the commissioners and thus discredit the potential leaders of the opposition in those parts. (A further precaution taken by John on the same day was to appoint Alexander of Pointon, also among the rebels of 1215, as sheriff of Lincolnshire.) Similar motives presumably lay behind the summons of four knights from each shire to a gathering at Oxford in mid-November 1213, especially since it was provided that of the others then summoned the knights were to come armed and the barons unarmed. Moreover the agenda for this gathering was significant: the four knights of each shire were to talk with the king concerning the business of the realm. They were not as in August 1212 merely to hear and to do; this time they were invited to speak, and in the encouraging presence of armed fellow knights and unarmed barons.[17]

---

13 *Pipe Roll 6 John*, 85; *Pipe Roll 10 John*, ed. D.M. Stenton (PRS, 1947), 66; *Rotuli Chartarum, 1199–1216*, ed. T.D. Hardy (London, 1837), 152.

14 '*ad faciendum hoc quod eis dicemus*', anticipating the '*ad audiendum et faciendum*' of some later parliamentary writs of summons to the representatives; *Rot. Lit. Claus.*, 152; writs of summons in 1282 and 1294, *Select Charters*, ed. Stubbs, pp. 458, 477.

15 *Rot. Lit. Pat.*, 97.

16 Robert de Ros and William de Albini among the twenty-five barons of the Charter – Holt, *Magna Carta*, 558; Simon de Kyme and Thomas of Moulton listed by Wendover, ii. 114–15.

17 *Select Charters*, p. 282.

For these reasons the baronial leaders of rebellion in 1215 had to frame their programme very widely if they were to counter the concessions, promises and propaganda of King John, and if they were to retain any control over and support from the men of their own localities. Moreover we should not underestimate the articulate political consciousness within the local communities, a consciousness which had been greatly strengthened and stimulated by the war controls and agencies of Hubert Walter's administration: not merely the operations of the sheriffs and itinerant justices but the escheators, justices of the Jews, exchequer of the ransom, committees for the enforcement of the Assize of Weights and Measures and the officers of the national customs, the whole host of officials who had been compared by Peter of Blois to an army of locusts.[18] By 1200 the port of Ipswich had had much experience of these officials and their demands. Accordingly its burgesses purchased a charter from King John giving them a measure of self-government. Fortunately there survives an unusually detailed account of the steps the burgesses took to give effect to their new constitution. One entry explains that Roger Bigod, earl of Norfolk and marshal of England, who had been of great assistance in procuring the charter, was admitted as a burgess of Ipswich on a country-member basis. It was provided that he and his villeins should in future be exempt from toll in Ipswich in respect of their own produce; that the earl should pay 4d rent a year for his quay in Ipswich; but that if his villeins should be merchants (i.e. trading with other men's produce) they should pay towards the farm of the borough. Here we have an earl using his political influence and access to the king to procure a borough charter and himself becoming a burgess; and we have villeins who are also merchants.[19] Bigod's interest is clear enough: Ipswich was an important port and one through which much of the surplus produce of the Bigod estates was exported. Two years previously Ipswich had been fined 200 marks for exporting corn to Flanders in breach of the royal embargo.[20] But it is also clear that Bigod had no aristocratic contempt for trade, no sense of demeaning himself by becoming a burgess, that he had indeed worked closely with the burgesses and was concerned, if only on grounds of self-interest, with the economic welfare of his villeins. Bigod was one of the twenty-five barons of Magna Carta, and he brought a great deal of experience to Runnymede in 1215. He had his interests as an earl: indeed his earldom had been withheld from him during the last twelve years of Henry II's reign. With his 162½ knights' fees he had ample experience of the incidence of scutage. His estates in East Anglia gave him, as we have seen, familiarity with the needs of traders and burgesses. In 1194 he had headed the itinerant justices in East Anglia, and in the following year took over the northern circuit of Northumberland, Cumberland, Copeland, Westmorland, Yorkshire and Lancaster. Few men can have rivalled his long experience of Angevin government as one who had experienced its vagaries, administered its laws and taken advantage of its readiness under pressure to sell concessions.

---

[18] Ep. 95 in Migne, *Patrologia Latina*, ccvii, 298.
[19] *Rotuli Chartarum.*, 65; C. Gross, *The Gild Merchant*, ii. 114–23.
[20] *Pipe Roll 10 Richard I*, 92.

The antecedents of Magna Carta of 1215 can be traced far back into the past. There had been a dress rehearsal for it in 1191, directed by John himself who was making a bid for power by acting as leader of the opposition to William Longchamp, Richard's minister. Against Longchamp John organized a coalition of the excluded and the malcontents and, with the help of Hugh of Nonant, bishop of Coventry and John's propaganda agent, endowed it with a plausible programme. Longchamp was accused of acting by his own arbitrary will without common counsel, of reducing the church to ignominy and the people to poverty. He was charged with disparaging the magnates by marrying his own base-born relatives into the families of earls and barons, with despising the English and with ignorance of the English language; and he was condemned for his knowledge and use of Roman law.[21] Against this John set the demand for common counsel and for judgement by the *curia regis* in accordance with the lawful customs and assizes of the kingdom.[22] Just as in May the dissident barons gained the vital control of London and allied themselves with the mayor and ruling citizen oligarchy, so in October 1191 John and his allies entered London and won the support of the ruling oligarchy by the grant of the commune.[23] John was well placed to organize this coup. He had close connections with the London merchant, Richard fitz Reiner, who led the demand for the commune and from whom John had borrowed money;[24] and it was in fitz Reiner's house that John stayed on the night before the grant of the commune.[25] The opposition to King John in 1215 had learned much from the political dexterity of Count John in 1191.

But Magna Carta was the product of King John's wars in two senses: it was the reaction to the measures of the war administration in the years down to the eve of the battle of Bouvines; and, as Jolliffe suggested, the fact that John's financial reserves were exhausted when he returned to England in October 1214 enabled his opponents to act against him with growing confidence.[26] One instance of John's financial difficulties in the spring and summer of 1215 may be given. He had borrowed from the Templars to finance the passage of troops from Poitou and was evidently pressed to repay the loan. On 11 April he ordered the exchequer to repay to the Temple 1,100 marks (suggesting that he had borrowed 1,000 marks.[27] The order was ineffective, and on 9 May he visited the New Temple in London and deposited gold there (possibly part of his regalia) as security, undertaking that if by 1 January 1216 he had not repaid the loan the Templars could do what they liked with the security. John granted Magna Carta. And on 22 July, anxious not to forfeit his security, John ordered the exchequer to

---

21 Howden, *Gesta*, ii. 215–20; *Gerald of Wales, Opera*, ii. 549.
22 Howden, *Gesta*, iii. 156.
23 *Wendover*, ii. 116–17; Walter of Coventry, ii. 220.
24 Page, *London, its Origin and Early Development*, p. 109.
25 *Diceto*, ii. 99.
26 J.E.A. Joliffe, 'The Chamber and the Castle Treasures under King John', in *Studies in Medieval History presented to F.M. Powicke*, 155–7.
27 *Rot. Lit. Claus.*, i. 194.

hand over to the Templars small or large sums as the money came in until the whole debt should have been repaid.[28]

Clearly the impact of war on English society and government in the reigns of Richard and John was different from that under the Conqueror and his sons. But how different? Had the demands of war in the intervening period helped to transform a feudal kingdom into a bureaucratic and autocratic state? It does not appear to me that the composition and structure of military forces, as distinct from the formal obligations of tenure, underwent any such dramatic change. Elsewhere I have tried to show that we hear as much of paid troops under the Norman kings as we do in the reigns of Richard and John. If Richard I ordered the raiding of the treasure and plate of churches as a contribution towards the raising of his ransom,[29] the Conqueror had similarly, in February 1070, ordered the treasures of the English monasteries to be ransacked in order that he might pay off the army which had carried out the arduous and destructive campaign of 1069–70 where the order is merely for the confiscation of the deposits in the monasteries made by the richer Englishmen.[30] The use of paid troops, the scale of war expenditure and the corresponding fiscal pressures were as much commonplaces to William of Malmesbury, Orderic Vitalis and Lawrence of Durham as they were to Richard fitz Nigel, Roger of Howden and Gerald of Wales. Gerald of Wales was however wrong when he contrasted the Welsh with the English, writing that the English fight for greed, the Welsh for liberty; the English for profit, the Welsh to avoid loss; the English paid troops for money, the Welsh fought for their fatherland.[31] Not all the Welsh had been actuated by such impeccable motives. Welsh princes had been won over by gifts and promises to Henry I's service in 1102; they served under Ranulf of Chester and Robert of Gloucester in the civil war of Stephen's reign.[32]

I have also tried to show elsewhere that the royal military household, that powerful instrument of war and government under Edward I and, as Jolliffe demonstrated so tellingly, equally influential under the Angevin kings, was potent and prominent under the Norman kings, organized in the same way, exercising the same functions and offering to its abler members the same opportunities for acquiring wealth, power and titles.[33] This is not to say that the strictly feudal obligations of tenure were never exacted or fulfilled, though it is inconceivable that any feudal summons ever produced in the field the 5,000 knights calculated by Round to be the total *servitium debitum* of the lay and clerical fiefs in England. Round made justifiable fun of Orderic Vitalis's statement that England under the Conqueror could produce 60,000 knights, and he had no difficulty in showing that this figure was widely used by chroniclers and his-

---

[28] *Rot. Lit. Pat.*, 135a; *Rot. Lit. Claus.*, i. 221.

[29] e.g. Howden, *Gesta*, iii. 211; Newburgh, i. 400; Diceto, ii. 110.

[30] Florence, ii. 4–5; but see *Annales de Wintonia*, in *Ann. Mon.*, ii. 29 – *quicquid auri vel argenti in ecclesiis fuerat, abstulit rex*; and *Chron. Abingdon*, i. 486, ii. 495–4.

[31] *Opera*, vi. 226.

[32] *Orderic*, vi. 26, 540, 547; *Gesta Stephani*, 110, 172; Huntingdon, *Historia*, 268, 273; *Rot. Lit. Claus.*, i. 210.

[33] J.O. Prestwich, 'The Military Household of the Norman Kings', *EHR* xcvi (1981), 1–35.

torians whenever they wished to convey the impression of a great number.[34] But Round did not care to notice Orderic's accounts of actual forces in the field in his own region and in his own day. He once credited Henry I with 1,000 knights and Fulk of Anjou with 500, and he believed that 900 knights in all had clashed in the battle of Brémule.[35] Ordinarily Orderic mentioned much smaller forces of knights in action: Reginald of Warenne attempting to take Rouen with 300 knights in 1090; Gilbert de Laigle operating with 80 knights in 1091; Ralph the Red, one of Henry I's household knights, attacking 300 knights with an inferior force in 1119; 80 knights being captured at the battle of Bourg Théroulde in 1124.[36] Writers who gave more comprehensive figures made it clear that in their opinion the knights, who anyway ordinarily dismounted for action, were greatly outnumbered by the infantry and other services, men who, by definition, were not performing knight service. For example the priest of Fécamp gave Robert Curthose 700 cavalry and 6,000 infantry at the battle of Tinchebray, while Henry I, in his despatch to Anselm on this same battle, claimed to have captured 400 knights and 10,000 infantry, and to have killed countless more. For what they are worth the proportions given indicate that the cavalry ordinarily formed between 5 and 10 per cent of the total; and Sir Steven Runciman found very similar proportions in the First Crusade.[37]

It may however be considered that what distinguished the Anglo-Norman state of the late eleventh and early twelfth centuries from the Angevin state is that the former was guided, if not controlled, by the influence of the king's feudal tenants-in-chief, his natural counsellors, whereas the latter was served by ministers of the king's own making. Roger Wendover provides a helpful list of John's counsellors in 1211, not his natural counsellors but his very wicked counsellors, *consiliarii iniquissimi*.[38] There are thirty-two names on this list. Of the three earls one was William earl of Salisbury, the king's half-brother, and another, Geoffrey fitz Peter, was the justiciar, leaving only the relatively poor and insignificant earl of Oxford as the son of an earl created by Stephen. The three bishops were all curialists, two being John's nominees and the third, Philip of Durham, Richard's old clerk and crusading companion. Almost all the rest were John's creatures, and they included his alien mercenary captains, Philip Mark, Peter de Maulay, Gerard d'Athée, Ingelard de Cigogné and Fawkes de Breauté, all highly unnatural counsellors.

Now it is a commonplace among historians of the later Middle Ages that the barons of England claimed to be the king's natural counsellors and that this claim was of the highest political importance. Adams, Baldwin, Powicke, Jacob, Storey, Brown, McFarlane and their younger colleagues or successors have all reminded us of this. Powicke for example wrote of the barons of Henry III reflecting on the barriers which separated the king's council from the larger

---

34 Round, *Feudal England*, 289–93.
35 *Orderic*, vi.194, 200, 240.
36 *Orderic*, iv. 200, 222; vi. 222, 350.
37 H.W.C. Davis, 'The Battle of Tinchebrai: a Correction', *EHR* xxv (1910), 296; Eadmer, *HH*, p.184; Steven Runciman, *History of the Crusades*, vol. 1, appendix II.
38 Wendover, ii, 59–60.

body of his natural advisers, and McFarlane of 'the feudal duty which made the greater barons the king's natural councillors'.[39] It seems that it was not until the reign of Henry III that the feudal nature of true counsel was expressed in the militant phrase, 'natural counsellors'; but the linking of the natural counsellors with feudal duty takes us back to the Conqueror's reign at least, to his three annual crown-wearings when, as Douglas put it, the members of the curia regis attended by reason of a military tenure.[40]

These are familiar truths, so familiar that none of the historians I have cited has thought it necessary to cite any evidence for the barons' claim to be the king's natural counsellors. But they are evidently translating the sources: the phrase 'natural counsellors' is frequently placed in quotation marks to make it plain that they are reporting claims made at the time, not reminding their readers of a necessary truth about the nature of councils. Here I must confess a failure, and perhaps my ignorance: I have been unable to find in the sources before Fortescue in the fifteenth century any Latin or French phrase for 'natural counsellors'. I began my search with Wendover and Matthew Paris, as likely to report baronial claims in the thirteenth century. Wendover tells us that at Christmas 1232 Henry III removed from office *omnes naturales curiae suae ministros* and set in their places *Pictavenses extraneos*, and he goes on to describe how troops from Brittany and Poitou oppressed the *homines Angliae naturales et nobiles*.[41] Matthew Paris reports Richard of Cornwall's vehement protest in 1238 about the marriage of Simon de Montfort to the king's sister since this had been done without *consilium naturalium hominum suorum* and Henry III had indeed been contumaciously *utens consiliis alienigenarum*.[42] In all these and in numerous other passages the contrast is between the natural-born or native-born Englishmen and the aliens or foreigners, not between the natural political rights inhering in baronies by tenure and the improper claims of those lower down the tenurial ladder. Clearly the magnates were taking the lead; but they were understandably careful to exploit and to stimulate anti-alien sentiment and understandably anxious not to use arguments based on the narrow and treacherous grounds of tenurial status. Hence in the Petition of the Barons of 1258 they were careful to define disparagement not in feudal, tenurial or even class terms but in national terms – *videlicet hominibus qui non sunt de natione regni Angliae*. Louis IX in his Award of Amiens expressly annulled *illud statutum factum quod regnum Angliae de cetero per indigenas gubernetur* and ruled that the king could safely summon both aliens and natives to his counsel.[43] Anti-alien sentiment had played a greater part in politics during the late twelfth and for much of the thirteenth century than many historians allow. It had been exploited against William Longchamp in 1191 when he was accused of using foreign troops,

---

[39] F.M. Powicke, *King Henry III and the Lord Edward* (Oxford, 1947), i. 154; K.B. McFarlane, *England in the Fifteenth Century*, ed. G.L. Harriss (London, 1981), 29; McFarlane, *The Nobility of Later Medieval England*, 119–20.
[40] Douglas, *William the Conqueror*, 285.
[41] Matthew Paris, *Chronica Majora*, iii. 240–1.
[42] Ibid., iii. 475–6.
[43] *Documents of the Baronial Movement of Reform and Rebellion*, ed. R.F. Treharne and I.J. Sanders (Oxford, 1973), 80, 288.

despising the English and being totally ignorant of the English language. It had been used by King John in his total mobilization order of 1205 against invasion, when he deliberately referred to the contingency of aliens landing.[44] And it was turned against John in Magna Carta when he was required to remove from the kingdom all the alien troops who had come with horses and arms to the hurt of the kingdom, *Naturalis* meant, and had long meant, native-born, as when Orderic Vitalis referred to the Conqueror's oppression of the *naturales regni filios*, the native-born sons of the kingdom. When Enoch Powell encountered the word *naturalis* in connection with his work on the origins of the House of Lords he correctly translated it as 'native-born'; though whether we should ascribe his accuracy to his early training in the classics at Cambridge or to his later interest in the supposed conflict of interests between those citizens of this country with lighter and those with darker skins I am unsure.[45] What matters is that he got his Latin right. Here I may be allowed to express my hope that in this university, whatever view may be taken elsewhere, we shall continue to recognize that a knowledge of Latin is essential for any really serious study of medieval history and that to rely on translations is to rely on fallible interpretations which undergraduates should be criticizing and not merely absorbing.

There was then no doctrine of natural counsellors under the Norman or the Angevin kings. The Conqueror did not make his tenants-in-chief his counsellors: he made his counsellors his tenants-in-chief in England. And if it is objected that these men were already great magnates in Normandy it should be remembered that, as Douglas pointed out in his Ford Lectures, most of these owed their rise in Normandy to their services to Duke William, and some, like William I de Warenne, a second son, to their services after the battle of Hastings. Had Duke William considered himself bound by any doctrine of natural and irremovable counsellors the Norman Conquest would never have taken place. And had his successors on the English throne considered themselves so bound they would not have achieved what they did. We have been taught that what the barons fought for and what the barons won in Stephen's reign was the principle of hereditary succession. If this had been so, and if these barons were also claiming to be the king's natural counsellors, the Angevin kings would have been saddled with an aristocracy and counsellors not of their own making. But it was not so. Henry II did not respect the principle of hereditary succession in 1175 when he annexed all the lands of the earl of Cornwall in England, Normandy and Wales, reserving them for his youngest son, John, fobbing off two of the co-heiresses with small portions (£100 per annum each) and disinheriting the third. Other male claimants were consoled by a grant of Limerick in Ireland, though with the disadvantage that Limerick had not yet been conquered from the Irish; and in 1177 the grantees sulkily resigned their rights in Limerick, complaining that they were wrongfully deprived of their inheritance.[46] Similarly in 1176 Henry II insisted that William earl of Glou-

---

44 *Foedera*, i. 92.
45 J. Enoch Powell and K. Wallis, *The House of Lords in the Middle Ages* (London, 1968), 160.
46 Torigny, p. 268; Howden, *Gesta*, i. 172–5; and see Gillingham, *Richard the Lionheart*, pp.

cester, who had already been deprived of his castle of Bristol, should grant his daughter and heiress in marriage to John. It was expressly provided that even if the earl should produce a son half the great inheritance should nevertheless go to John.[47] And we have already seen how Henry II in 1177 refused to allow Roger Bigod to inherit the earldom of Norfolk.[48]

Of course sensible kings frequently brought their magnates together, partly to keep an eye on them, partly to publicize their orders, partly to impress visiting dignitaries, partly, and sometimes chiefly, for conviviality. And some great magnates became trusted counsellors, constantly at the king's side and exercising a dominant influence in the making and execution of policy: such a man was Robert of Beaumont, first earl of Leicester, described, as one of Rufus's chief counsellors as early as 1093, a member of his military household, and recognized by both friends and critics as the dominant member of Henry I's court down to his death in 1118. Nor was it supposed that able and loyal fathers necessarily had stupid or disloyal sons: the second earl of Leicester was Henry II's hard-working justiciar for the first thirteen years of his reign and praised in the Dialogue of the Exchequer as of sound judgement, well educated, skilled in legal matters and diligent.[49] Work of this kind was not however to the taste of the great bulk of the earls and barons, and they neither wished nor claimed to be the king's natural counsellors; nor indeed was any such claim made in Magna Carta.

There is much more to be said on the place of war in English history between the battles of Hastings and of Bouvines: I should have liked to discuss the Oath of Salisbury, but shall now content myself with saying that the best source for this is not, as has been assumed ever since Stenton wrote, the Anglo-Saxon Chronicle but the Worcester Chronicle which is independent and is probably based on the Latin writ of summons sent to Wulfstan of Worcester. On this, as on the siege of Exeter and the rebellion of 1075, the Worcester chronicle has the further merit of making good straightforward sense. We need not make the history of this period more difficult than it is by dismissing good evidence as a late translation, especially when we can compare the Worcester version with what was the undoubtedly late and faithful translation of the Anglo-Saxon Chronicle's entry on the Oath of Salisbury by Henry of Huntingdon. I should also have liked to discuss more fully the civil war of Stephen's reign and especially the evidence showing that Stephen's financial position in 1139, like that of King John in 1215, was extremely weak. But I shall keep to my stint of six lectures.

I should however, in deference to my short title for this last lecture, offer some conclusions. The first is negative: the concept of feudalism, which is nowhere to be found in our sources, is of no help in considering the evidence for the conduct and consequences of war in this period. Maitland was right when he said that feudalism was first introduced into England by Sir Henry Spelman in

---

72–5 and 84–5 for the effect of Henry's confiscation on Aimar of Limoges, husband of Sarah of Cornwall.

[47] Howden, *Gesta*, i. 124–5.

[48] Howden, *Gesta*, i. 145–4 and cf. *Pipe Roll 2 Richard I*, 101.

[49] *Dialogus*, 57–9.

the seventeenth century; and I trust Marc Bloch who was unable to find any reference to feudalism in France earlier than 1727 and who pointed out that it was the decree of the National Assembly on 11 August 1789 solemnly enacting the entire destruction of the feudal regime which made it impossible thereafter to doubt the reality of a social system whose ruin had cost so much effort. Medievalists may therefore gratefully hand over problems about the nature and working of feudalism to their colleagues concerned with the early modern and modern periods. My second conclusion is that war had no single place in the history of this period. It occupied the minds and energies of the rulers of England more continuously and directly than it did those of their subjects in England for long periods. In conducting their wars these rulers exhibited both ruthlessness and cruelty, but their aims were limited and intelligible; and both they and their lieutenants commonly deployed both intelligence and administrative ability in the management of their campaigns – intelligence in the technical sense of military intelligence as well as in its general meaning.

My third and last conclusion is that although war had an important and often destructive place in the history of this period it also had a limited and often constructive place: limited because of the long years of internal peace in England under Henry I and Henry II, occupying almost half our period; and constructive because of the energies released within English society. Despite the disruption of war and the costs of war the English economy and English society showed an extraordinary resilience. Nor do I believe that the rulers and magnates of England enjoyed fighting for its own sake. It was dangerous and expensive. All the evidence indicates that Henry II for example greatly preferred to spend his time in hunting, in settling disputes in the courts and in diplomacy, and in the company of Rosamund Clifford and the agreeably named Bellebelle who makes her brief and tantalizing appearance in the Pipe Roll for 1185 when Henry spent lavishly on her clothes.[50]

Note on further reading

There has been surprisingly little work published on Magna Carta since this lecture was written. A new edition of J.C. Holt's classic work on the Charter contains an additional chapter dealing with the law.[51] A number of important articles by the same author were published in his *Magna Carta and Medieval Government* (London, 1985). R.V. Turner, *King John* (Harlow, 1994), provides a useful account of John's reign, and contains a chapter on the Charter.

The question of 'natural counsellors' is not one which has received much attention for the twelfth century. The role of 'aliens' in English politics is one which has proved to be of much more concern to historians of the thirteenth century; for a convenient summary, see D. Carpenter, *The Reign of Henry III* (London, 1996), 260–79.

[50] *Pipe Roll 30 Henry II* (PRS, 1912), 154.
[51] J.C. Holt, *Magna Carta Second Edition* (Cambridge, 1992).

Appendix I
Feudalism: A Critique

Ever since the great rationalizing historians of the eighteenth century devised and applied the concept of feudalism it has provided a singularly capacious category. To David Hume what he called 'the vast fabric of feudal subordination' was 'quite solid and comprehensive' and 'formed everywhere an essential part of the political constitution'. In his opinion feudalism was introduced into England by the Normans, 'who could scarcely form an idea of any other species of civil government', and hence 'England of a sudden became a feudal kingdom'.[1] But to his contemporary and remarkably intelligent critic, Gilbert Stuart, the comprehensive structure of feudalism, which in his view bound together government and property, the maxims of public and private life, inheritance and estates, justice and courts, the royal palace and the households of gentlemen, all the natural modes of thinking and acting, could not possibly have been, as he put it, 'the operation of one man and of one reign'.[2] He supported this general consideration by making a distinction between the introduction of fiefs and the introduction of knight-service and, more weightily, by the extensive quotations from and commentary on sources which formed two-thirds of his book. Since the time of Hume and Stuart the apparent power of the concept of feudalism to expose and explain the whole structure of society, to bring together in an intelligible scheme the whole range of human activities, is precisely what has commended it so strongly. To the social historian feudalism has meant a graded society of dependants, of lords and men; to the economic historian it has meant the exploitation of land by lords exercising their coercive authority over their tenants and villeins; to the legal historian it has meant a set of contractual relationships, the terms of the conditional tenure of land; to the military historian it has meant a system in which land was held on condition of rendering unpaid military service, the production of knights and the garrisoning of castles; and to the constitutional historian it has meant government by lordship, the greater lords being the natural counsellors of the greatest lord of all, *dominus rex*.

Historians have disagreed about the details of these definitions, about what is fundamental and what derivative in the interlocking system of feudalism, and about the value judgements which should be passed upon it; but there has long been wide, though not universal, agreement that the concept is comprehensive and indispensable. This agreement extends to the Marxists, for whom feudalism is one of the stages on which their whole scheme of history depends. If, but only if, society and government were monolithic in this way we shall be less troubled

---

[1] D. Hume, *The History of England* (London, 1792), ii. 107–8.
[2] G. Stuart, *A View of Society in Europe, in its Progress from Rudeness to Refinement* (2nd edn, Edinburgh, 1792), 90.

by the uneven and often inadequate evidence: if one element in the structure of feudalism can be taken as established the rest can be inferred or imposed on weak and scanty evidence. Postan, for example, took it as established by Stenton that during the greater part of the twelfth century England suffered from 'the seizure of land by turbulent neighbours and all other incidents of feudal and civil war, 'a *malaise* which affected England as a whole', and he used this to support his view that the system of estate management during this period 'was everywhere inimical to expansion'.[3]

There have however been difficulties in applying this concept of feudalism to the evidence. There is the problem of chronology: when, very approximately, did it flourish, decline and end? It is unreasonable to ask that its origins should be dated since the evidence is likely to be very scanty. But we shall learn more about the use of the concept if we consult historians on the decline and disappearance of feudalism. Gilbert Stuart held that the knight's fee, for him the foundation of what he termed 'the mighty edifice of the feudal strength', was no sooner invented than it was to suffer. He was impressed by the early evidence for the division of fees, the leasing of land for rent, the sale of land, the commutation of military service for money, the hiring of mercenaries, and the 'killing blow' given by the rise of commerce. It is clear from his notes that he saw these corrosive forces at work at least as early as the twelfth century.[4] A.L. Poole was rather more precise. Using the same classes of evidence as Stuart he observed of the late twelfth and early thirteenth centuries that 'already in this period a society based on tenures and services is beginning to pass into a society based on money, on rents and taxes'; and he found that by the turn of the century 'the feudal levy had ceased to be an effective fighting force . . . it was superseded by an army chiefly composed of men paid to fight'.[5]

For Powicke the change came almost a century later: he held that Henry Ill's armies were based upon the feudal levy until 1257, whereas under Edward I the feudal levy became subsidiary to the paid forces or was not summoned at all. And he linked the changes in military organization with social changes and with the appearance of a co-ordinated Parliament.[6] So too did Jolliffe who counted it to Edward I's merit that he had the courage or the indifference to break with the feudal past.[7] It was however Cam's view that Edward I 'found in the maxims and ethics of feudalism an entirely adequate support for his policy', and she attributed the death of feudalism to the legislation of Henry VII and Henry VIII, followed by the suppression of the two great northern rebellions.[8]

Allied to these difficulties of establishing the chronology of feudalism have been those of determining its nature. Many historians have adopted the Aristote-

3   M.M. Postan, 'Glastonbury Estates in the Twelfth Century: A Reply', *EcHR*, 2nd ser., ix (1957), 117–8.
4   Stuart, op. cit., 102–9, 379–87, and especially 384, n. 8.
5   A.L. Poole, *The Obligations of Society in the XII and XIII Centuries* (Oxford, 1964), 3–4, 52.
6   F.M. Powicke, *The Thirteenth Century* (Oxford, 1953), 554, 556.
7   J.E.A. Joliffe, *The Constitutional History of England* (London, 1937), 331.
8   H.M. Cam, *Liberties and Communities in Medieval England* (London, 1963), 207, 222.

lian method, constructing a model of ideal feudalism and describing actual societies as approximations to, or deviations from, this ideal. Some supposed that the Latin Kingdom of Jerusalem and its *Assises* conveniently embody such an ideal model.[9] Others rejected this identification of feudalism with what they took to be an instance of weak and decentralized government. For Stenton feudalism was a form of social order, a complex of rights and duties uniting barons and king. Hence, in passages unnoticed by Postan, he held that the conditions of Stephen's reign 'cannot fairly be regarded as the expression of feudal ideas', and it was Henry II's reign which saw 'the re-establishment of an effective feudal monarchy'.[10] It is at this political or constitutional level that the differences about the nature of feudalism are most clearly exhibited, and some historians have been content to weaken the explanatory force of the concept by treating it as politically neutral. It is not surprising that some scholars considered rejecting the concept of feudalism entirely. Maitland once described the task set before the word 'feudalism' as impossible since it was that of making a single idea represent a very large piece of the world's history.[11] Powicke told us with surprising firmness that 'the feudal system, in short, never existed', and he added, more characteristically, that 'the relations which we call feudal did not exclude relations of a different kind, and they were consistent with either a state of order or a state of chaos'.[12] More recently Cronne suggested that perhaps the concept of feudalism is becoming less and less meaningful and correspondingly valueless.[13] Still more recently Elizabeth A.R. Brown in a combative and persuasive article urged us to depose 'the tyrant feudalism'.[14] The majority of historians have however been reluctant to abandon a traditional term. Two modifications of the general theory of feudalism have proved particularly successful.

First, given agreement that feudalism was dynamic rather than static, the general stage of feudalism could be broken up into several phases. The awkward questions of chronology could then be dismissed, at least by medievalists. The origins of feudalism could be pushed back into the late Roman empire; the end of feudalism could be advanced into the seventeenth or eighteenth centuries, or even later.[15] For English history T.F.T. Plucknett evolved what he called 'a very neat chronological table': the first century of English feudalism runs from 1066 to 1166; the second from 1166 to the Statute of Marlborough in 1267; while the

---

[9] For the prevalence of this supposition and a criticism of it see J. Prawer, *Crusader Institutions* (Oxford, 1980), first section and especially chap. 1.
[10] Stenton, *First Century*, 4, 219, 256.
[11] F. Pollock and F.W. Maitland, *The History of English Law* (2nd edn, Cambridge, 1898), i. 67.
[12] F.M. Powicke, *Medieval England* (London, 1931), 173.
[13] Cronne, *Reign of Stephen*, 4–8.
[14] E.A.R. Brown, 'The Tyranny of a Construct: Feudalism and Historians of Medieval Europe', *American Historical Review* lxxix (1974), 1063–88.
[15] e.g. A. Dopsch, *The Economic and Social Foundations of European Civilization*, trans. M.G. Beard and N. Marshall (London, 1937), 301: 'the late Roman period saw a feudalization of public authority'; F.L. Ganshof, *Feudalism*, trans. P. Grierson (London, 1952) 152: 'Feudal institutions lasted in western Europe to the end of the *Ancien Regime*, and in some countries elements of them survived into the 'nineteenth and even twentieth centuries'.

third stage is 'not one century but four, consisting of a slow decline until 1660 when military tenures were converted into common socage'.[16] Many continental scholars would prefer to place the origins of feudalism much earlier; but if Plucknett's divisions are treated as the three phases of Boutrouche's second age of feudalism they are in exact accordance.[17] Thus the chronological difficulties disappear, and with them most of the difficulties about the nature of feudalism: within the Middle Ages there were various ends, not of feudalism but of its various phases; and there was no fixed and ideal nature of feudalism but various natures as feudalism changed.

The second modification has proved deservedly popular. Scraps of evidence obtruded which could not readily be reconciled with the required monolithic structure of society at the particular point of time under examination. But it was realized that if there have been stages and phases of development there must necessarily have been periods of transition in which there would be survivals from the old phase and anticipations of the new, momentarily destroying the symmetry of the evidence. Stubbs identified one such period in the Conqueror's reign,[18] while Vinogradoff treated the whole eleventh century as transitional in the history of English government.[19] Stenton observed of the whole of his first century of English feudalism that the ancient simplicity of social relationships had been destroyed while the evolution of a new order was slow.[20] Painter, in a work designed as a preliminary study for his admirable history of the reign of King John, prudently declared in advance that 'the reigns of Richard, John and Henry III were a period of transition'.[21]

For the individual specialist the device of the period of transition is invaluable: it allows him to delineate with care the deviations from the norm, the survivals, anticipations and local peculiarities encountered in the evidence, and at the same time to proclaim his orthodox belief in distinct stages and clear-cut systems, and thus in the general concept of feudalism. But the reader of specialized works on successive periods is awkwardly placed: he is left with a closely jointed series of transitions presenting no interstices large enough to accommodate the monolithic phases or stages required by the general concept.

If however we distinguish between the wide or 'continental' definition of feudalism and the narrow definition as adopted by Stenton, it may seem that the latter still provides the best model available to us for interpreting the evidence for the place of war in English history in the years between Hastings and Bouvines. The essential elements of the model, stated in the simplest terms, are as follows. First, English society in the century after Hastings was a society organized specifically for war on the basis of the conditional tenure of land. Knights trained to fight on horseback and castles were the indispensable and dominating instruments of war and coercive rule. From the territorial magnates,

---

16 T.F.T. Plucknett, *The Legislation of Edward I* (Oxford, 1949), 23.
17 R. Boutrouche, Seigneurie et Féodalité (Paris, 1959), i. 211–12, and especially n. 52.
18 W. Stubbs, *The Constitutional History of England* (5th edn, Oxford, 1891), i. 313.
19 P. Vinogradoff, *English Society in the Eleventh Century* (Oxford, 1908), 208.
20 Stenton, *First Century*, 8.
21 S. Painter, *Studies in the History of the English Feudal Barony* (Baltimore, 1943), 193.

the tenants in chief, kings obtained unpaid military service both in the field and in garrisoning the royal castles, and they governed with the advice of the magnates, their natural counsellors. Military and political power lay preponderantly in the hands of the magnates: they were the immediate lords of the knights; their castles greatly outnumbered those of the king; and in their honours, feudal states in miniature, they held courts for their men. Hence, as Stenton put it, the work of the Norman kings depended to a great extent on baronial loyalty, and the feudal army remained the ultimate defence of the land.[22]

Second, the model is comprehensive. Older historians linked the military system of feudalism with a very rudimentary economy. The landed estate by which soldiers were maintained was, Vinogradoff held, 'the most usual and convenient form of economic organization in those days of natural husbandry'. For him feudalism was 'an attempt to connect military organization directly with agricultural husbandry', while the state was 'a federation of feudal potentates' and the country 'a territorial union of baronies'.[23] Vinogradoff's use of the term 'natural husbandry' may suggest that economic historians would not now accept the material foundation of his argument. But Postan held that in the late eleventh century and during the greater part of the twelfth the economic conditions were those of stagnation or slump, the product of feudal or civil war, difficult communications and the disruption of the great estates by the need to carve out knights' fees to provide the manpower for war. Moreover feudal restraints on personal mobility, the disposal of property and freedom of contract greatly impeded the pursuit of trade: hence towns were 'non-feudal islands in the feudal seas'.[24] Others have contended that this is too pessimistic, that the period was one of economic expansion. But, it has been argued, the greater landlords were unaffected by this: they were monks with their minds on higher things, or great earls and barons devoting themselves to war and politics, or bishops ruling their dioceses and, very often, helping kings to rule their kingdom. Only towards the end of the twelfth century did they wake up to discover that they had been missing their economic opportunities for a century and, impelled by rapidly rising prices and debts, turn to become improving landlords engaged in the direct and rational management of their estates. What Postan had taken to be a sign of economic stagnation was merely a sign that the great landlords had not been economic men, a symptom of 'the non-economic mentality of those feudal and ecclesiastical classes from which the lords of the countryside were drawn'.[25] But this view implies that the pace of economic expansion had been almost imperceptible if for so long it was unperceived by the greater lords. And it is widely accepted that the very rapid inflation of the years 1180–1220 was linked with economic and social changes of a hitherto unprecedented magnitude.[26]

---

[22] Stenton, *First Century*, 216.
[23] Vinogradoff, *Eleventh Century*, 39, 213–14.
[24] *Cambridge Economic History of Europe*, i. (2nd edn, Cambridge, 1960), 585; M.M. Postan, *The Medieval Economy and Society* (London, 1972), 96–9, 212.
[25] E. Miller, 'England in the Twelfth and Thirteenth Centuries: An Economic Contrast?', *EcHR*, 2nd ser., xxiv, 8, 13.
[26] P.D.A. Harvey, 'The English Inflation of 1180–1220', *Past and Present* 61 (1973); E.

This model of strict feudalism should be valid for the century after Hastings. It should also be serviceable for the following fifty years since the extent to which it was distorted or corroded should help us to assess the nature and strength of the forces which acted upon it. To turn from this model of a society organized for war on feudal principles, however refined and qualified, to the annals, histories and biographies written in this period is to experience surprise and even shock. One occasion of surprise is to find that so much of the language employed is classical rather than susceptible of a feudal interpretation. William of Malmesbury tells us of the arrangements made in 1085 for the defence of the *respublica* against the barbarians, not of a feudal kingdom against the Danes.[27] William of Poitiers, who had served as a soldier before becoming one of the Conqueror's chaplains, drew extensively on the works of Sallust, Cicero, Caesar, Virgil, Lucan and Statius.[28] William of Malmesbury played with the notion that the soul of Julius Caesar had passed into the physical frame of William Rufus.[29] Orderic Vitalis put his Normans into Roman dress, and we read of Rufus's cohorts in 1097 being led by consuls, tribunes and centurions.[30] The *Gesta Stephani* even had the citizens of Exeter wearing togas in 1136.[31] And in the mid-twelfth century a poet claimed that Rouen was the new Rome to which empire had passed.[32]

It may be that much of this classical language is purely decorative, the product of a desire of authors to parade their learning and to flatter their patrons. But some of the language has to be taken more seriously as evidence of how men thought about government and its responsibilities. There is the word *respublica* and the terms associated with it: *publica potestas, utilitas publica, pax publica, publicus hostis* and *disciplina publica*. When William of Malmesbury reported that at the beginning of Rufus's reign the *administratio rerum publicarum* was entrusted to William of St Calais, bishop of Durham, he was apparently describing an appointment to a definite office, a delegation of wide general authority such as the chief justiciars were later to enjoy.[33] Both Orderic and the Worcester chronicler report Henry I proceeding against Robert of Bellême in 1102 as a public enemy, not as a contumacious vassal.[34] In the

Miller and J. Hatcher, *Medieval England: Rural Society and Economic Change, 1086–1348* (London, 1978), 68–9.

[27] *The Vita Wulfstani of William of Malmesbury*, ed. R.R. Darlington (Camden Soc., 3rd ser., xl (1928), 56.

[28] See R.H.C. Davis, 'William of Poitiers and his History of William the Conqueror', in *The Writing of History in the Middle Ages, Essays presented to Richard William Southern*, ed. R.H.C. Davis and J.M. Wallace-Hadrill (Oxford, 1981).

[29] Malmesbury, *Gesta Regum*, ii. 374. He later compared Robert of Gloucester to Julius Caesar, *Historia Novella*, 34–5.

[30] *Orderic*, v. 214.

[31] *Geta Stephani*, 32.

[32] Cited by C.H. Haskins, *Norman Institutions* (Cambridge, Mass., 1918, repr. New York, 1967), 144; and see J. Le Patourel, *The Norman Empire* (Oxford, 1976), 353–4. Orderic had claimed Julius Caesar as the founder of Rouen, *Orderic*, iii. 36.

[33] Malmesbury, *Gesta Regum*, ii. 360.

[34] *Orderic*, vi. 20; Florence, ii. 50.

second quarter of the twelfth century there emerged both in France and England the concept of the crown, the abstract notion of the rights and powers considered essential for the peace and defence of the realm and independent of the person of the ruler. Very early in Henry I's reign he spoke of the liberties, dignities and forfeitures belonging to the crown,[35] and later in the reign we learn of the large profit anticipated from the keeping of the pleas of the crown in Norfolk.[36] Henry II's treasurer wrote of the crown lands, and the London version of the *Leges Edwardi Confessoris* dwelt on the comprehensive duty of the king to recover, maintain and defend all the lands, honours, dignities, rights and liberties of the crown in their entirety.[37]

When William of Newburgh wrote of Henry II as zealous for the public peace and public discipline, and as ordering the new coinage of 1180 as necessary for reasons of public utility, or when Ralph of Diceto described Henry II's itinerant justices as agents of the *publica potestas* concerned with public utility, we may be inclined to dismiss these phrases as the rhetoric of sycophants.[38] But they have to be taken more seriously when we find them used so frequently by Henry's critics. Smalley noted the repeated use by Becket and his friends of the terms 'public power', 'public money', 'public edict', and 'public crimes'.[39] And they have to be taken yet more seriously when we encounter the same phrases in the same contexts in the *Dialogue of the Exchequer,* the work of Henry II's treasurer, written, as he claimed, in ordinary and straightforward language.[40] This is the language of a state and its subjects, not of a suzerain and his vassals; of executive decrees, not of feudal counsel; of impersonal authority allegedly directed to the public good, but capable of being overriden by prerogative on the grounds of urgent necessity. Richard Fitz Neal in the *Dialogue* had been uneasy about the king's right to the chattels of fugitive villeins, overriding the rights of their lords, and offered in explanation the doctrine of urgent necessity and the interests of peace.[41] A little earlier Henry II himself, writing to the pope, had invoked this same doctrine of urgent necessity in order to justify his much more lucrative retention of the revenues of vacant archbishoprics, bishoprics and abbeys for more than a year.[42]

These concepts of an impersonal crown, public power, public utility, prerogative and necessity entered largely into the practice as well as the theory of the Angevin state in the second half of the twelfth century; and they had a long history before them. They had also a history behind them. Some of these concepts were familiar to those who wrote about the Anglo-Norman state, and they were sometimes expressed in identical language. Orderic Vitalis repre-

---

[35] *Feudal Documents from the Abbey of Bury St Edmunds*, ed. D.C. Douglas (London, 1932), 62.

[36] *Pipe Roll 31 Henry I*, 91.

[37] *Regesta*, iii. no. 274; *Dialogus de Scaccario*, ed. and trans. C. Johnson (London, 1950), 14, 93.

[38] Newburgh, i. 102, 140–1, 225, 282; Diceto, i. 434–5.

[39] B. Smalley, *The Becket Conflict and the Schools* (Oxford, 1973), 228–9.

[40] *Dialogus*, 27, 43, 46, 84, 94, 100.

[41] Ibid., 102.

[42] Diceto, i. 410.

sented the Conqueror as claiming in 1082 that his continental campaigns had been conducted for the public good.[43] And he described the measures of the council of Lisieux in 1107 as Henry I's edicts for his subject peoples, commending them on the grounds of necessity and utility.[44] When Rufus taxed England to pay for his wars it was, according to William of Malmesbury, by an *edictum regium*, and when, a century later, Hubert Walter issued a measure for the greater internal security of England as a war base, this too was an *edictum regium*.[45] Sometimes the language varied. Anselm told Rufus plainly that he prolonged vacancies in the church for the sake of his campaigns and wars: Henry II justified the same practice in the more decent language of urgent necessity.[46] For the Worcester chronicler Henry I's currency reform of 1108 was a great benefit for the whole kingdom. William of Newburgh was less enthusiastic about Henry II's recoinage of 1180, but accepted it as necessary for the public good.[47] These accounts reflect at least an element of propaganda, and sometimes this was recognized. When in 1190 William Longchamp instructed the sheriffs to retain bands of armed men in their service, he justified this according to William of Newburgh, by the pretext of providing for the interests of the state.[48] But the language of the *respublica* and all the associated terms of public power, public good, public enemies, necessity and prerogative, and whether expressing policy or propaganda, was not the language of Vinogradoff's 'federation of feudal potentates'.

To those accustomed to employ the model of feudalism in describing and explaining society and government in this period these are discordant notes. It is equally disturbing to discover how largely the use of money was believed at the time to enter into the conduct of war and diplomacy.[49]

Historians have experienced no difficulty in accepting that some of the larger transactions of this period were effected through the agency of money. Robert Curthose sold, or perhaps mortgaged, western Normandy to Henry after the Conqueror's death, the sum being put at £3,000 and in 1096 he mortgaged the whole of Normandy to Rufus for 10,000 marks.[50] In March 1101 Henry I concluded a treaty whereby the count of Flanders, in return for a pension or money fief of £500 per annum, agreed to make available to Henry a thousand knights in England or Normandy or five hundred knights in Maine. In 1110 Henry I sent 10,000 marks to Germany as his little daughter's marriage portion after her betrothal to the Salian king Henry V. For Henry V of Germany this marriage portion meant that he could finance his Roman expedition of 1110 on a lavish scale, as Leyser has shown; to Henry I of England the alliance brought

---

[43] *Orderic*, iv. 42.

[44] *Orderic*, vi. 138.

[45] Malmesbury, *Gesta Regum*, ii. 369; Howden, *Chronica*, iii. 299–300.

[46] Eadmer, *Historia Novorum*, 49–50; Diceto, i. 410.

[47] Florence, ii. 57; Newburgh, *Historia*, i. 225.

[48] Newburgh, *Historia*, i. 334.

[49] For further examples, see above, 12, 20, 42.

[50] *Orderic*, iv. 118–20; Robert of Torigny, interpolation in William of Jumièges, *Gesta Normannorum Ducum*, ed. J. Marx (Soc. de l'histoire de Normandie, 1914), 269; C.W. David, *Robert Curthose* (Cambridge, Mass., 1920), 91 and n. 16.

prestige and was of considerable military value in 1124; and ultimately the marriage enabled the girl herself, Matilda, to claim the title of empress of which she made so much even after her second marriage to Geoffrey count of Anjou.

Less notice has been taken of the constant and pervasive influence of money in the day-to-day conduct of war. In his Ford Lectures McFarlane observed that with few exceptions historians had failed to grasp the first essential point of warfare in the later Middle Ages, the opportunities for profit presented by pay, ransoms and booty. The same observation holds good for this earlier period. The pages of Orderic Vitalis contain many detailed accounts of the traffic in ransoms in the reigns of the Conqueror, Rufus, Henry I and Stephen. When Henry I captured Pontaudemer in 1123 his hired Breton troops were richly rewarded by digging up the treasure chests which the citizens had buried, chests stuffed with gold, silver, precious clothes, cloaks, pepper and ginger. Nor was it merely the rank and file of the armies who served for pay. Hugh the Great, count of Vermandois and brother of the king of France, crossed the Channel in 1085 to take the Conqueror's pay. The counts of Flanders and Maine were hired by Henry I, and if William of Malmesbury can be trusted the arrangement with Flanders went back to the Conqueror's time and had been revived by Rufus. In 1136 the two brothers, Waleran count of Meulan and Robert earl of Leicester, hired the services of Theobald count of Blois for 100 marks in pursuit of the long feud between the Beaumonts and the Tosnys.[51] And in 1139 Rotrou count of Mortagne was similarly taken into King Stephen's pay.[52]

In the writings of William of Malmesbury, Orderic Vitalis and their contemporaries the role of money in war and diplomacy was conspicuous, so conspicuous that we must guard against accepting their exaggerations of it in their more cynical or pessimistic passages. Yet to those brought up to interpret this period in terms of feudalism the evidence on the scale and pervasiveness of monetary transactions in the Anglo-Norman state, so destructive of traditional views, is not easily accepted. Sometimes it has been ignored; sometimes minimized; and sometimes misinterpreted. Painter held that the first care of the Conqueror and his barons was to establish an effective military system and that this system 'was bound to be feudal in nature', partly because it is unlikely that there was enough money in circulation to maintain an adequate hired army, but chiefly because William and his men 'were deeply steeped in feudal tradition'.[53] Since Painter was an admirably realistic historian his belief that the military expedients of the Conqueror conformed to a uniform system and his failure to notice the evidence for the frequency and scale of the use of paid troops by the Conqueror is striking testimony to the hold of traditional teaching upon him. If we take the evidence of one contemporary literally we should conclude rather that Duke William set out in 1066 as a believer in a system of paid troops, for William of Poitiers says of the invasion forces awaiting the opportunity to embark that 'After forbidding all plunder, he supported 50,000 men-at-arms at

---

[51] *Orderic*, vi. 464, again using the verb *conducere*.
[52] *Orderic*, vi. 534.
[53] Painter, *Feudal Barony*, 20.

his own expense while unfavourable winds delayed him for a month at the mouth of the Dives.'[54] Unluckily for the historian the Conqueror, like his successors, was more concerned with effectiveness than with devising and enforcing any simple system. Nevertheless the testimony of William of Poitiers, often overlooked, should carry some weight: he had served the Conqueror in his campaigns before entering the church.

Stenton recognized that the Conqueror's introduction into England of very large paid forces from the continent in 1085 showed that 'in a great emergency the knight-service due to the king from his tenants in chief was obviously unequal to the defence of the land'. He also noted Henry I's treaties with Flanders.[55] And when he printed a mid-twelfth-century agreement between two Lincolnshire barons redolent, as he put it, of 'the authentic atmosphere of feudalism', he added a footnote to point out that the arrangements in question 'give a remarkable illustration of the influence of money on feudal relationships, an influence which is often underestimated'.[56] Nevertheless the central thesis of his Ford Lectures was that feudalism was a military as well as a social and political reality, that throughout the reign of Stephen and even after the troubles of Stephen's reign 'the feudal army remained the ultimate defence of the land, and the chief royal castles continued to be garrisoned by knights who were the tenants of baronial lords'. This structure was remarkably durable, for 'in the thirteenth century the king was still using the feudal army as a military reality'.[57]

On the 'feudal army' it is enough to observe here that the feudal obligation of knight-service could produce only knights, and that when contemporaries attempted to give comprehensive figures for combatant forces, they made it clear that in their opinion the knights were greatly outnumbered by the infantry.[58] Moreover campaigns were not conducted merely by combatant forces. When Rufus warned Hélie that if he wished to keep the county of Maine he would have to fight for it, he told him to send for masons and stone-cutters, greedy for gain, to repair his crumbling castles. And though Rufus boasted of the lances and banners of his own forces, he also pointed out that they would be backed up by his ammunition wagons laden with bolts and arrows.[59]

Castle-guard may well have been, as Stenton suggested, a more onerous obligation than knight-service. It is possible to reconstruct in some detail the groupings of baronies and fees to provide the garrisons of some royal castles and to show how the turns of duty were arranged. But, as Stenton pointed out, most of

---

[54] *Gesta Guillelmi*, 102–3.

[55] Stenton, *First Century*, 151, 216.

[56] Ibid., 47–9, and 50 n. 3.

[57] Ibid., 216, 179.

[58] In the account of the battle of Tinchebray written shortly after the event by a priest of Fécamp, the proportions of cavalry to infantry were 1 to 16 for Henry's forces and 1 to 9 for those of Robert Curthose (*EHR* xxv, 296). Henry's dispatch to Anselm on this engagement gave a proportion of 1 to 25 for the prisoners he had taken (Eadmer, *Historia Novorum*, 184). For the forces with which Henry of Anjou landed in England in 1153 the proportion given is 1 to 21 (Newburgh, 1. 88).

[59] *Orderic*, v. 230–2.

our knowledge about castle-guard comes from documents which are not earlier than the thirteenth century, by which time 'castle-guard had long lost its first military quality and had normally been commuted for a cash payment'.[60] The difficulty is to find clear evidence for castle-guard operating to provide actual garrisons in royal castles rather than money rents in lieu. When Rufus acquired Carlisle in his campaign of 1092 and constructed a castle there, he might have been expected at this early date to have imposed the duty of guarding it on a group of baronies. Instead we are told that he garrisoned the castle with his men and colonized the city with peasants drawn from southern England.[61] This suggests that Rufus was relying on the combination of castle and walled town defended by a royal garrison and English settlers, the combination later used so effectively by Edward I to hold down North Wales. The Pipe Roll of 1130 shows that money was still being spent on the city wall of Carlisle and that a paid royal garrison of knights and sergeants was being maintained there.[62] Sometimes a scrap of evidence seems unambiguous in isolation. The royal castle of Rockingham is known to have been the centre of a group of baronies owing castle-guard, and among these baronies was the abbey of Peterborough. There survives an order of Henry I ordering all who owed castle-guard at Rockingham to come into residence when summoned by its keeper. However a charter of Richard I to the abbot of Peterborough granted that the knights who owed castle-guard at Rockingham should be quit for four shillings each per annum in time of peace as they had been in the time of Henry I.[63] It is possible therefore that Henry I's order had been merely designed to secure the payment of castle-guard rents. Jocelin of Brakelond wrote of knights entering on their turn of castle-guard in the 1190s when referring merely to the term at which their rent was due.[64]

For Stenton the arrangements whereby tenants in chief provided the garrisons of royal castles supplied the clearest illustration of what he called 'the essential fact in the history of English feudal society, the original interdependence of king and baronage'. Before we accept this dictum it is instructive to consider some evidence on Norwich castle. During the rebellion of 1075 Norwich castle was held by the wife of Ralph earl of East Anglia, with a Breton garrison which included paid troops. After the castle was surrendered it was occupied by Geoffrey of Coutances, William I de Warenne and Robert Malet with a garrison of three hundred men-at-arms and a large force of crossbowmen and engineers. Castle-guard can have made little if any contribution to either of these garrisons. Nor was it effective in 1088 when Roger Bigod seized the castle and made it the base for his depredations.[65] Henry I began to break up the scheme of castle-guard at Norwich, first exempting the abbey of St Benet's Holme and then, for a fine of £1,000 (of which £364 was paid promptly) allowing the

---

[60] Stenton, *First Century*, 209.
[61] *Anglo-Saxon Chronicle, s.a.* 1092.
[62] *Pipe Roll 31 Henry I*, 140–1.
[63] Stenton, *First Century*, 213–14, 284; *Cartae Antiquae Rolls 1–10*, ed. L. Landon (PRS, 1939), no. 214.
[64] *The Chronicle of Jocelin of Brakelond*, ed. and trans. H.E. Butler (London, 1949), 67.
[65] *Anglo-Saxon Chronicle, s.a.* 1088.

bishop of Ely to transfer the guard service of his knights to the Isle of Ely.[66] The process was continued by Stephen who freed the abbey of Bury St Edmunds from the obligation to send its knights to do castle-guard at Norwich and allowed them to do it at Bury instead.[67] There was no castle at Bury to be guarded, and it seems more probable that Stephen was making a grant – or sale – of rents than that the abbot was seriously expected to require such of his tenants as Hugh Bigod to produce a guard outside the abbey's gates. Henry II ignored this grant, but it does not appear that any actual guard-service was demanded: Abbot Samson was left disputing with his knights about the precise number of pennies owed for castle-guard rent.[68] Henry also ignored Stephen's grant of Norwich castle, and when he forced Stephen's son, William, to surrender it in 1157 he put in a paid royal garrison. Again when invasion threatened in 1193 Norwich castle was garrisoned by a paid royal force of 25 knights, 25 mounted sergeants and 25 foot sergeants.[69]

It would be strange if the feudal obligation of castle-guard never produced a garrison at Norwich castle, but no evidence of it has survived. There is evidence of exemptions being granted, in one case for a large capital sum; and there is evidence of the obligation being commuted for a rent. In emergencies, as in 1075, 1157–58 and 1193, Norwich castle was held by substantial royal forces. And as for Stenton's hypothetical interdependence of king and baronage, members of the Bigod family in particular showed little sense of this relationship. A Bigod seized Norwich castle in the rebellion of 1088. Another Bigod seized it temporarily in1136, was a consistent opponent of Stephen during the civil war from 1141, at one time throwing in his lot with Geoffrey de Mandeville, and was induced to rebel in 1173 by the promise of the honour of Eye and the custody of Norwich for himself and his heirs. With the help of Flemish mercenaries he succeeded in capturing and sacking Norwich in the summer of 1174.[70] Even Abbot Samson failed to compel the next Bigod, Roger, second earl of Norfolk, to contribute to the castle-guard rent owed by the abbey of Bury St Edmunds to Norwich castle. And in 1214 King John was very careful to ensure that Norwich castle remained in his hands after the death of its custodian.[71]

We cannot even assume that there was a smooth and uniform movement from service to commutation. Indeed the story of the garrisoning of royal castles begins after Hastings with the employment of paid royal forces; and it ends, paradoxically, in the spring and summer of 1215 with both King John and his opponents asserting the duty and the right of discharging castle-guard in person. William of Jumièges described the construction of castles on the Conqueror's orders, and added that he garrisoned them with picked knights and very large

---

[66] *Regesta*, ii. nos. 1306, 1656; *Pipe Roll 31 Henry I*, 44.
[67] *Regesta*, iii. no. 757.
[68] *Jocelin of Brakelond*, 66–7.
[69] Torigny, 192–3; *Pipe Rolls 2, 3 and 4 Henry II*, ed. J. Hunter (London, 1844), 126; *Pipe Roll 5 Richard I*, ed. D.M. Stenton (PRS, 1927), 13.
[70] Huntingdon, *Historia Anglorum*, 259; *Gesta Stephani*, 166; Howden, *Gesta*, i. 45, 68.
[71] *Pipe Roll 16 John*, 175.

numbers of paid troops.[72] Between mid-April and mid-May 1215, when King John was uncertain whether he faced war or negotiations with his baronial opponents, he issued several orders from Wallingford to named knights of the honour of Wallingford to report for castle-guard duty.[73] Personal service with horses and arms was required. In the last of these orders John made it clear that he was reviving an old claim: the knights were to prepare to reside as they had been accustomed to do long ago, *antiquitus*. And in another order John relied on very ancient claims indeed; the sheriff of Berkshire was to summon all in his county to turn out without delay and to repair the ditch and ramparts of the castle and vill of Wallingford, again as they had been accustomed to do long ago. Here we seem to be taken far back into the Anglo-Saxon past.[74] A month later the Articles of the Barons demanded and Magna Carta granted that no knight should be compelled to give money for castle-guard if he was willing to do it in person or by a reliable deputy. It is however unlikely that there was any general enthusiasm for garrison duty at this time, and perhaps the intention behind this clause was to frustrate the normal royal preference for regular cash rents and to substitute for it the occasional appearance in person of politically unreliable and inadequately trained troops. The explanation of the apparently paradoxical chronology of royal policy is that after Hastings the Conqueror was, or believed himself to be, rich in the spoils and loot of conquest, whereas after Bouvines John was, and knew himself to be, poor.

The general or wide concept of feudalism is too loose and vague to be serviceable for descriptive or explanatory purposes, while the various devices adopted to solve the problems of the chronology and the nature of feudalism have led to confusion and contradiction. The strict or narrow concept of feudalism as applied to England in the century following Hastings is a highly artificial abstraction. It tells us how a small proportion of the army should have been raised and how some castles should have been garrisoned: it does not tell us how land and sea forces as a whole were raised and supplied, and it does not tell us how in practice English castles were garrisoned and defended. It deflects our attention from the politically crucial question of the control of castles, disposing us to think of royal castles as a fixed category throughout the period. Stenton conceded that 'Henry I . . . in England as in Normandy may sometimes have treated as his own, baronial castles which for any reason came into his hand.'[75] But this ignores the earlier evidence on the scale of the Conqueror's control of baronial castles in his continental dominions; and it ignores too the drastic change in the balance of castle-power between 1154 and 1214 in favour of the Angevin kings, a change convincingly established by R. Allen Brown.[76]

---

[72] William of Jumièges, 142.
[73] *Rot. Lit. Pat.,* i. 132b, 134b, 135b.
[74] *Rot. Lit. Claus.,* i, 199b. The reference to the vill in addition to the castle makes it tempting to link the *antiquitus* of this order with the place of Wallingford in the Burghal Hideage of the early tenth century.
[75] Stenton, *First Century*, 216.
[76] *Orderic*, iv. 152; C.H. Haskins, *Norman Institutions*, 38, 282; R.A. Brown, 'A List of Castles, 1154–1216', *EHR* lxxiv (1959), 249–80.

Use of the same concept of feudalism has commonly led historians to under-estimate the scale and volume of production and exchange in this period. If rulers relied so largely on unpaid feudal troops, on feudal counsellors in central government and on baronial honours in local government, the economy must have been relatively undeveloped, or its progress checked, even reversed, by feudal warfare, its potentialities ignored by a governing class with a non-economic mentality. And if feudalism provided the framework of government the language of the *respublica* must be dismissed as a literary exercise irrelevant to practical affairs.

Moreover the effect of applying the strict concept of feudalism to English history in this period is to divorce it from developments elsewhere. The Normans themselves were thoroughly familiar with the use and exploitation of money in their other theatres of operations. The Norman adventurers who first gained a foothold in Italy in the first half of the eleventh century did so as mercenaries, living on pay and pillage; and the great Guiscard began his career by hiring out his services. As they established themselves first in Italy and then in Sicily the Normans passed from taking pay to giving it. There were indeed feudal tenures in the established Norman kingdom, but they were neither universal nor generally effective; indeed Cahen observed that 'for a campaign of any length, the army became a genuinely paid army and no longer, to speak strictly, a feudal one'.[77] And, accepting the orthodox view of English history, he went on to contrast England, an essentially feudal state, with the Norman kingdom in the south where the monarchy was only very partially feudal and relied very largely on mercenary troops.[78] But it is doubtful whether Geoffrey of Coutances or Thomas Brown and the many others who knew both lands would have recognized so sharp a difference in military practice and political structure. Similar evidence comes from the First Crusade and the early history of the crusading states. Raymond of Toulouse offered to take the other leaders into his pay even before the capture of Jerusalem.[79] William of Tyre tells the story of how Baldwin of Edessa, unable to pay the wages of his many knights, tricked his rich Armenian father-in-law into coming to his rescue.[80] Baldwin I of Jerusalem found it equally difficult to meet his expenses and pay his troops, and he was ready to sell the succession to the Kingdom of Jerusalem to Roger II, the future king of Sicily, in return for the hand and fortune of Roger's rich and widowed mother.[81]

Similar evidence can be accumulated for Germany, the Low Countries and France. In 1075 only a sudden and unexpected windfall of treasure enabled Henry IV of Germany, whose reserves had been exhausted by very heavy military expenditure, to satisfy the demands of his troops.[82] His Italian expedi-

---

[77] C. Cahen, *Le Régime Féodal de l'Italie Normande* (Paris, 1940), 64.

[78] Ibid., 136.

[79] For this and other examples of pay given by the leaders of the First Crusade, see R.C. Smail, *Crusading Warfare* (Cambridge, 1956), 93.

[80] William of Tyre, *Historia Rerum in Partibus Transmarinis Gestis*, xi, 11.

[81] Ibid., xi, 21.

[82] *Lamperti monachi Hersfeldensis opera*, 230.

tion of 1081 depended largely on the service of paid troops and *ministeriales*.[83] The imperialist Benzo, bishop of Alba, writing in about 1089, told Henry IV that if he could not pay his troops he would alienate his own supporters; and he gave Henry elementary but vague advice on recovering dues and enforcing taxes.[84] Walcher, a claimant to the bishopric of Cambrai in the 1090s, furthered his cause both by placing his trust in God and by hiring mercenaries; and when his own resources were exhausted he melted down the treasures of the church, just as Pope Gregory VII melted down the church treasure of Canossa in 1082 for use in his campaign against the anti-pope.[85] Suger, who had much to say about Rufus's use of paid troops, was himself praised for ensuring that knights received their due wages, robes and gifts while Louis VII was absent on crusade.[86]

The Anglo-Norman state of the late eleventh and early twelfth centuries was not therefore a feudal state in a non-feudal sea. Indeed it was looked to in western Europe as a source of military leaders, treasure and technical advice on taxation. It was to the steward of the Conqueror's household that the widowed countess of Flanders turned for military help in 1071;[87] it was from Henry I's household that the leaders of the crusading states obtained a prince of Antioch; and it was from Henry I that the emperor Henry V obtained treasure in 1110 and advice on taxation in 1124.[88] Suger enviously contrasted the wealth and military resources of Rufus, whom he described as 'a wonderful merchant and paymaster of troops', with the poverty and attenuated forces of Louis of France.[89]

The problem of interpreting the evidence for the place of war in English history during this period has therefore to be approached without the help of the concept of feudalism either in its wide or narrow form. Nor can we hope to replace the supposed feudal system by any other monolithic system, agreeable as it would be to find one. Men could be mobilized for war by a feudal summons, by the offer of pay, by a general levy, by simple coercion, and by a promised remission of sins. These were not always mutually exclusive categories. Men might do paid service in response to a feudal summons, either

[83] K. Bosl, *Die Reichsministerialität der Salier und Staufer* (Stuttgart, 1950), ii. 90.

[84] *Benzonis Albensis Episcopi as Henricum IV Imperatorem Libri VIII, Monumenta Germaniae Historica, Scriptores*, xi. 600–1. Erdmann referred to this as a project to replace the feudal system by a mercenary army with the help of an imperial tax: C. Erdmann, *Die Entstehung des Kreuzzugsgedankens* (Stuttgart, 1935), 250, n. 2. But Benzo never mentioned the feudal system, took the need to pay troops for granted, and offered only the general advice that '*provideat sibi rex suisque successoribus investigando sepius de regalis fisci publicis pensionibus*'.

[85] *Gesta Episcoporum Cameracensium, Monumenta Germaniae Historica, Scriptores*, vii. 505; Erdmann, op. cit., 144 and n. 45.

[86] *Sugerii Vita*, in *Suger, Oeuvres*, ed. F. Gaspari (Paris, 1996, 2001), ii. 337: *Et ne propter regis absentiam regno quicquam deesset honoris, ab hoc milites solita consequabantur stipendia, et certis diebus vestes vel dona regia.*

[87] *Orderic*, ii. 280–2; Malmesbury, *Gesta Regum*, ii. 314–15; D.C. Douglas, *William the Conqueror* (London, 1964), 224–5.

[88] J.O. Prestwich, 'The Military Household of the Norman Kings', *EHR* xcvi (1981), 8; K.J. Leyser, *Medieval Germany and its Neighbours, 900–1250* (London, 1982), 205.

[89] Suger, *Vie de Louis VI*, 8.

from the outset or after a fixed period. It is ironic that the document chosen by Stubbs in his *Select Charters* to illustrate knight-service should have been a return to the inquest of 1166 in which it is specified that the service should be performed at the king's expense.[90] Men might volunteer for a crusade, serve under their lord, be maintained by pay and hope at the same time for spiritual rewards. The phrase which Orderic Vitalis applied to the Norman adventurers in southern Italy, *stipendiarii contra paganos*, linked the motive of gain with the cause of the Holy War.[91] Contemporaries distinguished certain troops as *solidarii* or *stipendiarii* because their chief and obvious bond with their masters was that of their wages. But these terms were applied to many different kinds of troops: to those temporarily brought together and hired for a campaign, to members of standing bands available to any paymaster, and even to permanent members of a king's household. No general political tendency was imputed to the use of paid troops.

Why then has the concept of feudalism for so long and so widely been accepted as a valid account and analysis of England as a society organized for war, above all in Stenton's first century? One reason is that most historians are commendably concerned to discover patterns in the past, and feudalism offers just such a pattern, allowing us to detect and admire what has been called 'the logic and symmetry of Anglo-Norman feudalism'.[92] Certain categories of evidence which had long been easily accessible, wide or general in their coverage, and satisfactorily firm in quality, appeared to exhibit the pattern of feudalism. First there was Domesday Book arranged to show the estates of the king, the estates held of the king by his tenants in chief, and below them those on the lower rungs of the tenurial ladder. Next there were the returns of the tenants in chief to the inquest of knight-service of 1166 from which Round was able to work out the *servitia debita,* the numbers of knights which tenants in chief owed to the king, and the knights' fees which supported them. Bridges could be thrown across the intervening gulf of eighty years enabling Round to claim that 'the Domesday under-tenant proves to be a feudal *miles*' and indeed that the whole system of knight-service was introduced by the Conqueror within a few years of the battle of Hastings.[93] Hence, as a modern historian expressed it, the Norman land settlement led 'to a revision of social relationships at all levels, to a regrouping of land and men into units with a prime responsibility for maintaining the members of the feudal army'.[94] Finally the evidence of charters, legal records and treatises threw into prominence the feudal aids and incidents –

---

[90] *Select Charters*, ed. W. Stubs (9th edn, Oxford, 1921), 174.

[91] *Orderic*, ii. 58

[92] Frank Barlow, *The Feudal Kingdom of England, 1041–1216* (London, 1955), 111. However he later rejected the formula of 'the introduction of feudalism into England', and noted that by the time of Domesday Book 'there had arisen every kind of tenurial complexity which can be imagined'; *The Norman Conquest: Its Setting and Impact*, ed. C.T. Chevellier (London 1966), reprinted in Frank Barlow *The Norman Conquest and Beyond* (London, 1983), 164–5.

[93] J.H. Round, 'The Introduction of Knight service into England', in J.H. Round, *Feudal England* (London, 1909), 307.

[94] E. Miller, *The Abbey and Bishopric of Ely* (Cambridge, 1951), 70.

escheat, wardship, marriage and relief – designed to maintain the whole structure in working order and cementing together the individual units.

More detailed scrutiny of this and associated evidence revealed awkward anomalies and gaps. Round noted that Hugh de Port, the greatest lay tenant-in-chief in Hampshire, was unorthodox by strict feudal standards: he also held land as a sub-tenant under five different tenants in chief in Hampshire; some of his own demesne manors were let out at farm; and he took over other manors in the county at farm from the king, while he was also farming crown lands in Rutland. Commercial dealings of this kind led Round to write of 'a complexity of relations, foreign in spirit to the feudal system'.[95] But as long as Hugh de Port could be treated as exceptional his dealings proved the feudal rule. So too did the comment that it was somewhat curious in a feudal society that the Conqueror should have bequeathed £5,000 in silver to his youngest son, Henry;[96] no general inferences can be drawn from a curious act, even if it was the act of the king. Where the evidence was reticent or silent on important aspects of feudalism in action its deficiencies could be supplied. Although Stenton found it necessary to point out that 'it is remarkable how little we really know about the nature of military service in the century after the Conquest', he had no doubt that the age was one 'when knight-service was a military reality'.[97] Some weaknesses in the evidence were candidly admitted. Barlow found it difficult to extend his 'logic and symmetry of Anglo-Norman feudalism' to royal government. He doubted whether the composition of the king's council could at any time be fully explained by tenure; he held that the feudal doctrine of counsel only found logical expression in Magna Carta when feudal government was already in decay; and he pointed out that the Anglo-Norman kings retained most of the rights of their English predecessors and added procedures that came from the Roman empire by way of the Franks.[98]

The power of the concept of feudalism to resist the discovery of gaps and anomalies in the evidence was seldom more clearly revealed than in Stenton's *The First Century of English Feudalism*. That work rested on his incomparable knowledge of the charters, writs and records, examined with exact scholarship and considered largely in isolation from the more general evidence of the chronicles and histories. Many of Stenton's comments on specific documents indicate his scepticism about the validity of the general concept of feudalism. He noted that Domesday Book tells little, and that indirectly, about feudal organization, and commented that 'to an extent which is not always realized our conception of the feudal society of King William's day rests on a series of uncertain inferences'.[99] One document led him to call attention to the volume in which money circulated in the middle of the twelfth century.[100] Another, requiring a tenant to compound for all his military obligations by an annual payment in money,

95 *Victoria County History, Hampshire* (Oxford, 1900), 1. 414, 422–4.
96 G.W.S. Barrow, *Feudal Britain* (London, 1956), 54.
97 Stenton, *First Century*, 168, 170.
98 Barlow, *Feudal Kingdom*, 112–13.
99 Ibid., 8–9.
100 Ibid., 109.

provoked him to comment on the very great difficulty of enforcing general military service and to note the early imposition of scutage on lay as well as on ecclesiastical tenants in chief.[101]

Nevertheless in the *First Century* itself the general validity of the concept of feudalism was asserted without qualification. Of post-Conquest society it was laid down that 'the precise definition of service was a result of the feudal conception of society'; that this was 'a society organized essentially for war'; and that 'the most important of all forms of service was the plain duty of attending a lord in war, mounted and equipped as a knight'.[102] Here Stenton was ignoring evidence he had himself provided. In his general argument he drew the sharpest possible distinction between the vague and miscellaneous services required before the Norman Conquest and the closely defined services demanded according to feudal notions of tenants by knight-service. He illustrated the former from the terms on which Bishop Oswald of Worcester leased land to his tenants in the tenth century. These included 'the law of riding', the payment of dues, burning lime for the work of the church, and bridge-building.[103] Much later he selected a mid-twelfth-century charter granted by Walter de Aincurt as an analysis of a knight's duty deserving of respect. This specified 'the army, castle-guard, scutage, riding, work, and all the service pertaining to a knight'.[104] There are important differences between the two documents, in particular the reference to castle-guard; but on this evidence tenth-century Worcestershire is brought inconveniently close to twelfth-century Lincolnshire. Moreover both documents merely record obligations and provide no evidence on how far and in what ways the obligations were discharged in practice.

Keynes once described his long struggle of escape from habitual modes of thought and expression. In the preface to his *Rural England, 1086–1135* Lennard described with characteristic moderation his own escape from the traditional conception of English society at this period. 'I have certainly learnt', he wrote, 'that money played a larger part in agrarian affairs than I had supposed and that the farming-out of manors on stock-and-land leases was so common that this mode of estate management, which was inherited from Anglo-Saxon England, must at least rank in importance with the system of tenure by knight-service introduced by the Normans.' Careful scrutiny of Domesday enabled Lennard to show that the practice of farming out royal manors for a money rent can be traced in twenty-five of the thirty-four counties surveyed and that the same practice is found on the estates of ninety-five tenants in chief.[105] Lennard further showed that where Domesday can be compared with other and fuller records its bare valuations often corresponded with farms or rents paid in money.[106] The fortunate pertinacity of the commissioners for the south-eastern

---

101 Ibid., 179, 184.
102 Stenton, *First Century*, 130–1.
103 Ibid., 124.
104 Ibid., 172.
105 Lennard, *Rural England*, 123–5.
106 Ibid., 118ff.

circuit revealed that within their counties the cash nexus was extensive and reached far down the social scale. At East Clandon in Surrey the villeins were paying £6 for a whole manor valued at £4.[107]

The importance of these findings is that the practices which struck Round as foreign in spirit to the feudal system have turned out to be widespread, and that alongside the instances which justify his maxim that the Domesday undertenant proves to be a feudal *miles* are to be set those in which he proves to be a rent-paying farmer. We are also led to doubt the comprehensive validity of Stenton's statement that at this time 'the service of a knight was the most valuable return which could be made for a grant of land'.[108] Lennard quoted with great effect the passage in which the Anglo-Saxon chronicler described how the Conqueror 'gave his land as dearly for rent as he could possibly could', and showed that this was not a rhetorical accusation but was strikingly confirmed by the evidence of Domesday both for the royal estates and others, lay and ecclesiastical.[109] When men granted their lands at farm the returns they required were financial, and these were commonly high. The royal manor of Merton in Surrey was valued at £25 in King Edward's time and at £35 in 1086; but it was noted that the holder was actually paying £43.[110] Fulbert held Chilham in Kent of the fee of Odo of Bayeux, and it was valued in 1086 at £30; but it was noted that Odo himself had been drawing £82 from the estate.[111] When men granted land for knight-service the return they expected and received was not exclusively personal service. Henry I was aided by his knights, but the aid, *auxilium militum,* of which we read in the Pipe Roll of 1130, was purely financial.[112] In Henry's reign Eustace of Boulogne spoke of his knights serving, specifying the form of service as 'in cash, or in the army, or in castle-guard', and it is interesting that he set it out in that order.[113] A lord might grant some land to a tenant for knight-service and other land to the same tenant for rent. Under Rufus, Godfrey of Malling owed the service of three knights to the archbishop of Canterbury and he also paid £90 a year as rent for the manor of South Malling. Godfrey's role as a rent-paying farmer was far more important to Canterbury than his role as a tenant by knight-service.[114]

Modern historians have found it helpful to calculate from Domesday the value of the great estates in England and to show for example that the Warenne estates were worth c.£1,165 a year in 1086.[115] But it does not follow that the lords of these estates themselves thought in these terms, or that such men as

---

[107] *DB*, i. 34a.

[108] Stenton, *First Century*, 131.

[109] Lennard, *Rural England*, 156–7.

[110] *DB*, i. 30a.

[111] Ibid., i. 10a.

[112] *Pipe Roll 31 Henry I*, 49, 84, 89, 128, 153–4.

[113] Cited by Round, *Feudal England*, 270.

[114] F.R.H. du Boulay, *The Lordship of Canterbury* (London, 1966), 100, 203. Godfrey's rent would have enabled Canterbury to hire 45 knights for 60 days at 8d each a day.

[115] C.W. Hollister, 'The Anglo-Norman Civil War: 1101', *EHR* lxxxviii (1973), 220, n. 2 (given as a very approximate figure of landed revenue in England, including the subinfeudated portions).

Godfrey of Malling balanced their obligations as knights against their obligations as rent-paying tenants. It is therefore especially significant that when William II de Warenne complained in 1102 of his loss of the earldom of Surrey he should have done so, according to Orderic Vitalis, not in terms of status or of his knightly following, but simply of the loss of an estate 'which produced an annual revenue of a thousand pounds of silver for him'.[116] Orderic is likely to have been well informed, for Roger of Warenne, the earl's cousin, was for many years Orderic's fellow monk at St Evroul.[117]

There are indications that wealth and power had not always been reckoned in cash terms. Orderic himself, writing earlier, reported that Geoffrey bishop of Coutances had been given 280 manors by the Conqueror as a reward for his spiritual and military services.[118] Maitland found indications in Domesday Book that the Conqueror had in some cases made promises to his followers of ten or twenty manors; and he pointed to one entry strongly suggesting that Eustace of Boulogne had been promised a hundred manors.[119] It would in any case have been difficult in the early part of the Conqueror's reign to have established firm cash values for grants of land. But it was soon discovered that the counting of manors was unsatisfactory. Just as Orderic reported the monetary value of the Warenne lands, so William of Malmesbury gave cash figures to illustrate the inequity of the division of lands between the bishop of Ely and his monks.[120] Stenton called attention to the many charters which from the mid-twelfth century onwards defined grants of land in monetary terms, so many *libratae, marcatae* or *solidatae terrae*; and he was especially interested in those which equated the knight's fee with a valuation of £20 or, more commonly £10.[121] Certainly in Stephen's reign some very large grants or promises of land were expressed in monetary terms. Stephen granted £700 worth of land to his son, William.[122] The empress granted or confirmed £400 worth of land to Geoffrey de Mandeville, £200 worth to his son, Ernulf, and £100 worth to his half-brother, William fitz Otuel.[123] Henry of Anjou's extensive confirmations and grants to the earl of Chester in 1153 were reinforced by the promise of £100 worth of land to each of six of the earl's barons.[124] Five years later Henry II mobilized his troops in Normandy and compelled Conan IV of Brittany to

---

116 *Orderic*, vi. 12.

117 Ibid., iii. 228–30.

118 Ibid., ii. 266, and n. 3, pointing out that Domesday Book shows Orderic's figure to have been remarkably accurate.

119 F.W. Maitland, *Domesday Book and Beyond* (Cambridge, 1897), 127–8.

120 Malmesbury, *Gesta Pontificum*, 324, where William, writing in 1125, gave the bishop's annual revenue as £1,400 and the monks' share scarcely £300. These figures presumably include spiritualities, but seem high as compared with the vacancy accounts of Henry II's reign: see M. Howell, *Regalian Right in Medieval England* (London, 1962), 35.

121 Stenton, *First Century*, 165–9.

122 *Regesta*, iii. no. 272.

123 Ibid., no. 275. Stephen's second charter to Geoffrey had granted him even more, £600 worth, according to R.H.C. Davis ('Geoffrey de Mandeville Reconsidered', *EHR* lxxix (1964), 203), but this rests on a misunderstanding, and the figure is £300, together with £100 from escheats.

124 Ibid., no. 180.

surrender the county of Nantes. It is significant that when Robert of Torigny reported this he should have added that the county was said to be worth 60,000 shillings in Angevin money, or £750 sterling.[125]

In considering the place of war in English history during this period it is desirable to consider how in practice wars were fought, and for what ends. Men did not fight for monetary gain alone. But in considering these questions the evidence for formal military obligations, which has been held to give body to the concept of feudalism, is of little value, and it will be necessary to turn to the chroniclers and historians who, though guilty of some anachronisms, never employed the gross anachronism of feudalism.

Note on further reading

Susan Reynolds, in her *Fiefs and Vassals* (Oxford, 1994), set out to challenge the orthodoxies of feudalism in a most important book. In a letter of 1995, JOP commented 'I share her scepticism about feudalism. . . . Reynolds excludes the Latin Kingdom, though it would have strengthened her case.'[126] A detailed study based on the 1166 returns, which are a key source, is T.K. Keefe, *Feudal Assessments and the Political Community under Henry II and his Sons* (Berkeley, 1983). See also the note on further reading at the end of chapter eight, for work on the introduction of knight-service into England. JOP's plea to historians to abandon use of the 'feudal' model may perhaps now find an increasingly sympathetic audience. It is interesting that in the six hundred pages of *A Companion to Britain in the Later Middle Ages*, ed. S.H. Rigby (Oxford, 2003), which covers the period from 1100 to 1500, there are a mere six entries for feudalism in the index, and in most of them it is dismissed. In a recent article, however, 'The Second Century of English Feudalism', *Past and Present* 168 (2000), 30–71, David Carpenter has argued for the 'immense social and political significance' of 'fiscal feudalism', and suggests that 'For a long time it was difficult to envisage a society organized on anything but feudal lines' (pp. 70–1).

[125] Robert of Torigny, 197. It seems that in France under the Capetians the practice of defining grants of land in monetary terms did not appear until the last quarter of the twelfth century (Josette Metman, 'Les infeodations royales d'apres le "Recueil des actes de Philippe Auguste" ' in *La France de Philippe Auguste: le temps des mutations*, ed. R.H. Bautier (Paris, 1982).
[126] Letter to Ralph Bennett, dated 6 September 1995.

Appendix II

The Composition of Military Forces, 1066–1135

When we turn back from the England of Edward I to the reigns of the Conqueror and his sons we find ourselves, it seems, in a very different and a much simpler world: different because more rudimentary and simpler because simplified by conquerors with a genius for organization. No historian would now say with Hume that 'England of a sudden became a feudal kingdom'. But even those historians most concerned to emphasize the achievements of the Old English State and to set limits to the innovations of the Normans have stressed the importance of the military reorganization which followed the Conquest. Sayles wrote of 'the easy imposition of a new order upon the old society', and the essence of this new order was that 'a professional army was constructed and based firmly on the soil'.[1] Barlow wrote of 'the complete feudalization of England' and of the way in which feudal tenure provided the king with castle garrisons and a field force, with revenue and, in part, with counsel.[2] Round long ago taught us of the introduction of knight-service by the Conqueror. Stenton, though warning us that the influence of money on feudal relationships has often been underestimated, has emphasized that down to and even after Stephen's reign 'the feudal army remained the ultimate defence of the land', and that for over sixty years after the Conquest the monarchy therefore 'depended in the last resort on the loyalty of individual barons and the knights of their honours'.[3] Painter was even more emphatic when he wrote of the Conqueror that even if there had been sufficient resources to maintain an adequate hired army, the fact that William and his men were deeply steeped in feudal tradition would have made the adoption of such a military system out of the question.[4] Both Domesday Book and the Oath of Salisbury have been placed firmly in this feudal context. Of the former Galbraith concluded that 'the Normans were never so feudal as when they first arrived in England, and Domesday Book was their supreme and successful effort to wrest the intractable material of OE tenures into the feudal form in which alone they could understand it'.[5] Of the latter Stenton argued that the Conqueror required the feudal act of homage as well as an oath of fealty from the honorial baronage in addition to the tenants-in-chief.[6]

The introduction of knight-service and the process of subinfeudation disrupted the greater estates; the scattered holdings discouraged centralized

1   G.O. Sayles, *The Medieval Foundations of England* (London, 1948), 222, 225.
2   F. Barlow, *The Feudal Kingdom of England, 1042–1216* (London, 1955), 110, 112.
3   Stenton, *First Century*, 50, n. 1, 214, 191.
4   Painter, *Studies*, 20.
5   V.H. Galbraith, 'The Making of Domesday Book', *EHR* lvii (1942), 177.
6   Stenton, *First Century*, 111–13.

management and production for the market; and feudal particularism prevented the administrative order in which economic enterprise could flourish. The succeeding period when the Angevin kings were able to finance a war effort vastly greater in scale and different in kind coincides with a period of rapid economic expansion. The profits of high farming, industry and international commerce could be tapped to pay troops and officials. The 'age of Glanvill' and the 'age of Bracton' were a period of internal security encouraging further productive investment and bequeathing a rich legacy to the organizing hand of Edward I. Thus we have the earliest mention of paid knights, *milites solidarii*, in 1162, just at the time when Henry II was inaugurating his legal and administrative reforms.[7] 'Money', wrote Richard Fitz Neal in about 1179, 'appears necessary not only in time of war but also in peace. In war it is poured out in fortifying castles, in soldiers' wages and in numerous other ways depending on the nature of the persons paid, for the preservation of the kingdom.'[8] This comment can be interpreted as the recognition of a recent change and as pointing forward to the extensive use of mercenaries and the mounting costs of building castles and subsidizing allies in the reigns of Richard and John.

This view of military organization in the century after the Conquest carries implications for political history. If the field armies and castle garrisons were largely composed of tenants-in-chief and their knights performing their due service, then the survival of the monarchy must have depended on the loyalty of these men. Historians have come to reduce the importance formerly attached to the frequent revolts and rebellions of the Norman period and to lay much more stress instead on the co-operation between the crown and the baronage. It is significant that Stenton should have attributed the disorders of Stephen's reign not to any 'deliberate opposition to royal power' but to the 'unprecedented situation created by a disputed succession' and to Stephen's personal failings.[9] It is also significant that he should have argued that baronial revolts only acquired a genuine political character in the thirteenth century. For only then did the monarchy cease to be dependent on feudal military resources and only then did 'the king's development of his household organization' lead to 'the struggle between the barons and the king for the control of those formidable instruments of government'.[10] This is a very different reading of the revolts and rebellions from that of Stubbs, for whom the rebellion of 1173–74 was 'the last which the feudal baronage undertook in arms against the royal power' and for whom Magna Carta was the first great public act of the nation'.

Nevertheless, despite the agreeable harmony between these various interpretations of the period, it is worthwhile re-examining the evidence for the composition of military forces under the Conqueror and his sons. Richard Fitz Neal's remark about the pouring out of money on castles and soldiers' wages was not meant to call attention to a new development under Henry II; he intended the remark as a commonplace, made familiar and respectable by long practice.

---

7 A.L. Poole, *Obligations of Society in the XII and XIII Centuries*, 52.
8 *Dialogus de Scaccario*, ed. C. Johnson (London, 1950), 2.
9 Stenton, *First Century*, 216–17, 221.
10 F.M. Stenton, 'The Changing Feudalism of the Middle Ages', *History* xix (1935), 293.

Writing of the period immediately following the Conquest, Richard tells us that coined money for the wages and rewards of knights, *stipendia uel donativa militum*, was derived from the profits of royal justice, from voluntary payments for privileges and from the urban communities; and he added that this payment of troops persisted under the Conqueror's sons.[11] Perhaps it would be unwise to make too much of this, for the treasurer could make mistakes, and we have been warned that 'he is a very unsafe authority for anything that had happened more than a generation before his own time'.[12] The older historians, who had read the chronicles, were not very confident in using the concept of feudalism. 'The word *feudal* is bad in every way', Freeman observed in a parenthesis, adding 'but I know no better.'[13] Stubbs's common sense told him that the requirements of knight-service were designed to produce merely mounted knights and he concluded that 'the infantry must have been furnished almost entirely by the more ancient fyrd system, or by mercenaries'.[14] Vinogradoff pointed out that mercenaries were employed after as well as before the Norman Conquest, though he dismissed them as 'merely casual combinations of men' and considered that the social importance of this expedient was not great.[15] Then there are the qualifications and silences of the more recent historians. Round was concerned with the introduction of knight-service, not with its enforcement; and he was able to cite only three instances of the summoning of the feudal under the Conqueror and his sons. He did however observe that 'from the very commencement of knight-service the principle [of payment in lieu of military service] must have prevailed'.[16] Stenton, commenting on the paucity of the evidence, wrote that 'to an extent which is not always realized our conception of the feudal society of King William's day rests on a series of uncertain inferences'; that 'it is remarkable how little we really know about the nature of military service in the century after the Conquest'; and that 'no chronicle professes to enumerate all the occasions on which the feudal army was called into being'.[17]

Another reason for re-examining the evidence is that as McFarlane pointed out, the origin of the practice of substituting paid for unpaid service remains untraced in detail; and indeed he left open the question whether even military service was ever wholly or mainly a matter of tenure.[18] Moreover the orthodox military organization of the Anglo-Norman state presents anyone seeking to understand the political history of the period with difficulties. If military service was wholly or mainly a matter of tenure, unpaid service produced by the tenants-in-chief, the rebellions against Rufus and Henry I must be reduced to

11 *Dialogus de Scaccario*, 40.
12 V.H. Galbraith, *Studies in the Public Records* (Oxford, 1948), 48.
13 E.A. Freeman, *The History of the Norman Conquest of England* (London, 1867–79), v. 128.
14 W. Stubbs, *Constitutional History of England*, i. 469.
15 P. Vinogradoff, *English Society in the Eleventh Century* (Oxford, 1908), 15, 21.
16 Round, *Feudal England*, 270, 305.
17 Stenton, *First Century*, 9, 168, 177.
18 K.B. McFarlane, 'Bastard Feudalism', *Bulletin of the Institute of Historical Research* xx (1945), 162.

minor episodes and only a strong sense of solidarity between the bulk of the baronage and the crown can explain the survival and strengthening of the monarchy down to 1135. But it is difficult to find sufficiently strong grounds for these assumptions in the accounts of the chroniclers; and in particular it becomes necessary to hold that Orderic Vitalis was guilty of a hysterical overdramatization of the political and military conflicts of this period. Nor is it easy to explain the outbreak and course of the civil war of Stephen's reign. Above all it is peculiarly difficult to fit in what we know of financial policy and institutions under Rufus and Henry I. Jolliffe contrasted the scale, severity and cost of the wars fought by Henry II, Richard and John with what he called 'the comparative modesty of the wars of the first century after the Conquest', and wrote of the Norman monarchs as 'burdened with nothing but the Household expenses, the outlay of the great feasts and an occasional foray into the Welsh Border or Maine'.[19] Perhaps contemporaries exaggerated the financial greed of the Conqueror. Perhaps Rufus's extravagance on dress and on the building of Westminster Hall together with the need to raise the money for granting the mortgage on Normandy, largely explain the exactions of which contemporaries complained. But if Henry I fought his campaigns with unpaid feudal service only pointless avarice can have driven him to levy the great sums of money accounted for in the solid and impressive evidence of the Pipe Roll of 1130. For Henry appears to have regulated and restricted the expenses of his household, and is even reported to have dropped the three annual great feasts held by the Conqueror and Rufus.[20] Constitutional historians have unravelled the introduction and development of knight-service, and they have thrown much light on the origins and structure of the exchequer; but they have not shown how the working of these two institutions can be intelligibly related to each other.

There are other and more general reasons for approaching the study of Anglo-Norman society and government from the point of view of military history. It is seldom profitable to consider English history in isolation; and the late eleventh and early twelfth centuries formed a period when warfare was of peculiar importance to men in western Europe. We are likely to learn more about them if we attend to what seemed to them of such importance. During the lifetimes of William the Conqueror and Henry I western Europe produced a remarkable number of men of a self-confident, aggressive and exceptionally ambitious temper, a temper sustained and disseminated by the successes they enjoyed. Some of them, such as Robert of Bellême in Normandy and England, Thomas of Marle in France and Ekbert of Meissen in Germany, were almost entirely destructive in their careers; but many were able to see more profitable fields of action and to direct the predatory energies of western society into more constructive courses of conquest and expansion. It was during this period that England was conquered, defended and held under Norman leadership, while Norman arms and influence made headway in both Wales and Scotland. There were the Hungarian campaigns of Henry IV, following the plans of his father;

---

[19] J.E.A. Joliffe, 'Magna Carta', *Schweizer Beiträge zur allgemeinen Geschichte*, x (1952), 95.
[20] Malmesbury, *Gesta Regum*, ii. 335, 483, 487.

though during the greater part of this period German military energies were absorbed in the struggles in Germany itself and in Italy.[21] But it was in the Mediterranean that the most striking successes were won. In Spain the reconquest from the Moslems gathered powerful momentum. Toledo was won in 1085, Saragossa in 1118, while north of the Tagus the Christian kingdoms were consolidated. And it was in this period that the deeds of the Cid supplied the material for a native romantic and heroic literature. In the central Mediterranean the Genoese and Pisans had already passed to the offensive against Sardinia, Palermo and Bone; and in 1087 they captured the city of Mehdia, gaining spoils and an advantageous commercial treaty. By the close of this period the Norman conquests in southern Italy and Sicily had been welded into a powerful kingdom under Roger the Great, threatening the papacy, north Africa and Byzantium. In the eastern Mediterranean the First Crusade had led to the establishment of a chain of states extending from the Euphrates to the Red Sea; and by the end of this period Fulk of Anjou, king of Jerusalem, was the suzerain of the principality of Antioch and of the counties of Edessa and Tripoli.[22]

It was not merely a period of vigorous and successful expansion and aggression; it was a period which saw a change in men's attitude towards war and the profession of arms. 'The habits of mankind, and the interest of religion,' Gibbon observed of the age of Constantine, 'gradually abated the horror of war and bloodshed, which had so long prevailed among the Christians.'[23] But in the west these sentiments of horror endured much longer: it was less easy to justify or to glorify war when war meant the division and weakness of western Europe, the plunder of the church and sufferings at the hands of Viking, Saracen and Magyar invaders. War, in the eyes of most churchmen, was at best a necessary evil: the clergy were forbidden to bear arms and were required to impose penances on those who killed in battle.[24] But in the late tenth and early eleventh centuries, as the external threats receded and as the church came to have a greater material stake in the security of its possessions, individual reformers sought to enforce order or to mitigate strife through the Peace of God and the Truce of God. Well-meaning decrees were not enough, and it became necessary to organize peace militias. Their action could be only local and was sometimes disillusioning. In the second half of the eleventh century, under the reforming popes, more ambitious plans could be formulated, plans for the organization and use of force against the enemies of reform within Christendom and against the infidel without. Thus the church came to revise and indeed almost to reverse its old atti-

---

[21] However, the period after the death of Henry V in 1125 saw a vigorous German expansion eastwards across the Elbe and along the Baltic coastline.

[22] It was no more than a fragile suzerainty, especially over Antioch, in 1135: see J.L. La Monte, *Feudal Monarchy in the Latin Kingdom of Jerusalem* (Cambridge, Mass., 1937), 190–3.

[23] E. Gibbon, *The History of the Decline and Fall of the Roman Empire*, ed. J.B. Bury (London, 1896–1900), ii, 298.

[24] For this change in the attitude to war, oversimplified in the text, see in particular G. Erdmann, *Die Entstehung des Kreuzzugsgedankens* (Stuttgart, 1935); also P. Alphandéry, *La Chrétienté et l'idée de Croisade* (Paris, 1954), and P. Rousset, *Les Origines et les Caractères de la Premiere Croisade* (Neuchâtel, 1945).

tude towards war; the *Sanctum Bellum* became the necessary preparation for the *Pax Dei*. During Gregory VII's struggle to make Europe safe for theocracy this new military ethos was defined much more clearly and criticized much more sharply. Gregory conducted or threatened war against Henry IV, Robert Guiscard, Philip of France and Alfonso VI of Castile. He dated his letters from the camp (*data in expeditione*), promised the remission of sins in return for military help, and gave a literal meaning to such expressions as *militia sancti Petri* and *servitium sancti Petri*. Gregory's methods made many observers suspicious and many participants in the conflict bitterly hostile; but under Urban II it was possible to divert much of the religious and militant enthusiasm of the west into the external channels of the First Crusade.

Not all the reformers were persuaded by the propaganda in favour of the new concept of war. Peter Damian was shocked by the spectacle of Pope Leo IX leading his troops against the Normans. If it had never been lawful to take up arms for the faith of the church, how, he asked, could slaughter be justified for the terrestrial and transitory interests of the church? He accumulated embarrassing quotations from the New Testament and argued for a policy of nonviolent resistance to evil.[25] Anselm wrote of the bloody confusion of wars, stigmatizing as iniquity; and he would not accept the church as militant in any but a metaphorical sense. '*Non militia sed malitia*', he insisted, but Damian and he were old-fashioned.[26] During this period the cult of saints long valued in Byzantium for their efficacious intervention in battle was imported into Europe. Military banners, once profane symbols, were now sanctioned and employed by the church, and that sent to the Conqueror is but one example among many. Dubbing to knighthood became a solemn religious rite; and it was from the hands of Lanfranc that the Conqueror's son, Henry, received his arms in 1086.[27] And with the foundation in this period of the military orders of the Templars and the Hospitallers, combining the discipline and centralized rule of the monastic orders with the military training and strength of professional soldiers, the fusion of secular and ecclesiastical ideals was complete. The realities of war remained very different, and it is hard to know how far contemporaries were touched by the new ideals. The knighting of the future Henry I may have been a solemn religious act; but his own attitude towards war was singularly careful and controlled. The First Crusade, which Orderic Vitalis knew only at secondhand, appeared far more dramatic and romantic to him than the fighting in Normandy from which his own monastery suffered. The Pisan sailors may have seen the Archangel Michael and St Peter in the sky when they attacked Mehdia in 1087,[28] but the Venetians appear to have been less privileged. During the First

---

[25] Ep. lx in Migne, *Patrologia Latina* cxliv, cols 311–18.

[26] Ep. ii in Migne, *Patrologia Latina* clviii, col. 1168; ep. i, ibid., col. 1147; ep. iv. ibid., clix, col. 212. These passages are quoted and discussed by Erdmann, op. cit., 252, and by Marc Bloch, *La Société Féodale*, ii. 54–55.

[27] *Orderic*, iv. 120. According to William of Malmesbury, Rufus was also knighted by Lanfranc: Malmesbury, *Gesta Regum*, ii. 360.

[28] 'Carmen in victoriam Pisanorum. Genuensium et aliorum Italorum de Timino', quoted by H. Pirenne, *Economic and Social History of Medieval Europe* (London, 1936), 30, from the edition by E. Duménil, *Poésies populaires latlnes* (Paris, 1842).

Crusade the Genoese went on to take part in the siege of Jerusalem, a town of little commercial importance, while the Venetians concerned themselves with the more valuable coastal ports.[29] Godfrey of Bouillon's chaplains might complain of his excessive piety but his brother Baldwin was of a much more secular disposition.[30] Germany was less affected than France, the Low Countries and northern Italy. Yet it would be dangerous to underestimate the release of energy and enthusiasm produced by the new ideals and the propaganda for the Holy War, and the *chansons* testify to their effect upon laymen. To some, Gregory VII was a saint, to others a devil, and to Peter Damian, who knew him, a holy Satan.[31] To the author of the *Chanson de Jerusalem* Thomas of Marle was a hero of the First Crusade: to Suger, who knew his destructive career in France, he was a ravening wolf, *deo et hominibus infestus*.[32] It was possible to hold different views about the military organizers and leaders of this period; it was impossible to ignore their dramatic quality and the energies they inspired or manipulated.

The personalities and events on this wider stage were not ignored by the English chroniclers and historians. We ordinarily read them to learn what we can of English history; but it is instructive to notice how much William of Malmesbury, for example, included in his account of the deeds of the kings of the English.[33] He attributed to the Conqueror a desire not to be outdone by Guiscard, *terror mundi*: and this gave him an opportunity to summarize Guiscard's career and conquests. He reported the plans of Odo of Bayeux to acquire the papacy, and followed him to his death at Antioch. He retailed anecdotes of Hildebrand and gave an account of his conflict with Henry IV. He marked the year of the Conqueror's death by noting that in the same year Cnut of Denmark was killed and Alfonso VI drove back the Moslems in Spain. He emphasized the importance of the military help which the countess Matilda gave to Urban II; he told the story of the First Crusade, *Europa contra Turcos*, at length; and he used the lost work of David the Irishman to give an account of the conflict of Henry V with the papacy. What was achieved during this period by arms was dramatic enough; but what was planned or rumoured is also indicative of the contemporary climate of opinion. It was rumoured in 1074 that the Conqueror was about to seize Aachen;[34] it was believed in 1082 that Odo of Bayeux was preparing to seize the papacy; and in the same year it was believed or feared, with more cause, that Guiscard was about to seize Constantinople. It was believed in 1085 that England was about to be invaded by a great force

[29] Raymond of Agiles in *Recueil des Historiens des Croisades* (Paris, 1841–1906), *Historiens occidentaux*, iii, 898.

[30] William of Tyre, 'Historia rerum in partibus transmarinis gestarunt', in Migne, *Patrologia Latina* cci, col. 435.

[31] Ep. I. xiv, Migne, *Patrologia Latina*.

[32] A. Hatem, *Les poèmes épiques des Croisades* (Paris, 1932), 264, 272, 374; Suger, *Vita Ludovici Grossi*, ed. H. Waquet (Paris, 1929), 30.

[33] Malmesbury, *Gesta Regum, passim*.

[34] Lampert of Hersfeld, *Annales*, ed. O. Holder-Egger, *Scriptores Germanicarum in usum scholarum* (1894), 195.

under Cnut of Denmark assisted by Olaf of Norway and Robert of Flanders.[35] Both the Conqueror and Rufus were credited with schemes for the conquest of Ireland; and Suger repeats the story that Rufus was aiming to make himself king of France.[36] Shortly before his death Rufus was planning to acquire Poitou from its count, who needed to raise money on mortgage for his crusading expenses; and a little later this same count of Poitou was besieging Constantinople.[37] And in 1124 it was believed in France that German forces under Henry V were about to attack Reims.[38] It is difficult to accuse the men of the time of undue credulity. These were plans or possibilities; and it is not surprising that even monks followed the news and rumours of war with fascination.

Against this background the Norman Conquest of England and the consolidation of the Anglo-Norman state under the Conqueror and his sons appears almost inevitable; and historians with constitutional preoccupations have stressed the development of ordered feudalism, the cooperation of the various orders of society, the gradual fusion of Normans and English in a uniquely law-abiding community. The record evidence of Domesday Book and of the surviving Pipe Roll of Henry I appear as powerful testimony to the strength and grip of the conquerors and of the royal administration. But the Normans were not primarily concerned with the English constitution; and both Domesday Book and the Pipe Roll of 1130 give a misleading impression of strength. Domesday Book shows us Odo of Bayeux as the most powerful landlord in England after the king, dominant in Kent, influential in almost every county, and as the Conqueror's half-brother reinforcing the power of the royal family. But at the time of the Survey Odo was not enjoying the profits of his great estates and the confidence of his royal half-brother; he was a prisoner in the tower of Rouen and had been there ever since his arrest in 1088. Two years after the making of the Survey Odo was out of prison, planning and directing a major rebellion against Rufus. Both Geoffrey bishop of Coutances and William bishop of Durham were Domesday commissioners; and both were also implicated in the rebellion of 1088.[39] Similarly the entries of the Pipe Roll of 1130 conceal tensions and conflicts which, within a few years, caused Orderic Vitalis to observe of the Normans that 'though they conquer other peoples they defeat themselves, and as their hostile neighbours look on with scorn they belabour and mercilessly butcher each other'.[40] There were many points at which the enterprise might have foundered: indeed if some of the Norman leaders had had their way in 1066 it would never have been launched. They pointed to the dangers of the Channel; and they reminded William that the Normans were few and the

---

[35] e.g. *Anglo-Saxon Chronicle, s.a.* 1085.

[36] Ibid., *s.a.* 1087. The tradition about Rufus's designs on Ireland was preserved by Gerald of Wales in his *Itinerarium Kambriae (Opera*, ed. J.S. Brewer and J.F. Dimock, Rolls Series, vi. 109–10); Suger, *Vita Ludovici Grossi*, 10.

[37] Malmesbury, *Gesta Regum*, ii. 379; *Orderic*, v. 330.

[38] Suger, op. cit., 218.

[39] Round, *Feudal England*, 134; V.H. Galbraith, 'The date of the Geld Rolls in Exon Domesday', *EHR* lxv (1950), 6.

[40] *Orderic*, vi. 456–7.

English were many. How then did the Conqueror, Rufus and Henry I mobilize and maintain the troops which enabled them to overcome the successive doubts and dangers, crises and rebellions of this period?

Henry of Huntingdon considered the Conqueror as the instrument of divine vengeance on the English. 'For', he wrote, 'God had chosen the Normans to exterminate the English people, because he saw that they surpassed all peoples in the prerogative of unparalleled cruelty.'[41] William of Malmesbury gave a more secular explanation. Commenting on the Conqueror's avarice he wrote: 'But it will easily be excused, because it is impossible to rule a newly won kingdom without a great deal of money.' The Conqueror, he continued, 'for fear of his enemies, cheated his territories of money in order that with it he might either delay or even repel their attacks . . . and this shameful evil still endures and daily increases, vills and churches being subjected to payments'.[42] How then did the Conqueror spend this money? Largely, it seems, on paying and rewarding his troops. The Conquest army which assembled at the mouth of the Dives was neither wholly feudal nor wholly Norman. It is clear from the combined evidence of William of Poitiers, a contemporary, Orderic Vitalis and Henry of Huntingdon, that many of William's own men offered strong opposition to the enterprise;[43] and according to Wace, writing a century later, the Norman barons raised the formal objection that their obligation to service did not extend across the Channel. Nor was it an exclusively Norman force: Flanders, Picardy, the Boulonnais and above all Brittany produced large contingents. As William of Poitiers put it, 'a large number of foreign knights came to assist William, some attracted by his well known generosity and all by their confidence in a just cause'. But this confidence had to be maintained for a month while the expedition awaited a favourable wind; and William of Poitiers continues: 'They were forbidden to steal, and fifty thousand knights were maintained by William's pay (*stipendio ipsius alebantur*) while unfavourable winds delayed them.'[44] William of Malmesbury adds something to this. 'All that year', he wrote, 'the duke prepared what was needed for the war, keeping his own knights together by lavish expenditure and inviting foreign knights.'[45] Indeed this historian attached more importance to William's generosity and to the change in the wind than to the general belief in the justice of his cause; for he represents the mass of the knights as grumbling in the taverns and alleging that William's ambition was madness.[46]

Thus the Conqueror realised that the motive of religions, enthusiasm and the more material incentive of promised estates in England were not sufficient to mobilize and hold together an army during the period of concentration and waiting. It is unlikely that all the troops received regular pay from the Conqueror; but contemporaries and the writers of the next generation thought that pay

---

[41] Huntingdon, *Historia Anglorum*, 208.

[42] Malmesbury, *Gesta Regum*, ii. 379.

[43] Poitiers, *Gesta Guillelmi*, 156; *Orderic*, ii. 142; Huntingdon, 199.

[44] Poitiers, *Gesta Guillelmi*, 150.

[45] Malmesbury, *Gesta Regum*, ii. 298.

[46] Ibid., ii. 300.

and financial inducements played a large part in the enterprise. Two further scraps of evidence can be cited. William of Malmesbury tells us that in return for help in counsel and in knights which the Conqueror received in 1066 from his father-in-law Baldwin count of Flanders, he paid him an annual grant of 300 marks.[47] It is possible that under this arrangement William contracted to pay the Flemish knights, for we know that when the treaty was renewed in 1101 the Flemish knights were to be maintained at Henry I's expense. Then there is an extremely interesting though tantalizingly cryptic document to which Stenton called attention in connection with the reorganization of the English church.[48] This sets out the penances imposed on the Conquest army by the Norman bishops sitting in council in 1070, presided over by the papal legate, Ermenfrid. It may seem odd that penances should have been imposed at all for an enterprise represented as a just war and blessed by the dispatch of a papal banner. It seems that the church was hesitating before committing itself fully to the new doctrine which taught the desirability of shedding the blood of erring Christians: Hildebrand was not yet pope. And in 1070 the Normans, fresh from the devastation of the north and the midlands, could afford to take out an insurance policy. The penitential code was applied to those whom William had armed on his own orders, to those who were armed without his orders, and to those who owed him service as a matter of duty. It is perhaps significant that the bishops placed this category last. After prescribing penalties for men in these categories and for clerks and monks who had fought, the code deals with those who had 'been induced only by rewards' (*tantum praemio adducti*). Stenton rendered this as 'all who served the duke for hire' and he is probably right, since the code deals separately with those who went off in search of booty. The code ends with the clause: 'In respect of the spoliation of churches the violators are to restore the goods to the church from which they took them, if possible; or, if this is impossible, to another church. If they are unwilling to restore the goods, the bishops have decreed that the thieves shall not sell them and others shall not buy them.' This attempt to put down the traffic in ecclesiastical loot suggests that William's troops were not as unfamiliar with commercial intercourse and money dealings as Vinogradoff and others have suggested.[49]

Paid troops continued to be employed in England after the battle of Hastings. When William returned to Normandy in March 1067 he gave liberal pay to the knights who accompanied him. William fitz Osbern and Odo of Bayeux were left in charge of England. It was probably on the occasion of the Conqueror's return at the end of this year that he rebuked fitz Osbern so roughly for having wasted 'treasure by excessive expenditure on the wages of knights'. It may have been for reasons of financial prudence, or out of over-confidence, or even because touched by the sufferings of the conquered English that the Conqueror summoned his paid knights, *solidarios milites*, in 1068, rewarded them liberally and allowed them to return across the Channel. But they, or replacements, were

---

[47] Ibid., ii. 478.
[48] F.M. Stenton, *Anglo-Saxon England* (Oxford, 1943), 653–4.
[49] Vinogradoff, *English Society*, 87.

soon required again for the winter campaign of 1069–70. William spent Christmas at York, completed the harrying of the north in January, and then crossed the Peak country to put down the Welsh and the men of Cheshire, Staffordshire and Derbyshire. During this arduous march the troops drawn from Anjou, Brittany and Maine sought to be released; but William held his forces together, and when he reached Salisbury he was able to reward his knights liberally.[50]

But the Conquest was the result of an exceptional military effort, achieved, it may be thought, by forces raised and rewarded in exceptional ways. During the first difficult and dangerous years the Norman leaders and their allies found it necessary to keep their knights together and to pay them; but as conditions became more settled and secure these stipendiary knights were dispersed and quartered out on lands which they held in the familiar way. We have accounts of this process at Abingdon, Ely and Peterborough, for example.[51] And we know from a letter of Lanfranc that the followers of Ralph Guader, earl of East Anglia, in the rebellion of 1075, were composed partly of Bretons who held lands in England, partly of landless men who served for pay. The Conqueror's own son, Robert Curthose, complained that he was being treated as just such a landless knight when he told his unsympathetic father: 'I do not want to be your mercenary always. Sometime I want to have something of my own, so that I may be able to give proper pay to my followers.' And when the Conqueror put down the subsequent rebellion of Robert and his associates, he confiscated their lands and, with, characteristic economy, applied the rents to paying the mercenaries he had employed in the campaign. It was also in this campaign that the Conqueror hired the services of Rotrou count of Perche. The invasion threat of 1085 led William to bring over from France what was probably the largest paid force of his reign. It was drawn from Normandy, Brittany, Maine and France, and included Hugh count of Vermandois, brother of the king of France, who was later to take part in the First Crusade. Contemporaries marvelled at the size of this force and wondered how it could be fed. Part of the force was dismissed by William when he considered the immediate danger over; but he retained part of it during the winter of 1085–86. On Lanfranc's suggestion the troops were quartered out on the magnates. This had unfortunate results at Worcester, where Bishop Wulfstan paid the knights well and entertained them lavishly until the knights got out of hand in a drunken brawl.[52] Some of these men may even have left traces in Domesday Book. At Southampton sixty-five Frenchmen and thirty-one Englishmen were quartered in the town (*postquam rex Willelmus venit in Angliam sunt hospitati*).[53] It seems natural to read this as referring to

50 *Orderic*, ii. 236.
51 *Chron. Abingdon*, ii. 3; *Liber Eliensis*, ed. D.J. Stewart (1848), 275; *Chronicon Johannis Abbatis S. Petri de Burgo*, ed. J. Sparke (London, 1727), 47.
52 William of Malmesbury, *Vita Wulfstani*, ed. R.R. Darlington (Camden Soc., xl, 1928), 56. According to Florence of Worcester (ii. 18) not only the bishops, abbots, earls and barons but also the sheriffs were ordered to maintain the army.
53 *DB*, i. 52a. English troops had been employed by William in Maine in 1073 (*Anglo-Saxon Chronicle* and Florence of Worcester, ii. 10). They may have been employed in the Maine campaign of 1083–85 and brought back to England to meet the threatened invasion.

William's recent crossing to England in 1085. Possibly the thirty-four French and English knights who were lodged in the town of Bury St Edmunds in 1086 can be explained in the same way.[54] Close by the abbey of Westminster there were twenty-five houses occupied by knights and other men at the time of the Domesday Survey; and it is just possible that these too may reflect the billeting arrangements made by the Conqueror for his mercenaries.[55]

Commenting on the army of 1085 Stenton wrote that 'in a great emergency the knight-service due to the king from his tenants-in-chief was obviously unequal to the defence of the land'.[56] But, as the evidence for the earlier part of the reign shows, it was not only in a great emergency and as a wholly exceptional measure that the Conqueror employed mercenary troops. In this connection the terms and tenses of the section of Domesday Book which deals with Colchester are interesting. From each house, it is said, there is due each year 6d which can be paid to maintain the king's mercenaries or for an expedition by land or sea (*quae redderi potest ad victum soldariorum regis vel ad expeditionem terrae vel maris*). And, it is added, this shall be so if the king shall have employed mercenaries or shall have summoned the host (*hoc sit si rex soldarios habuerit vel expetitionem fecerit*).[57] Commenting on this Stephenson wrote that 'the entry is given in the present tense, but the reference to *soldarii* clearly indicates a custom T.R.E'.[58] It is reasonable to suppose that this Colchester payment is based on pre-Conquest precedents, as at Exeter which had paid geld of half a mark *ad solidarios*, and for a land or sea-fyrd had served 'to the amount of five hides'.[59] But it is difficult to believe that such a payment was a matter of merely antiquarian interest in 1086 when in 1085 the Conqueror had ordered his men to maintain his mercenaries (*solidariis . . . victum praebere*).[60]

William Rufus had neither the temperament nor the secure position which would have allowed him to regard the use of paid troops as an outmoded and expensive expedient. He had to put down the great rebellion of 1088 and to deal with Robert Mowbray and his supporters in 1095. He engaged in repeated campaigns for the acquisition of Normandy until he was able to acquire it on Robert Curthose's departure for the crusade in 1096; and he then used

---

[54] *DB*, Ii. 372. Douglas has discussed these knights in the introduction to *Feudal Documents from the Abbey of Bury St Edmunds* (London, 1932), ed. D.C. Douglas, cvi–cviii. He regarded them as part of the household retinue of the abbey, like those at Worcester and Ely. William of Malmesbury mentions those at Worcester as having been quartered on Wulfstan by royal orders to meet the invasion threat of 1085 (*Rex Willelmus ita fieri preceperat*), while those at Ely had also been installed *secundum jussum regis*, shortly before William left England for the last time in 1086. It may well be that the thirty-four knights in Bury St Edmunds were also mercenary troops who had been brought over in 1085 and retained over the winter.

[55] *DB*, i. 128b.

[56] Stenton, *First Century*, 150.

[57] *DB*, ii. 107.

[58] C. Stephenson, *Borough and Town* (Cambridge, Mass., 1932), 98 n. 4.

[59] *Exon Domesday*, 8. For *ad solidarios* Domesday Book itself has *ad opus militum* (*DB*, i. 100a).

[60] *Florence of Worcester*, ii. 18.

Normandy as a base for operations against France and Maine. He led two expeditions against the Scots and was finally able to install Edgar Atheling on the Scottish throne. And in 1095 and again in 1097 he led expeditions into Wales, though with less success than he had enjoyed in Scotland. William of Malmesbury has a revealing account of Rufus's method of raising troops. 'At the very outset of his reign, fearing disorders, he had assembled knights, denying them nothing and promising more for the future. And so, because he had energetically exhausted his father's treasures, and limited revenues were left, his resources ran short; but he continued to be extravagant, for this had become second nature to him. He was a man who did not know how to beat down the price of anything or to get proper value in his dealings (*aestimare commercium*). Sellers sold to him at their own prices and knights fixed their own rates of pay (*pro libito venditor distraheret mercimonium, et miles pacisceretur stipendium*).'[61]

There was a sellers' market for mercenaries in England. Meanwhile Robert Curthose was preparing to intervene in England by lavishing his treasure on knights; and when these were exhausted he raised more by selling territory to his younger brother Henry. The proceeds of this sale, variously estimated at £3,000 or 3,000 marks, were also expended on the wages of troops.[62] Nor was the power to raise paid troops a monopoly of princes and magnates at this time. In the autumn of 1090 the leading citizen of Rouen, Conan, arranged to hand over the city to Rufus and employed his own great wealth to mobilize a large force for use against Robert Curthose.[63] But it was Rufus's war expenditure which astonished and dismayed contemporaries. In 1094 he is described as raising mercenaries on all sides in Normandy and showering gold, silver and lands on those whom he detached from Duke Robert.[64] In 1095 he sent his brother Henry into Normandy with ample funds; and in the campaigns of 1097 and 1098 he spent lavishly on troops drawn from France, Burgundy, Brittany and Flanders, and on subsidies to Robert of Bellême.[65] Suger, a practical statesman with much experience of the problems and methods of war and finance, described Rufus in striking terms as 'that rich man who poured out the treasures of the English, a wonderful merchant and paymaster of knights (*mirabilisque militum mercator et solidator*).[66] It is revealing that William of Malmesbury should have used the words *commercium* and *mercimonium* and that Suger should have chosen the term *mercator*; for to Rufus war was a trade and troops, castles and allies its merchandise.

Soldiers were stimulated not only by pay, rewards and the prospect of booty but also by the hope of ransoms. Orderic Vitalis explains Rufus's relative lack of

---

61 Malmesbury, *Gesta Regum*, ii. 368.
62 *Orderic Vitalis*, iv. 118–20; Malmesbury, *Gesta Regum*, ii. 468. Henry bought the lands in eastern Normandy from the legacy of £5,000 given him by the Conqueror. Henry is said to have weighed this out carefully and placed it securely away even before his father died.
63 *Orderic Vitalis*, iv. 220.
64 Florence, ii. 18.
65 Huntingdon, *Historia Anglorum*, 218.
66 Suger, *Vie de Louis VI*, 8

success in the campaigns of 1097–98 by the fact that the French were spurred on by their handsome gains from ransoms.[67] According to Suger the balance of payments on this account was wholly in favour of the French, for Rufus's knights soon ransomed themselves, while the French were released only after a long imprisonment, in severe conditions.[68] It was in the early 1090s that, according to Orderic Vitalis, William of Breteuil ransomed his castle for £1,500 and himself on three occasions for sums totalling £7,000.[69] It is no wonder that Orderic should have described him as '*dives herus intrinsecus nimio dolore punctus*'. William of Malmesbury has an interesting passage which throws some light on the contemporary attitude towards ransoms. Describing Rufus as liberal to a fault he found it necessary to define his terms;

> There are two kinds of generous men, the one being called prodigal, the other liberal. The prodigal are those who so pour out their money that they leave behind but a brief memory of themselves or none at all, and have no almsgiving to their credit which would avail them before God: the liberal are those who redeem prisoners from their captors, or relieve the poor, or take on themselves the debts of their friends.[70]

Moreover others besides those actively engaged in fighting drew wages; much was spent on the construction and repair of castles and, as Rufus reminded Hélie de la Flèche when calling attention to his own superior resources, masons and stone-cutters were anxious for monetary gain.[71]

Rufus's only mourners may have been the troops whom he had paid so well and the loose women, uncharitably linked together by Orderic Vitalis.[72] But the mercenaries were not thrown into unemployment on Rufus's death. Valuable evidence of the value attached to mercenaries and of the numbers required is provided by the Treaty of Dover, concluded between Henry I and Robert count

---

[67] *Orderic*, iv. 216.

[68] Suger, *Vie de Louis VI*, 10. Cf. Florence, ii. 34, for the French king's capture of the castle of Argentan in 1094, when he took many captives whom he ordered to be held in captivity, until they could be ransomed.

[69] *Orderic*, iii. 209; iv. 289.

[70] Malmesbury, *Gesta Regum*, ii. 367. It is interesting that when describing William fitz Osbern's generosity to his knights William of Malmesbury should have used the phrase *pene prodiga liberalitas* (Malmesbury, *Gesta Regum*, ii. 314). The notions of prodigality and liberality were closely linked in William of Malmesbury's mind with pay and ransoms. Cf. *Historia Novella* for Stephen being stigmatized as *quod minime principem decet prodigus* in connection with the use of paid troops. Orderic Vitalis throws a different light on the practice of ransoms. In 1119 Richer de Laigle and his companions were engaged in looting in Normandy, when they turned aside to attack some peasants presumptuously hoping to recover their goods. The defenceless peasants took refuge by a wayside cross, whereupon Richer called off his men. Orderic's comment is 'So the honourable man, in awe of his Creator, spared about a hundred villagers, from whom he might have extorted a great price if he had been so irreverent as to capture them.' He considered the sparing of the peasants so remarkable that it deserved to be remembered to eternity (*Orderic*, vi. 250–1).

[71] *Orderic*, v. 230–3.

[72] *Orderic*, v. 293. Cf. the phrase in William of Malmesbury's obituary notice on Rufus: *stipendariis militibus pro copia donativorum mirandus* (Malmsbury, *Gesta Regum*, ii. 379.)

of Flanders on 10 March 1101.[73] By this treaty the count of Flanders agreed to make 1,000 knights available to Henry in England in the event of invasion, whether by the French or anyone else, or in the event of rebellions. Henry was to be responsible for providing the shipping, for maintaining the knights in England and for making good their losses. This last provision would apply particularly to horses, of which each knight was to have three. If Henry should require military help in Normandy the count was again to produce 1,000 knights, though in this case he was to maintain the knights for the first eight days and Henry for the next eight days. For campaigns in Maine 500 knights were to be provided for one month and wholly at Henry's expense. There remained the awkward fact that the count of Flanders was the vassal of the French king, who was unlikely to look favourably on these arrangements. Accordingly it was provided in the treaty that if the French king should invade England Count Robert should accompany him with the minimum number of men necessary to avoid forfeiture of his fief. If the French king should intervene in Normandy Count Robert was to join him with ten knights, leaving the other 990 in Henry's service. In return Count Robert was granted an annual money fief of £500 sterling. It is an interesting example of the way in which feudal forms were manipulated to meet military and diplomatic needs. And it is also significant that at a time when the total *servitium debitum* of England amounted to about 5,000 knights in theory, Henry should have been arranging for the service of 1,000 knights from one external source alone. It is also made clear in the treaty that the Flemish knights were to be hired (*conducere praedictos milites*), and that their wages were not included in the annual money fief paid to the count.

But the treaty is better evidence for Henry's attitude towards the problem of securing troops than it is for the composition of his armies. According to William of Malmesbury the first such arrangement with Flanders had been made by the Conqueror and had been renewed by Rufus.[74] Eadmer's report of a meeting between Rufus and the count of Flanders at Dover in 1093 lends support to this. And Henry I certainly renewed the treaty of 1101 on 17 May 1110, at Dover, with the difference that the number of knights to be provided was halved.[75] Henry I was not the man to make annual payments for no return. But while there is evidence that Rufus employed Flemish troops in Normandy there is no mention of Flemish troops in England in 1101 and 1102 (when the terms of the treaty would have justified their use), nor of their presence in Henry's forces in the campaigns which culminated in the battle of Tinchebray in 1106. Henry I is known to have planted a substantial number of Flemings in

[73] *Foedera*, i. 7; F. Vercauteren, *Actes des comtes de Flandre, 1071–1128* (Brussels, 1938), 88–95, no. 30. The treaty was correctly dated by W. Farrer, 'An outline itinerary of King Henry the First', *EHR* xxxiv (1919), 309–10. For a modern translation see E. Van Houts, 'The Anglo-Flemish Treaty of 1101', *Anglo-Norman Studies* xxi (1999), 169–74 [MCP].

[74] Malmesbury, *Gesta Regum*, ii. 478–9. See the discussion by B.D. Lyon, 'The Money-Fief under the English Kings, 1066–1485', *EHR* lxvi (1951), 178–9.

[75] *Foedera*, i. 6 (where the treaty is erroneously dated 1101) and Vercauteren, op. cit., 109–116 (no. 41)

Pembrokeshire at some date between 1105 and 1111, thus achieving the double purpose of ridding England of a potentially troublesome element and supplying an effective curb to the Welsh.[76] It is tempting to suppose that the Flemings were demobilized mercenaries, and perhaps some of them were. But the only source to mention their origin states that they were drawn from the Flemings who lived in Northumbria.[77] They certainly combined martial qualities with attention to material gains. Between 1113 and 1116 the bishop of St David's sent missionaries to this Flemish settlement to convert them, as he put it, 'to the spiritual pastures and away from the pastures of real sheep to which they devote their energies'.[78] The missionaries were unsuccessful in instilling mildness into the Flemings. Orderic Vitalis describes the Flemings as killing the Welsh like dogs.[79] And towards the end of the twelfth century Gerald of Wales, a good authority on this subject, described them as strong and robust people, fiercely hostile to the Welsh in the continual conflict of war, extremely familiar with weaving and trade, remorselessly seeking gain by land and sea whatever the efforts and dangers involved.[80]

Mercenaries were certainly employed in England in the early years of Henry I's reign and on one occasion the king himself paid tribute to their professional conduct. In 1102 Henry took action against the formidable Robert of Bellême, who had supported Robert Curthose's invasion of 1101. Robert of Bellême handed over the castle and town of Bridgnorth to three of his captains, placing under them eighty mercenary knights. Henry besieged Bridgnorth, detached the rebels' Welsh allies by bribes and promises, and then threatened that unless the garrison surrendered within three days he would hang every man whom he took. The captains and burgesses agreed to surrender and, when the mercenaries refused to collaborate, cooped them up in a corner of the castle and admitted the royal forces. 'Then', says Orderic, 'the king allowed the mercenary knights to leave freely with their horses and arms, because they had served their master as was right. As they rode out through the besieging forces they bewailed their fate, and called upon the whole army to witness the tricks of these plotters, so that their downfall might not bring contempt on other mercenaries.'[81] The loyalty of these mercenaries to their paymaster compared favourably with that of many vassals to their lords; and their sense of professional solidarity is very revealing.

After Henry had secured his position in England by buying off Robert Curthose's claims to the English throne with a grant of 3,000 marks a year and the surrender of Norman lands and by forcing Robert of Bellême into rebellion

---

[76] Malmesbury, *Gesta Regum*, ii. 365–6, 477 (*ut et regnum defaeceret, et hostium brutam temeritatem retunderet*). For other references and discussion of the date of the settlement see Lloyd, *History of Wales*, ii. 424 and n. 74.

[77] Florence, ii. 64.

[78] *Historia et Cartularium Monasterii Sancti Petri Gloucestriae*, ed. W.H. Hart (Rolls Series, 1863), i. 265.

[79] *Orderic*, vi. 442–3.

[80] *Giraldus Cambrensis, Opera*, ed. J.S. Brewer, J.F. Dimock and G.F. Warner (Rolls Series, 1861–91), vi. 83.

[81] *Orderic*, vi. 28–9,

and defeating him, he devoted himself to acquiring Normandy itself. In the two campaigns of 1105 and 1106 Henry's money and the hired troops of his allies played a decisive role. In 1105 he hired Hélie de la Flèche and the men of Maine and, as Henry of Huntingdon puts it, he took Caen with his money and Bayeux with his arms.[82] And in the decisive battle of Tinchebray in the following year it was the cavalry forces of the Manceaux under their count, Hélie de la Flèche, and of the Bretons under their duke, Alan Fergant, who won the day for Henry by their charge from the flank.[83] William of Malmesbury tells us that Henry had been familiar from his youth with the readiness of the Bretons to serve for foreign pay and that he, 'well aware of these characteristics, spent much on the Bretons whenever he needed paid knights, borrowing the faith of that faithless people with his coins'.[84] Robert Curthose had also been hiring troops. Henry I, writing to Anselm after the battle of Tinchebray, described Robert's forces as composed of all those *quos prece et pretio adunare potuit*.[85] And one of the duke's supporters, a certain Robert, who attempted to ambush Henry before Tinchebray, had bought the abbey of Saint-Pierre-sur-Dives for 140 marks and had then sold off the church plate to hire a band of mercenary knights.[86]

After Tinchebray it was both possible and expedient to reduce the scale of war expenditure. William of Malmesbury said justly of Henry that 'he preferred to fight with policy rather than with the sword: he triumphed, if he could, without spilling blood; if he could not, he spilt as little as possible'. So successful was this policy that whereas Rufus was mourned by the knights to whom he had given full employment and high wages, Henry's peace was hated by the knights of England, reduced thereby to a slender diet.[87] But although defence expenditure was reduced it was not abolished; and the comments of chroniclers show that Henry continued to employ paid troops as a regular practice. In 1118 his suspicions of Norman loyalty led him to take Bretons and English into his pay in Normandy; and in 1120, after the campaigning which had seen him victorious over the French at Brémule, he paid his troops liber-

---

[82] *Orderic*, vi. 78; Huntingdon, *Historia Anglorum*, 235. Eadmer describes almost all the barons of Normandy as running after Henry's gold and silver and handing over their castles and cities to him (Eadmer, *Historia Novorum*, 165).

[83] *Orderic*, vi. 88–90; Huntingdon, *Historia Anglorum*, 235. H.W.C. Davis, 'The Battle of Tinchebrai: a Correction', *EHR* xxv (1910), 296, giving the text of a letter from a priest of Fécamp reporting the battle. See the discussion of these sources by C.W. David, *Robert Curthose* (Cambridge, Mass., 1920), Appendix F. The first and third of these sources mention both the Manceaux and the Bretons, while the second attributes the cavalry charge to the Bretons alone. Orderic Vitalis mentions only Hélie de la Flèche as in command of the cavalry, while the priest of Fécamp adds Alan Fergant. Thomas Wykes, presumably using a source which has not survived, stressed Henry's use of paid troops in the Tinchebray campaign: *Henricus . . . congregato exercitu copioso ab Anglia, transfretavit in Normanniam, sibique in adjutorium innumerabilem stipendiariorum coepit adjungere comitivam, de pecunia quae sibi copiosus abundavit sufficienter stipendia subministrans . . . (Chronicon . . . Thomae Wykes*, in *Ann. Mon.*, iv. 15).

[84] Malmesbury, *Gesta Regum*, ii. 478.

[85] Eadmer, *Historia Novorum*, 184.

[86] *Orderic*, vi. 172–4.

[87] Malmesbury, *Gesta Regum*, ii. 488, 540.

ally.[88] On one of Henry's later campaigns the contemporary writers provide information which, though fragmentary, is more interesting on the composition of Henry's forces than that supplied in such conventional phrases as *exercitum rex aggregavit* or *cum magna militum copia*. In the autumn of 1123 a powerful group of Norman barons, headed by Waleran of Meulan and Amaury de Montfort, planned rebellion in the interests of William, the son of Robert Curthose. The threat was the more formidable since it was backed by the resources of Fulk of Anjou and Louis of France. Against the rebels Henry, always nervous of treachery, employed mercenaries, drawn largely from Brittany; indeed in this campaign he is said to have feared the treachery of his own men more than external attacks. The siege of Pontaudemer alone consumed six or seven weeks in October and November, though when it fell the Breton mercenaries were richly rewarded by the abundant loot. Digging in the ruins of the town they found in the cellars chests which the prudent citizens had filled with gold, silver, precious cloths, cloaks, pepper, ginger and other valuables.[89] The mercenaries had good reason to loot Pontaudemer, for Robert of Torigni tells us that during the campaign of 1123–24 the English moneyers issued coins of which scarcely a third was silver, the rest being tin. When Henry's knights in Normandy received their wages in this currency and discovered that they could buy nothing with it, they complained to the king; and, angry on account of the wrong suffered by his knights, Henry issued his savage orders for the mutilation of all the guilty moneyers, orders which Roger of Salisbury carried out at the end of December 1124 and early in January 1125.[90] Robert of Torigny took the occasion to praise Henry for his love of justice, since he could have allowed the moneyers to purchase their physical immunity at a high price; but to us the passage is more interesting as showing that the campaign had been financed with English treasure and as demonstrating the importance which Henry attached to keeping his paid troops contented.

From Orderic Vitalis we have another sidelight on this campaign. On 25 March 1124 a royal force consisting of knights and horsed archers under Ralph of Bayeux encountered the rebel leaders near Bourg Théroulde. Although the royal forces were superior in numbers they were uncertain whether to accept battle. Orderic Vitalis put into the mouth of one of their commanders, Odo Borleng, a speech in which he proposed his tactics and urged his men to fight. If they did not, he is represented as saying, how could they dare to face the king? They would deservedly lose their pay and their reputation and ought never to eat the king's bread again. On the other side Amaury de Montfort argued that battle should be avoided since the rebels were so inferior in numbers. But, according to Orderic, sentiments of snobbery prevailed over this prudent advice. Were not the rebels, it was asked, the flower of the knighthood of all France and Normandy? Were they so afraid of the peasants and common soldiers who faced them that they would turn aside and decline battle? This appeal was successful; and so

---

[88] *Orderic*, vi. 190, 294.

[89] Symeon of Durham, *Historia Regum*, ed. T. Arnold (Rolls Series, 1882–5), ii. 274.

[90] Robert of Torigny's interpolation in William of Jumièges, *Gesta Normannorum Ducum*, ed. J. Marx (Rouen, 1914), 297; *Anglo-Saxon Chronicle, s.a.* 1125.

were Odo Borleng's defensive tactics.[91] After the capture of the rebel leaders in the battle of Bourg Théroulde resistance to Henry in Normandy quickly collapsed. It is improbable that either Odo Borleng or the rebels made set speeches of the kind that Orderic attributes to them; but it is also improbable, especially in view of the other independent evidence on the composition of Henry's forces, that Orderic who knew these men, did not express their sentiments and their incentives.

Robert of Torigni emphasized that even in the relative tranquillity of Henry's last ten years his wealth allowed him to defend his frontiers with large numbers of knights whom he paid adequately and rewarded.[92] Henry fittingly remembered these men on his deathbed, ordering Robert of Gloucester to pay them their wages and rewards from the treasure at Falaise, recently replenished from England.[93] The use of paid troops was indeed a commonplace to writers of this generation. Orderic Vitalis described the monks who curried favour with the lay powers in order to gain abbeys or bishoprics as *stipendiarii non monachi*.[94] Lawrence of Durham, explaining in the preface to one of his poems that the poet, like other men, required an incentive, wrote of the farmer kept to his task by the prospect of harvest, of the trader driven to face dangers by the relentless lust for profit, and of the warrior urged into battle by the prospect of his wages.[95] When Richard Fitz Neal wrote of the wages and rewards of knights under the Conqueror and his sons his history was perfectly sound. Paid troops had helped to win, garrison and defend England for the Conqueror; they were the chief instruments of Rufus's ambitious schemes; and they were employed by Henry I to regain Normandy and to defend his territories. And they had also been employed by Robert Curthose and the rebel leaders, few of whom showed the social prejudice attributed to the followers of Waleran of Meulan. The frequency of their employment and the evidence for their professional pride and standing suggests that they were more than merely casual combinations of men. Nor was it only in great emergencies that they were called on to reinforce other methods of raising troops: Robert of Torigni mentions paid troops and paid troops alone as being responsible for the security of Henry's territories during the last ten years of his reign.

But armies had not been composed of paid troops alone during the whole of this period. Much of the evidence for the use of paid troops, especially in the reigns of Rufus and Henry I, relates to the campaigns in Normandy and on its borders. This is in part due to the fact that Normandy saw much more fighting and in part because the balance of evidence is tilted heavily in favour of Normandy by Orderic Vitalis. Little has so far been said about the composition of the forces employed against Wales and Scotland and against the rebels in England. Were not these forces provided by the system of knight-service supplemented by the fyrd? And even if, as Stenton argued, the feudal army of England

---

91   *Orderic*, vi. 348–50.
92   William of Jumièges, *Gesta Normannorum Ducum*, 296.
93   *Orderic*, vi. 448.
94   *Orderic*, ii. 268.
95   Laurence of Durham, 62 (from the preface to his *Hypognosticon*).

was only brought together for some especial purpose, did not the feudal obligation of castle-guard supply the permanent garrisons of baronial and royal
castles?[96] Unfortunately we know much more about the formal obligations of
knight-service in this period than about its practical operation. Round's famous
essay on the introduction of knight-service into England was not, and did not
claim to be, a study of the composition of military forces. He cited only one
royal writ of summons to the host, and it is still the only one known for this
period. And he mentioned only two other occasions on which the feudal host is
said to have been summoned. Indeed, much of Round's evidence for the early
existence of the obligation of knight-service is evidence not for its performance
but for its commutation.[97]

There is however rather more evidence than Round cared to cite for the
summoning of the feudal host in this period. In connection with the Conqueror's
Scottish campaign of 1072 the *Liber Eliensis* states that the abbots and bishops
of all England had been ordered to produce the military service due from them.
The same passage mentions the abbey's quota of forty knights though this was
to be maintained as a guard in the Isle of Ely and was not necessarily the contingent required for the host. This Ely evidence on the Scottish expedition was
linked by Round with the Conqueror's writ to abbot Aethelwig of Evesham
requiring him to summon all those who owed knights to the king to produce
them and also to produce the five knights owed from the abbey of Evesham
itself.[98] But as Darlington pointed out, this involves geographical improbabili-
ties. For the place of assembly specified by the Conqueror was Clarendon; and it
is unlikely that the Conqueror would have brought men south from Shropshire
and Staffordshire before marching them north to Scotland. Darlington's suggestion that Clarendon was the assembly point for the expedition to Maine in 1075
is plausible.[99] Almost all the knights of Abingdon abbey were ordered to serve
in the Conqueror's one expedition to Wales in 1081.[100] According to the historian of Ely Rufus summoned the *servitium debitum* in 1088. And from Eadmer
comes the well-known complaint made by Rufus about the equipment and
training of the knights whom Anselm had produced for the Welsh expedition of
1097.[101] For 1101 there is clear evidence from the Abingdon chronicle of Henry
issuing a formal feudal summons – *totius regni sui expeditionem dirigit*. On this
occasion the abbot of Abingdon was unable to obtain the service from one of his
fees and had to find a substitute. It was later established that this fee had found a
knight in the Conqueror's time; and the erring tenant was fined £10 and made to

---

[96] Stenton, *First Century*, 190.
[97] Round, *Feudal England*, 304–5, 268ff.
[98] *Liber Eliensis*, ed. E.O. Blake (London, 1962), 274–5; Round, *Feudal England*, 304. The
Ely account must be suspect since it is not contemporary and since it was not until late in
Henry I's reign that the castle-guard service of the Ely knights was transferred from Norwich
to Ely. The story that castle-guard in Ely was fixed in the Conqueror's reign may have been
concocted to support the negotiations with Henry I.
[99] R.R. Darlington, 'Aethlwig, Abbot of Evesham', *EHR* xlviii (1933), 17 n. 4.
[100] *Chron. Abingdon*, ii. 10.
[101] Eadmer, *Historia Novorum*, 78.

recognize his obligations.[102] The language of the chroniclers makes it probable that a feudal summons was issued in 1102 for the operations against Robert of Bellême and it is likely to have been repeated for Henry I's Welsh expeditions of 1114 and 1121.[103]

But the meagre evidence for the composition of the military forces on these campaigns shows that they were not wholly feudal armies composed of the full feudal quotas. The *Liber Eliensis* which describes the exaction of the *debita militiae obsequia* from the ecclesiastical tenants-in-chief for the Scottish expedition of 1072, also states that the campaign was conducted *cum navali et equestri exercitu*, the equivalent of the Anglo-Saxon chronicler's ship-fyrd and land-fyrd.[104] If Darlington was right in linking the writ to Aethelwig with the Maine expedition of 1073 it is noteworthy that the sources describe that army as partly, even predominantly, an English force. According to Orderic, William summoned the Normans and English and had a force composed of knights and infantry.[105] The D version of the Anglo-Saxon Chronicle refers to William leading the English fyrd and Frenchmen. Florence of Worcester attributes William's successes in Maine largely to the English, while William of Malmesbury mentions the English alone.[106] This combination of French and English was a common one. Lanfranc described the force which operated against Ralph Guader in 1075 as composed of French and English.[107] While the Ely historian stresses Rufus's exaction of the *servitium debitum* in 1088, Florence of Worcester describes Rufus as mobilizing an army consisting partly of Normans but chiefly of English, and William of Malmesbury represents Rufus as directing written summons to the English alone.[108] In the west the custody of the royal castle at Worcester had been entrusted to Bishop Wulfstan, who is known to have created 37½ knights' fees before his death in 1095. Yet it is not of these enfeoffed knights that we hear in the account of the defence of Worcester, but of the bishop's household troops and the citizens.[109] William of Malmesbury calls them *regii milites* and it is possible that they included some of the mercenary knights who had been quartered on Wulfstan in 1085.[110] In view of the

---

[102] *Chron. Abingdon*, ii. 128.

[103] Florence, ii. 50, 67; *Orderic*, vi. 20; Huntingdon, *Historia Anglorum*, 239; Symeon of Durham, *Historia Regum*, ii. 263.

[104] *Liber Eliensis*, 274; *Anglo-Saxon Chronicle, s.a.* 1072. In John's view the Anglo-Saxon chronicle referred to the fyrd 'when an expedition with the host is plainly meant', and he regarded these entries as evidence for continuity between the fyrd and the feudal host (E. John, *Land Tenure in Early England* (1960), 157, n. 3. I do not see the need for the assumption that the Conqueror raised only one kind of troops on only one principle; and the equation of the fyrd with the host is not easily reconciled with the mobilization of English infantry in 1094 (Florence, ii. 35). Some Englishmen were knights; and many Normans, Flemings and Bretons were infantry.

[105] *Orderic*, ii. 307.

[106] Florence, ii. 10; Malmesbury, *Gesta Regum*, ii. 316.

[107] *Letters of Lanfranc*, ed. Clover and Gibson, 124.

[108] Florence, ii. 22–3; Malmesbury, *Gesta Regum*, ii. 361.

[109] *Anglo-Saxon Chronicle, s.a.* 1088; *The Red Book of the Exchequer*, ed. H. Hall (Rolls Series, 1896), i. 300; Florence, ii. 25.

[110] Malmesbury, *Gesta Pontificum*, 285.

importance which has been attached to the Worcester evidence for the survival of the Anglo-Saxon five-hide unit and the Anglo-Saxon terms of tenure into the Norman period it is noteworthy that William of Malmesbury, keenly interested in the differences between English and Norman ways, should have stressed Wulfstan's adoption of Norman methods in this connexion. For, William tells us, Wulfstan maintained a retinue of knights who drew annual pay and a daily allowance of food.[111] The units and terms of tenure may have been little changed, but in William of Malmesbury's opinion the methods of maintaining troops were very different and distinctively Norman. Nor did the rebels in 1088 rely wholly on feudal forces. The rebel leaders who attacked Worcester did so with a force of English, Normans and Welsh.[112] Nor were those in the south-east under Odo of Bayeux merely mobilizing their tenants. According to Orderic Vitalis they had chosen to base themselves on Rochester partly because it was conveniently placed for raids on London and Canterbury and partly because, being near the coast, it was well placed for the despatch of messengers to hire support from across the Channel.[113]

Similarly in 1101 we are told that when Robert Curthose landed at Portsmouth Henry's support came largely from the bishops, the common knights (*milites gregarii*) and the English.[114] William of Malmesbury, interested as always in the part played by the English, lays particular stress on their participation: he represents Henry as mobilizing the local forces and in language which must remind many readers of 1940, as giving them personal and elementary instruction in the methods of dealing with the invading and armoured enemy.[115] In the following year Henry could expect a more satisfactory response to a summons of the feudal host for the operations against Robert of Bellême. We are told that Henry mobilized his full forces (*totius Angliae legiones*) and concentrated the greater part of these for the siege of Bridgnorth.[116] Orderic distinguished three elements in the royal army. First there were the earls and magnates, who feared that if Henry should defeat and exile Robert of Bellême he would be able to crush them as if they were unwarlike girls; and they accordingly sought to restrain Henry and to make peace. Next there were the country knights (*pagenses milites*) who urged Henry to act vigorously against the traitors. Lastly there was a large force of infantry, used by Henry to fell the trees and to clear a safe path for the army.[117] Perhaps Orderic was applying the term *pagenses milites* to the knights of the tenants-in-chief, whether enfeoffed or household retainers, though he made the rebels of 1124 call Henry's paid troops *pagenses et gregarii*.[118] But feudal obligation cannot account for the large numbers of infantry.

---

111 Malmesbury, *Gesta Pontificum*, 281.
112 Florence, ii. 24.
113 *Orderic*, iv. 126.
114 Florence, ii. 49.
115 Malmesbury, *Gesta Regum*, ii. 471–2.
116 *Orderic*, vi. 24; Florence, ii. 50.
117 *Orderic*, vi. 26–8.
118 *Orderic*, vi. 350.

In the rebellion of 1088 and the invasion of 1101 much of the feudal host was anyway denied to the monarchy, while its leaders were still unreliable in 1102. For the other campaigns especially those against the Welsh and the Scots the feudal summons may have produced a useful contingent of knights. But the large contingents, most of whom must have been infantry, were raised by other methods. Only one piece of evidence throws any light on the mobilization of the English. In 1094 Rufus is said to have summoned 20,000 English foot to Normandy. When they reached Hastings, Flambard, on Rufus's orders, took from each man the 10s which had been given him from his maintenance (*quae data fuerat eis ad victum*) and sent the proceeds across the Channel to the king.[119] This suggests that the force had been raised in the same way as the pre-Conquest fyrd as described in the Berkshire entry in Domesday Book. There it was laid down that one *miles* went from every five hides, and that from each hide he received 4s for his maintenance or wages (*ad ejus victum vel stipendium*) for two months. The entry stresses that the money went to the troops and not to the king, and perhaps this is why Rufus adopted this circuitous method of taking money instead of service.[120] Often the mobilization of the English is likely to have taken a rougher and more arbitrary form: Urse d'Abetot was not the man to have observed forms and precedents punctiliously when as sheriff of Worcestershire he raised local forces to meet the rebellion of 1075.[121]

That Rufus should have chosen to take money instead of service from the fyrd in 1094 is not surprising; in this year he had been hiring mercenaries on all sides in Normandy and showering gold, silver and lands on those whom he detached from Robert Curthose. How far was money taken instead of knight-service during this period? No precise and quantitative answer can be given; but it is significant that the evidence for scutage is almost as old as the evidence for knight-service. As Stenton has said, 'all the early evidence which we possess suggests that under Henry I a lord holding of the king by military service must pay scutage when he is called upon to do so'; and it was being imposed on both lay and ecclesiastical tenants-in-chief.[122] Evidence from Norwich and Ely suggests that Henry I was levying scutage at the high rate of 30s on the fee, though the rate cannot be established with certainty.[123] Payments for knights are mentioned in charters in ways which suggest that commutation of military service was common and familiar. A charter issued in the reign of Henry I by Eustace of Boulogne, referring to a suit settled in the count's court at Stafford, mentions the service of his knights 'whether in cash, or in the army, or in castle-guard'.[124] There is the more explicit charter of Henry's reign, cited by

---

[119] Florence, ii. 35.

[120] *DB*, i. 56b.

[121] Florence, ii. 35.

[122] Stenton, *First Century*, 182.

[123] The evidence was conveniently assembled by Round, *Feudal England*, 268–70, and has been conveniently discussed by Stenton, *First Century*, 179–81, and by E. Miller, *The Abbey and Bishopric of Ely: The Social History of an Ecclesiastical Estate from the Tenth Century to the Early Fourteenth Century* (Cambridge, 1951), 160–2.

[124] Quoted by Round in *Feudal England*, 270, from the charter printed by E.J.L. Scott in *The Atheneum*, 2 December 1893, 772–3.

Stenton, 'freeing a manor not only from every *expeditio*, within or without England', but also 'from pennies for knights, when or in whatever way they may be demanded'.[125] The Abingdon chronicle records a grant made in the first half of Henry I's reign of four hides of land as half a knight's fee. The service is specified as 'in castle-guard in the host on both sides of the sea, in giving money for a knight, in guarding the king, and in all other services as performed by the other knights of the church'.[126] Further, Stenton has shown that in the reign of Henry I lords were making enfeoffments for very small fractions of a knight's fee, fractions which can only have discharged their obligations in cash. Indeed in a charter granted by the son of a Domesday tenant-in-chief in about 1125 the tenant is to hold his land 'by the third part of the service of one knight so that he ought to redeem the whole of his service each year for twenty shillings'.[127]

There is a great deal about the composition of military forces in this period which remains unknown. In the absence of muster rolls and payrolls it is unsafe to make any statements about the number of troops mobilized or engaged in any particular battle. Probably the figure which has most influenced thinking about the size of military forces during this period is that of 5,000 knights, Round's estimate for the *servitium debitum*, calculated by working backwards from the returns to Henry II's inquest into knight-service. Round made justifiable fun of Orderic Vitalis's statement that England could produce 60,000 knights, and showed that this figure was widely used by the chroniclers and historians of the day when they wished to give the impression of a great number.[128] But Round was not concerned to estimate the number of troops actually mobilized at any one place and time and Orderic has been unfairly discredited. Orderic never mentions a force as large as 5,000 knights in the field in Normandy or on its borders. The priest of Fécamp, writing shortly after the battle of Tinchebray, estimated Henry's forces as about 40,000 infantry and 8,400 cavalry (of whom 1,000 were drawn from Maine and Brittany) while he gave Robert Curthose 6,000 infantry and 700 cavalry.[129] Henry himself claimed to have captured 400 knights and 10,000 infantry, and to have killed countless more.[130] It would be unwise to attach much importance to these totals; Edward I once put about 3,000 cavalry and some 25,700 infantry into the field in a single army, though

---

[125] Stenton, *First Century*, 176–7.

[126] *Chron. Abingdon*, ii. 135. The date of this grant is probably 1105. The grantee was Robert Mauduit, and the previous holder, his father, William Mauduit, had died in about 1105 (*Regesta Regum Anglo-Normannorum*, ii. nos. 697, 729). The chronicler adds that before this grant to Robert Mauduit the service on only three weeks a year had been done. Perhaps this represents half of forty days service, and the chronicler may mean that only castle-guard service (or commutation thereof) had previously been acknowledged. The passage is however consistent with, but does not entail, the view that the period of service at this time was greater than forty days.

[127] *Sir Christopher Hatton's Book of Seals*, ed. L.C. Lloyd and D.M. Stenton (1950), no. 528. There follows in the original typescript a section dealing with castle-guard; for discussion of this topic see above, 92–5.

[128] Round, *Feudal England*, 289–93

[129] Davis, 'The Battle of Tinchebrai: a Correction', 296.

[130] Eadmer, *Historia Novorum*, 184. See above, 78, for further figures.

this was exceptional.[131] But the proportions given, for what they are worth, indicate that the cavalry ordinarily formed about five per cent of the total and only once slightly exceeded ten per cent. In the earlier Edwardian armies the proportion of cavalry was about ten per cent, rising to twenty per cent in the later campaigns. The Norman armies included ordinary infantry, archers both foot and horsed, crossbowmen, mechanics and engineers in addition to cavalry; and Henry I used large numbers of woodmen just as did Edward I. Moreover many of the knights were men of relatively humble status, *milites gregarii*; the cavalry forces of this period were certainly not drawn exclusively from the 'flower of knighthood' which Waleran of Meulan's followers claimed to represent.[132]

Those historians who regard the history of war as largely a history of battles have but scanty and dubious material in this period: Hastings, Tinchebray, Brémule and Bourg Théroulde provide the only excuses for misleading diagrams. Rufus, for all his high reputation as a soldier with contemporaries, never fought a pitched battle. Much depended on bribery, diplomacy and the capacity to ransom prisoners. Much too depended on the capacity to mobilize, maintain and supply a superior number of troops in the field and in garrisons. And a great deal depended on the siting and strength of fortifications. Both Rufus and Henry were able to bring much Norman territory and many Norman castles under their control by bribery, diplomacy and manoeuvre without having to fight for them. Warfare was very largely a matter of marches, patrols, garrison duty, sieges, the burning of towns and the construction of castles. It was by these methods, not by sweeping cavalry charges, that Normandy was won and defended, Wales deeply penetrated and Scotland intimidated. Indeed Henry

---

131 Correction to original text, which cited figures from the Welsh wars. This is taken from M.C. Prestwich, *Edward I* (London, 1988), 479 [MCP].

132 The *milites gregarii* present a problem. Stenton quoted William of Poitiers on the *milites mediae nobilitatis atque gregarii*, adding 'They were dangerous servants, and the Conqueror had disbanded his own mercenary army as soon as it had done its work.' His references show that he was referring to the Conqueror paying off his mercenaries in 1067 and again in 1070. They had also been paid off in 1068, and the Conqueror had had to restrain his *milites gregarii* from looting Exeter earlier in that year (*Orderic*, ii. 214). But although the Conqueror paid off his mercenaries after campaigns this was merely due to his business-like ways: he had reproached William fitz Osbern for extravagant expenditure on troops, and when he could he made his enemies pay. The Conqueror and his sons continued to take these mercenaries back into service into campaign after campaign. And if Stenton's identification of the *milites gregarii* with paid knights could be accepted, the evidence of the use of paid troops in this period would be yet further extended. Henry I enjoyed the support of the *milites gregarii* in 1101, when there is no other direct evidence of his use of paid troops. There is evidence from Stephen's reign that *milites gregarii* were hired (*Gesta Stephani*, 85), while another reference to these troops describes them as *milites gregarii et conductitii* (Florence, ii. 133). Henry I's opponents at Bourg Théroulde were described by their opponents as *pagenses et gregarii* (*Orderic*, vi. 350). Of itself the word gregarius means 'common, of the rank and file'. But writers of the eleventh and twelfth centuries may also have been using the word in its primary sense to describe knights who were banded together, landless and dependent on pay or booty. It may be significant that William of Poitiers should mention the *milites gregarii* in connection with the Conqueror's strict discipline and measures against quarelling, murder and looting, and that Orderic should describe the Conqueror's measures to prevent the looting of Exeter by the *milites gregarii*.

appears to have reflected that the horse which could carry a knight against the enemy could also carry him away from the battlefield, if the rider judged this to be the more prudent course. He made many of his knights dismount both at Tinchebray and at Brémule, *ut constantius pugnarent*, and his knights who won the victory of Bourg Théroulde similarly dismounted for action.[133]

If it is impossible to give even approximately reliable figures for the numbers engaged in military operations it is also impossible to give any precision to the obligations of knight-service and fyrd service. There is evidence that knight-service was owed for forty days, both in the host and for castle-guard, in Normandy under the Conqueror.[134] As Round pointed out this figure is suggestive of commutation, since forty is a convenient fraction of both the mark and the pound, though bearing no direct proportion either to the week or the month.[135] When personal service alone was required it would be natural for the tenants to seek its limitation and for it to be defined in weeks or months. But if money was taken in lieu of service it would be administratively convenient to take a mark or pound or multiple thereof from each knight's fee. If a mark was taken the knight would argue that the duke had obtained forty days service at 4d a day; if a pound, forty days service at 6d a day. However, the period of service due from fees in England cannot be established for this period. The Berkshire entry in Domesday Book defines the period of fyrd service as having been two months and the sum needed to maintain each man as a pound, giving a rate of 4d a day. But there is no evidence on the period of service demanded from the English after the Conquest, and, if the Anglo-Saxon Chronicle is to be trusted, each man had not a pound but only ten shillings in 1094. The only evidence for wage rates in this period comes from a single entry in the Pipe Roll of 1130, suggesting that on garrison duty a knight received 8d a day and a sergeant ½d.[136] Scraps of evidence suggest that it would be wrong to look for precision and definition in this period, or at least in the Conqueror's reign. The enfeoffment of a certain king's knight called Peter as a feudal tenant of the abbey of Bury St Edmunds for the service of three or four knights in royal expeditions is curiously casual.[137] And there is a good deal of evidence to show that feudal tenure was not everywhere hereditary tenure in the earlier part of this period, though the hereditary principle was quickly established.[138] It was an easy matter to obtain personal service from an unenfeoffed knight who lived in his lord's household; it was, perhaps, not too difficult to obtain military service from a tenant enjoying only a precarious tenure and depending on his lord's favour for the re-grant of

---

133 For Tinchebray see the discussion of the evidence by David, *Robert Curthose*, Appendix F; for Brémule, *Orderic*, vi. 234–42; and for Bourg Théroulde, *Orderic*, vi. 348–52.

134 C.H. Haskins, *Norman Institutions* (Cambridge, Mass., 1918), 20.

135 Round, *Feudal England*, 270–1.

136 J.O. Prestwich, 'Anglo-Norman Feudalism and the Problem of Continuity', *Past and Present*, xxvi (1963), 46 [MCP].

137 Douglas, *Feudal Documents from the Abbey of Bury St Edmunds*, no. 168.

138 S.E. Thorne, 'English Feudalism and Estates in Land', *Cambridge Law Journal*, new ser., vi (1959), 193–209. See *Chron. Abingdon*, ii. 34–5, for a grant of land for the service of one knight, a grant restricted to the lives of the holders instead of *jure hereditario* as they had asked. This was before 1097.

his lands to his son; but it was less easy to enforce service when hereditary succession had been established, when the original ties of common loyalties and common dangers had been relaxed and when tenants were primarily concerned with organizing and managing their estates. One of the household knights of the abbey of Abingdon was granted land not to support him in his future military service but precisely because he was incapable of further service: he had had the misfortune to be captured by pirates in the Channel and to have had his hands cut off. Only the Conqueror's compassionate intervention secured this provision for the knight.[139]

In the absence of record evidence no precise and quantitative account of the composition of military forces under the Conqueror and his sons can be given. We cannot do for the Norman armies what Morris did for the Edwardian armies. But though the Norman armies were more lightly equipped than the Edwardian, and though the fortifications they had to defend and attack were much less elaborate, there was much the same variety of troops in the Norman armies as in the Edwardian, and they may even have been combined in much the same proportions. Certainly the Norman armies were no more mobilized and organized according to a definite and comprehensive feudal plan than were the Edwardian. Norman armies were not composed of knights alone, and the knights they contained were not wholly, perhaps not even mainly, the products of feudal tenure. As Maitland pointed out, to hold in fee was not necessarily to hold by knight-service: it might merely involve the payment of a rent. Maitland also observed of the word *feudum* at the time of the Domesday Survey that 'all sense of militariness, and all sense of precariousness, that the word has ever had in its continental history seems to be disappearing'.[140] Moreover tenure by knight-service did not guarantee the performance of knight-service. Failing the evidence which records could supply on the composition of military forces in this period it is necessary to use evidence of a less precise but still persuasive kind. We can turn to the chroniclers, historians and other writers of the late eleventh and twelfth centuries. And on the converging and independent testimony of William of Poitiers, Lanfranc, Orderic Vitalis, William of Malmesbury, Suger, Lawrence of Durham and Richard Fitz Neal the use of paid troops in general and of paid knights in particular was widespread and familiar.

Note on further reading

The central element in royal armies was not discussed by JOP in this chapter. The knights of the royal household provided the core of the armies, and would have been examined in a different chapter, which provided the basis for his article, 'The Military Household of the Norman Kings', *EHR* xcvi (1981), 1–35. S. Morillo, in his *Warfare under the Anglo-Norman Kings* (Woodbridge, 1997),

---

[139] *Chron. Abingdon*, ii. 6–7.
[140] F.W. Maitland, *Domesday Book and Beyond*, 152. Maitland quoted from Domesday Book the instance of William the Chamberlain, who had held a manor in Middlesex *in feudo* first from the queen and later from the Conqueror for £3 a year.

47ff, provides a valuable study of the Anglo-Norman military machine and its composition. For a brief survey of the role of mercenaries, see M.C. Prestwich, 'Money and Mercenaries in English Medieval Armies', in *England and Germany in the High Middle Ages*, ed. A. Haverkamp and H. Vollrath (Oxford, 1996), 129–50.

The question of the introduction of feudal service, given fairly short shrift in this chapter, has continued to interest historians. J. Gillingham, 'The Introduction of Knight Service into England', *Anglo-Norman Studies* iv (1982), 53–64, provided a dramatic challenge to existing views, suggesting that quotas pre-dated the Conquest, and pointing to the silence on the question of fifteen contemporary or near-contemporary writers who dealt with the consequences of 1066. J.C. Holt provided a more orthodox, and convincing, interpretation of quotas of service in 'The Introduction of Knight-Service in England' in his *Colonial England 1066–1135* (London, 1997), 81–101.

JOP's views on the importance of pay were questioned by S.D. Church in 'The Rewards of Royal Service in the Household of King John: A Dissenting Opinion', *EHR* cx (1995), 277–302, reprinted in his *The Household Knights of King John* (Cambridge, 1999). Church claimed that 'Prestwich's case for the regular payment of wages and money fiefs to household knights by Henry I rests in substantial part on the words of Walter Map writing between about 1181 and 1192', while 'The second linchpin of Prestwich's argument rested on a clause that appeared in a treaty between Count Robert of Flanders and Henry I at Dover in 1101.'[141] However, this chapter by JOP demonstrates that his evidence was rather more extensive than Church suggested. JOP had, in addition, other criticisms of Church's work, noting for example that far from William de Gamages having been granted the manors of Dymock in Gloucestershire and Meon in Hampshire, he was actually granted £7 in 'Muena' and £8 in Dymock, both places being in Gloucestershire. 'A Hampshire manor cannot turn up in the *terrae datae* of Gloucestershire.'[142]

For Anglo-Flemish connections in this period, see R. Nip, 'The Political Relations between England and Flanders (1066–1128)', *Anglo-Norman Studies* xxi (1999), 145–67.

---

[141] S.D. Church, *The Household Knights of King John* (Cambridge, 1999), 75, 77.

[142] S.D. Church, 'The rewards of royal service in the household of King John: a dissenting opinion', *EHR* cx (1995), 299; some of JOP's criticisms were set out in a letter to J.R. Maddicott, dated 6 May 1999, which appears not to have been sent. Unfortunately, it is impossible to reconstruct from the surviving notes the article that JOP intended to write.

Index

Warfare in History

Warfare in Medieval Brabant, 1356–1406
Sergio Boffa

Renaissance Military Memoirs:
War, History and Identity
Yuval Harari